DON'T AGONIZE, ORGANIZE!

YOUR LIFE IS YOUR BUSINESS

By
Regina Muster

DNA Press™

ISBN 1933255-12-9

Library of Congress Cataloging-in-Publication Data

Muster, Regina. Don't agonize, organize! : your life is your business / by Regina Muster.— 1st ed.
    p. cm. — (The Nuts & bolts series)
  ISBN 1-933255-12-9 (alk. paper)
    1. Home economics. 2. Time management. 3. Planning. I. Title. II. Series.
    TX147.M87 2005
    640—dc22

                                    2005003803

DNA Press, LLC
P.O. BOX 572
Eagleville, PA 19408, USA
www.dnapress.com
editors@dnapress.com

Publisher: DNA Press, LLC
Executive Editor: Alexander Kuklin
Art Direction: Alex Nartea
Cover & book layout: Studio N Vision (www.studionvision.com)

DON'T AGONIZE, ORGANIZE!

YOUR LIFE IS YOUR BUSINESS

Acknowledgements

This book is dedicated to my father, Majer Muster, who was meticulously organized and my mother, Yetta, who approached everything in life with a very positive and practical attitude.

I wish to give very special thanks to my dear friends - Dana Bare, Karen Farber, Tracy Ecclesine Ivie, Susan Hafford, Beth Harness and Adrianne Rowe who helped me edit the book and to Kenneth H. Dreyer for his technical assistance. They each provided me with ideas and suggestions on how to best present the subject matter.

Thanks to Jenna Mehler, my daughter, whose comments and positive feedback made the task of writing the book so much fun. I also wish to thank my husband, Eric Mehler, for his infinite patience and support while listening to my ideas.

TABLE OF CONTENTS

Introduction

A long time ago I heard someone say that you should run your life like a business. I found that strange since I viewed my life as almost the opposite of a business. Business is impersonal and 9 to 5 while my personal life goes into effect after work. A business is a tightly run activity that strives to make a profit or make a big difference in the world. It is a multi-faceted operation that can span the world. I think of a business as a corporation constantly growing bigger and more profitable. When I first thought about life as a business I did not see any relationship. The more I thought about it, the more I began to understand the correlation and it made sense. Just as a business, I too wish to be successful, possess many different abilities, and constantly gain maturity and financial security. I learned that I could apply many successful business methodologies and practices to my life. Now I run my life like a business. I have a plan for the future, my sights set on my goals and I am ready to make my mark on humanity.

Within a business each worker has a specific role and is assigned a series of tasks to perform. Management decides on the major goals and sets target dates for their completion. Employees are given smaller goals to complete within a given timeframe. Each employee is responsible for getting his or her work accomplished. To become successful, business management must act in an organized manner to get things done and become highly productive. Departments and sections are organized by function and one process usually operates concurrently with other processes. By combining the individual talents, experience and knowledge of the employees a team is built. The whole team works for the common goal; for the profitability and success of the business.

By looking at business as a model, you can learn how to successfully run your personal life. Organization is about systematically arranging and uniting to produce a specific result. It is about doing things the correct way, when the time is right and eliminating errors. It is about working on many tasks at once and getting them all done on time. It is about combining all your efforts and resources to complete a job with the least amount of effort. It is about being responsible to yourself and others you care about. You can simply look at the business model as a way to gain insight into how to organize your life, set personal goals, get things done, meet deadlines and stay on target, all at the same time.

Many people have been pushed to the point of acting in an organized manner while struggling to handle the stress and pressure of daily life. They have successfully introduced a sense of order to their lives. They plan and schedule the tasks and activities they choose to do. Those that choose not to be organized pay dearly for their disorganization and so do those closest to them. The level of disorganization of parents is costly to their children. The disorganization of managers, doctors, attorneys and teachers is costly to their employees, patients, clients and students. By failing to effectively deal with the daily stresses and pressures in their own lives, individuals unknowingly add stress and pressure to the lives of others as a result of their disorganization.

Some people are able to successfully live their lives with great results, on many dimensions, while others never seem to be able to accomplish what they want. *"Don't Agonize, Organize"* provides the information necessary to organize your life to achieve great results. Organizing your life is much more than making up a list of things to do for the next day. It is about gaining control of your time, balancing all the details in your life and setting and reaching your desired goals. No one can control what life presents us but we can control where our life is going. The book gives equal emphasis to the health, family, financial, social, intellectual and professional components in your life. Being able to spend quality time in the various areas of your life will give you a higher level of personal satisfaction and happiness.

If you are reading this book it means you probably want to change one or more patterns of behavior that doesn't work for you. If there is something you wish to change in your life you can either change what you do or how you feel about it. Change often gives us an opportunity to learn new things and experiment with new methods. Being conditioned by many of the obstacles we have faced in the past, we are often prevented from doing certain things today. Obstacles can stop us temporarily but only your attitude can permanently stop you from reaching your goals. We each choose how to think and how to act. By maintaining a positive attitude throughout your life, you will be increasing your returns in life. Becoming organized does not involve monumental changes, it is only a matter of learning new techniques, applying them and practicing them everyday.

Organization can help you reach your goals. This book will take you through many aspects of organization. You will learn how to plan ahead and set goals based on your needs and desires. You will learn how to manage your time and schedule all the incidental and important events in your life. You will learn how to manage paper and organize your affairs. Suggestions in the book will offer you alternatives to keeping every single thing that comes into your life. You will learn to buy what you need instead of always what you want. You will learn how to store your belongings so you can find them and you will not have to live with duplicates, broken items or things that need repair. It will teach you how to handle new situations under difficult conditions. This book will get you ready to face your future by getting the things done that are important to you.

Computers and the Internet are now a fact of life, not a fad or passing craze. They are like the telephone or automobile; you don't need to know how they work to appreciate their value. The ease of communications on the Internet has changed the way people conduct their business. Instant communication and access to information that once took weeks to gather has changed the pace of living. It has opened our eyes and made the rest of the world seem closer. It has given us masses of information on the most specific of topics allowing us to make better use of and save large amounts of time.

The use of technology, such as email, voicemail, PDAs (personal digital assistants), the Internet and personal computers provides unlimited resources for getting yourself organized. You can instantly create a list or a spreadsheet for any purpose. You can keep track of money, personal belongings, collections, budgets, schedule meetings and appointments and much more. The Internet provides a "24/7" medium to research any topic you wish to learn more about. The websites I have listed in Appendix 1 contain information about various topics discussed in the book. Scanning these sites will give you more detailed information and further resources to get you started on any new or existing project that you've had trouble finishing.

"Don't Agonize, Organize" details all the routines and methods that I have successfully tried to practice and use everyday. As you read through each chapter, try to gain an understanding of how each relates to the different aspects of your life. Sometimes you need to step out of the box, out of your usual behavior pattern and learn to listen to yourself. The book breaks down and separates the many routines and processes that you perform everyday. It will allow you to critically examine how well each fits into your life style. At times, you may be able to identify with some of the habits described or become aware of a new method you can use to improve yourself. Our habits are so frequently repeated and fixed by daily automatic performance that we never even think of stepping back to analyze them.

Everyone needs some sort of organization in their lives to get things done. Employed people, especially working parents, must be particularly organized as they need to stay on top of child care arrangements, help with household duties, assist with their child's homework, attend school meetings and be attentive to the needs of their own careers. Business owners need to be highly organized for they are responsible for handling the various functions of their business, making sure that they operate at peak efficiency. Students must be highly organized as they juggle their studies, after school activities and social schedules every day. Each set of circumstances is different but what they have in common is the need to be organized to accomplish the most in their lives.

I have an organized life style. Because of my sense of organization I have been able to accomplish many of my major and minor goals. I use various organizational methods and techniques in both my job and my personal life. They help me overcome the obstacles and excuses that prevent one from starting on new projects. I have developed my own style and learned to break large goals and tasks into sizeable, doable pieces. I am able to find specific documents in my files, at a moment's notice. I always carry my date book with me and do not forget birthdays or doctor appointments. I am rarely, if ever, late. When I say that I will do something I get it done, I keep my word. I can plan an entire day and stick to my schedule. I get a lot accomplished and I am not afraid to take on new responsibilities. In other words, I run my life like a successful business and you can too.

Good luck and get organized!

CHAPTER 1

WHY BE ORGANIZED?

"A man who does not think and plan long ahead
will find trouble right at his door."
Confucius (551 - 479 BC)

In my social circle, I was a normal teenager. I was rebellious and fought against authority. I resisted my father's precise manner of organization and viewed my mother's plastic sofa covers with disdain. I maintained a typical teenager's messy bedroom. It became worse each time I would get ready for a date or a party. I would throw each article of clothing onto the floor after trying it on. By the time I was dressed my room looked like a cyclone had hit. My school papers and books were scattered all around the house. I could never find anything without spending a great deal of time searching for it. Worst of all I kept misplacing money, leaving it in my pant's pockets, a different bag or just laying around my room. This was the lifestyle I maintained through my twenties. The life I led was fine until I married, had a child and became a working parent. I quickly realized that if I wished to live in a clean house, spend time with my child, enjoy an evening with my husband, prepare for work the next day, find my checkbook, have clean clothes and eat a healthy dinner - I had to get organized. That was the only way I could possibly attempt to do everything I wished to accomplish.

Order It Your Way

I found the solution to my messy life in the form of order. Order is what helps you function in an effective manner, towards a specific goal. The order you decide on needn't be too strict. What order does is establish a method for having things in the proper place. You design the rules of order to align with your personality. One important element of real order is your physical environment. You should aim to style your home and office as one that is easy to move around in, easy to look at and easy to function in. Design an organized environment to create an atmosphere that will accommodate your changing needs while remaining clutter free. Order is a simple technique to effectively handle the volumes of paper you must confront everyday. Order can control the arrangement of your personal affairs and money matters. It will produce a condition in which there exists a methodical and harmonious arrangement of all your things. It will allow you to get tasks done at your own pace.

Living In a Complex Society

Order is just the tip of the iceberg. Having the many parts of your life in order will lead you towards organization. Every action or decision you make will get you a step closer to a carefully chosen goal. As modern society becomes more complex, the need for organization increases. Everyday the world offers us more choices. It has become highly important to make decisions to advance carefully chosen objectives. Learning and practicing good organizational skills can help control the management of the complex problems and situations we face. We need to realize that we cannot do everything all by ourselves. It is okay to depend and rely on others. Being interdependent has replaced the need to be independent. For example, it is wise to delegate tasks that you dislike or those you do not have the time to do.

> **Hint:** *You need to develop good organizational skills to help manage your busy and active life.*

Reasons Behind It All

There are many reasons for not being organized. The most popular reasons are postponing what you dread or lacking the physical or psychological energy that you believe will be required. Procrastination is a really big thing that transcends many other reasons. But when you really think about it there are definite reasons why a person can feel this way. Procrastination pushes what you have to do into the future away from the present temporarily easing your mind and relieving you from responsibilities. The task at hand may be so overwhelming that your natural reaction is to delay it. You may be fearful of the effort required to devote to the task or it may simply be a matter of not knowing where or how to start. What you do is create obstacles for yourself and reasons and excuses to rationalize your inactivity.

Can You Identify Your Problem Areas?

- *Am I disorganized?*
- *Am I surrounded by clutter?*
- *Do I have a paperwork backup?*
- *Do I tend to put off doing things?*
- *Do I constantly search for things?*
- *Do I have an excuse for almost everything?*
- *Have I created obstacles to my own success?*
- *Have I done all I want to do so far in my life?*

• *Do I have many reasons for not doing things I really want to do?*
• *Am I unwilling to put in the effort needed for long-term projects?*
• *Am I am afraid to start something new because I do not know how?*
• *Do I tend to keep everything I've ever owned, even if I have no use for it?*

Pinpoint Your Problems

If any of the statements previously listed are true for you then you can benefit from the advice in this book. Not only will this book help you plan your personal and business affairs effectively, it will help plan your time, your future and even your closets. It will teach you how to standardize, file, customize, de-clutter, make decisions and fulfill your desires. It will help you define, prioritize and set your goals. It will help you to establish an organized way of life tailored to your own desires and needs. By pinpointing the problems in your life and learning how to bring them into manageable solvable proportions it will help get your life in order. Being ready for a sudden change in direction or new set of circumstances will not catch you off guard. Thinking ahead and being organized will give you the skills to make your future what you want it to be.

Educate Yourself

First, you need to get a handle on your concerns. How big are they? Do you see the end result but not how you are going to get to it? Are you afraid of failing? Learning how to break a big job into smaller pieces and getting satisfaction upon its completion is a major function of organization. Do you not know where to begin? Educating yourself and developing a plan or schedule of attack will start you off. When given a new assignment on my job, or when I begin a new project for myself, I am usually terrified. I first research and gather any information I can locate on the topic. I try hard to lessen my fear until I learn exactly what the new project is about. By the time I have learned what the task entails I have already begun the project and my fear is usually unjustified and never becomes reality. If I do not take that time to research, study or learn about the subject I begin to fantasize about how difficult it can be. After too much thinking my mind begins to create obstacles, excuses and reasons for not starting it. When I do research on a new topic and apply the rules of organization (that I have developed for myself) I know that I will be able to change my habits and control the outcome.

> **Hint:** *Your success or failure is up to you. You have the power to succeed.*

Organizing Yourself

You do not need any natural talents to be well organized. Anyone can learn organization by acquiring good habits and shedding undesirable habits, but it is a skill that requires practice and you have to practice all the time. You cannot be punctual some of the time. You have to be punctual all the time. You cannot organize your life by carefully planning some days and winging it on others. You have to work hard to plan every day. Organizing has a lot to do with getting your life in order. It helps you see where you have been and where you are going. It helps you identify where you need help and then gives you direction. If you are drowning in piles of paper and no longer able to find things, organizing helps get rid of what you do not need. It can help sort out what you really need and then place them where you can easily access them. If you find it difficult to start or to finish projects, organizing can give you the motivation to complete a task. If you never have enough time or are always late for appointments, organizing can keep you on track. It can help you make the best use of your time. Organization can help you transform what seems impossible to accomplish into attainable goals.

What Good Organization Can Do For You

- *Simplify*
- *Save time*
- *Be on time*
- *Start you off*
- *Get things done*
- *Help you prioritize*
- *Manage your schedule*
- *Plan on a regular basis*
- *Help you make decisions*
- *Transcend procrastination*

- *Get your possessions in order*
- *Overcome everyday obstacles*
- *Keep you on track and punctual*
- *Help you set and reach your goals*
- *Help you decide what you want out of life*
- *Complete big projects that are important to you*
- *Just go for it!*

Building Blocks

Life is a series of choices. Your basic values and principles are the building blocks upon which you shape your life. These lay the foundation for all your decisions and actions. Having goals allows you to use your mind and talents to work towards your maximum potential. Goals allow you to work towards something. A clearly defined target and set of priorities is essential to getting things done. They can step you through complicated processes and situations. Scheduling and planning activities and tasks leads to the accomplishment of goals and can help you work efficiently and effectively. By following your plans and keeping on schedule you will be able to put your choices, wishes and desires into action. Following these steps will help you to achieve personal organization.

Five Building Blocks of Personal Organization
(see next page diagram)

Getting Motivated

The conscious or unconscious thoughts that incite you to some action or behavior are called motivation. Businesses are motivated by profit and gaining success in their field. Motives and motivated behavior are selectively directed towards a specific goal. A highly organized person is someone who does things that make a definite contribution to a major goal. This motivated behavior tends to continue until the goal is reached or until another goal takes a higher priority. The strength of a motive depends on a persisting attitude that is dominant in your thoughts and actions. One of the first steps in getting organized is defining your objectives and purposes. This will allow you to set up a practical system to implement your goals, whether they are large or small. For organized behavior to occur you

FIVE BUILDING BLOCKS OF PERSONAL ORGANIZATION

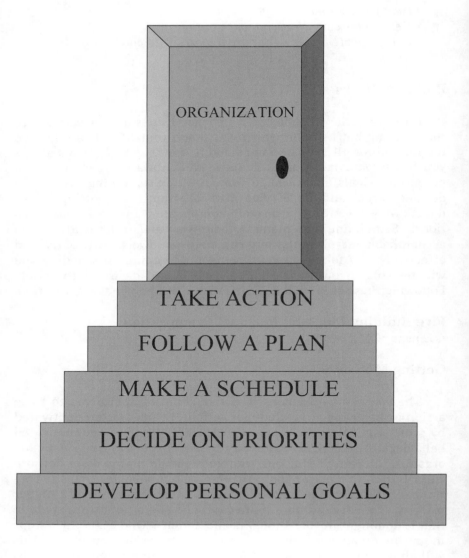

must focus your thoughts, feelings and behavior so that they are all directed towards the goal.

> **Hint:** *When you are asleep you need your dreams and when you are awake you need your goals.*

Attitude and Energy

You are motivated by both a state of energy and by behavior that is directed towards a goal. This goal has been selected in preference to other possible goals. All your psychological processes - perceiving, thinking, feeling and performing are directed towards the goal. The coordination of these processes in a common direction is *"organization"*. When your state of being is motivated, it is directed towards some purpose or end. This behavior is reflected in your attitude. As a reaction to the motivation you direct your actions to produce results. Motivation is a concept that joins a state of energy and a goal. Therefore, organization is a joint contribution of ones physical, mental and emotional states. Your energy and behavior are directed towards a positive attitude and outcome. A positive, winning attitude consciously directs a steady stream of constructive messages towards the outcomes you want.

Be Honest With Yourself

If you have a high expectancy that your behavior will lead to the satisfaction of a desired need then you will be motivated to pursue your goal. In order to define your needs and desires you must be willing to think hard and look inside yourself. You must be truthful and honest. Defining a need that someone else wishes for you will not give you the motivation to succeed. You need to exclude pipe dreams and stay within realistic expectations. The desire to go to college at Princeton or Yale when you have very low grades or buying a one million dollar house when you are heavily in debt are very unrealistic goals. Your personal needs and desires must be constantly analyzed. Getting married may bring up hidden desires of raising a family, going away to college may raise issues of independence or the threat of losing your job may increase your interest in financial security. Personal values can change at many points in your life and your needs and desires may accompany this change in attitude.

> **Hint:** *It is necessary to first discover what you really want out of life, what you value most and how far you are willing to go to get there.*

Simplify Your World

One easy way to focus on getting organized is to simplify many of the actions and routines you perform everyday. You probably lead a full and complicated life and should consider devoting some time to slowing it down. It takes less time and energy to deal with smaller simple units of work than ones that are larger and intricate. Here are some techniques you can practice to simplify your life and alleviate the stress and aggravation that goes along with complex situations.

Consolidate and Combine - The smallest number that you must consider, the less time and energy you will need to devote to managing it. Consolidate loans, credit cards, bank, checking and mutual fund accounts. Shop at one main center where you can combine many errands. Combine a visit with a friend with a night out.

Don't Over Analyze - When either making an initial decision or after reaching a decision, people keep thinking and analyzing a situation. Sometimes this brings about a change of heart but most often a headache. If you carefully weigh the pros and cons, then after you decide, go onto something else. Do not dwell on the notion that you may have made an incorrect choice.

Divide and Conquer - Break down any problems, situations and tasks you have to contend with into the smallest pieces. This way you can attack each item individually and really concentrate on it. Focus your attention so you can work on all the finer details. You will not feel overwhelmed and will be able to complete the entire task in a more logical unstressed manner.

Tell the Truth - Telling a lie and fabricating a story always becomes more complicated than you imagine. Telling your friend you are sick at home when you actually agree to meet someone else and getting caught is not a good thing. Not being honest on your taxes can end up more trouble than it's worth if you are audited. When dealing with others be honest about your feelings and actions. When dealing with data make sure you can back it up with facts or good documentation.

Always Be Prepared

People who are organized try to anticipate and be ready for any situation that occurs. Just taking a look inside my handbag and briefcase can give you a picture of what I mean. I try to be prepared by keeping emergency or useful supplies handy.

Besides a wallet, an address book, a date book and a comb, I carry:

- Mirror (so I always look great)
- Nail File (when I get that nick)
- Tissues (for the unexpected sneeze)
- Paper (to write notes and to-do lists)
- Safety Pins (for that unexpected rip)
- Reading material (for *"waiting time"*)
- Stain Remover (when I stain my shirt)
- Aspirin (when I get a sudden headache)
- Band Aids (for the unexpected paper cut)
- Pens (to write down all my notes and dates)
- Pre-Moistened Towelettes (when I get sticky)
- Stamps (when I need to mail a letter or card)
- Paper Clips (for attaching my notes together)
- Lifesavers or Mints (when I need fresh breath)
- Tape Measure (for measuring specific dimensions)
- Tiny Screwdriver and Screws (to tighten eyeglasses)

Hint: Keep an extra umbrella and flashlight in your office and car for emergencies.

Storing Information

Our minds have a large capacity to store information in memory. It is stored and organized in many useful ways. As you may have noted (now or in the past) when preparing for examinations, unorganized knowledge is quickly forgotten. The way we store information has to do with the properties of objects, the events surrounding the object and the relationships among the objects. Objects become associated with one another because we find it useful to group them together. This is a pretty common method of organization that we practice all the time. Writing information on cards that can be easily sorted to group certain cards together can help you to remember. Constructing an outline giving broad general headings for major categories of information and more specific headings for more detailed data is another method to aid memory. The organization should provide a scheme or order for the most specific elements in the array. Without our even noticing it, our minds assemble and sort things into categories for future reference. This order can be applied to storage control, paper control, planning and scheduling.

Value Your Time

Organization has a lot to do with time. You may think that it takes a lot more time to be organized. The truth is that you save time by being organized, time that you can use for things that you really enjoy. What organization does is to eliminate what you don't need and help you keep order among the things you must keep. Organizing is about creating simple, effective systems to help you function and save time on a daily basis. You will no longer need to search for misplaced items and will know exactly where to find what you need. To use your time more effectively look for ways to save time in little bits and pieces. Time is a valuable commodity. Each moment spent is gone forever. Learning to simplify and streamline your life by being organized will afford you extra time and increase your personal productivity. *"Working smart"* is the practice of leveraging your time for maximum results.

Hint: Making the most of your time and understanding how valuable your time is can help give you the rewards that you deserve in your life.

Time Is Money

We all know that time is limited and each minute counts. Your personal productivity is the measurement of what you accomplish each day. The value of your time is often translated into money and losing money on your job because of lateness or disorganization is curable. If you hadn't misplaced your uniform you would not have been late for your after-school job. If you hadn't spent one hour looking for your car keys you would have been able to make that appointment with your client or if you listened to the traffic report while getting dressed you would have taken a different route and not missed that important meeting at work. Time management is getting things done in the shortest amount of time, gaining control and increasing your productivity. Once good time and project management techniques are set up, they will save you both time and money. Hopefully, by the end of the book you will be richer by all the time you practice saving.

Saving Every Day

When you really get to think about the time you spend you can break it down into three big chunks: time spent at work, time spent doing things you like to do and time spent doing things you have to do. There is little you can do about your time at work except to improve your work habits and organizational skills or do more at work and bring less work home with you. We all want more time to spend on things we like to do, like relaxing, going on vacation and enjoying our hobbies. The most control we have in our lives is on the amount of time we spend doing things we have to do such as running errands, shopping, going to medical appointments, taking care of finances and getting all sorts of personal tasks accomplished. Dining out every night because you did not go grocery shopping can make a big dent in your wallet. Not going to the dentist for five years is very bad for your health. Your bank account can easily become overdrawn if you do not deposit your checks. Each day we spend a lot of our free time doing things we may not enjoy but have to do to live a comfortable and responsible life.

> **Hint:** *Saving time is just like saving money, after accruing a sizable amount you can use it to fulfill a goal.*

Small Ways to Be Organized

There are simple techniques for getting yourself organized. For now I will concentrate on the small ways we tend to spend our time. Not every day or every week will entail a doctor appointment or a major shopping adventure. However over the course of a month, following these suggestions will save you time and maybe even some money. See which of these ideas may work for you.

Appointments

• *Schedule appointments at the beginning or end of the day*
Having the first appointment of the day insures minimal or no waiting time. Having the last appointment is less stressful and allows you to be more relaxed because you do not have to rush to get back to work.

• *Call ahead or the day before to confirm your appointment*
Lots of doctor's offices call to confirm your appointment. If you forget, or do not show up, they lose money. If they do not call you, call them just in case you made a mistake and your appointment is on a different day or at a different time.

• *Always call before you travel*
Call the airport or train station to check if your flight or train is running late, or call the person you made an appointment with to see if they are running late. If they run late, you must wait. Your time is valuable too. You can save time by arriving later for your flight, train or appointment and still be on time for it.

• *Make reservations or appointments on the Internet*
Besides reserving airline flights and hotel rooms you can also save time my making your restaurant, car rental, hotel, museum, theater reservation or car inspection appointment on the web.

Telephone

• *Make calls during your lunch hour*
Make good use of short amounts of time. If you do not have enough time to go on errands during your lunchtime or free periods use the time to make some short telephone calls to take care of your personal business.

• *Invest in a cell phone*
If you do not own one already, buy a cell phone. You do not need to wait until you get home to make your daily telephone calls. You can use it wherever you are (providing you get service), when you have a few minutes to spare or while waiting for an appointment.

- **Make a telephone call instead of writing**

Some believe that writing is a lost art or a thing of the past. Many of us still enjoy writing; however, writing takes more time. Calling provides instant gratification assuming you can contact the party you are trying to reach. If you do not need something in writing, it is faster and cheaper to place a call to get information than it is to write a letter or type up an email. For any business transactions conducted over the phone, write down the person's name for future reference.

- **Place frequently dialed phone numbers on speed dial**

If you call the same people every day or several times a week purchase a telephone with a speed-dial feature. Once programmed, this feature will allow you to press one button to reach them instead of keying in the same phone number each time you call.

Shopping

- **Plan your weekly meals when preparing your grocery list**

By planning what you will be serving for the week you will know exactly what you need to buy and can check off what you already have. This can prevent you from buying items you do not need. Then you don't have to think about what to have for dinner every night when you arrive home, just glance at your weekly menu.

- **Grocery shop only once a week**

Keep a list handy for what you need. If you run out of an item, place it on your list. Review sales at your local supermarket when you are preparing your grocery list, not while you are walking down the aisles. Keep supplies on hand so you do not need to run out for one item at the last minute.

- **Always carry a shopping list**

When you go into a store you are at the advertiser's mercy if you do not have a plan. They aim to get you to spend money and to entice you to buy things you probably do not need. Following a well thought out list and not deviating from it should keep you from straying too far off your budget.

- ***Do shopping on your way home from work***

Grocery shop, pick up a birthday card or hunt for that special outfit on a weeknight on your way home from work. If you make it part of your route home, you do not have to go out of your way. By doing this you are saving the time of making a separate trip. Stores are generally less crowded closer to dinnertime and on days at the beginning of the workweek.

Errands

- ***Attend to all your errands in sequence by location***

Before you leave your home, think about all the places you must stop. Decide on a travel route that will pass each place and what direction you intend to travel. Start your errands at the stop furthest from your home and work back towards your home.

- ***Place your order by phone or Internet beforehand***

You save time if you place your order ahead of time and then pick it up. By having your order ready at the store you will save time by not having to wait for it. You can save money by not buying additional items that catch your eye, just because you are there. Many drugstores will let you call in prescriptions and many stores have websites that allow you to pre-order.

- ***Get your postage on the Internet***

What could be more convenient than printing postage from your computer? The U.S. Postal Service offers software-based postage solutions that can be downloaded on your computer and used for all mail classes with the exception of periodicals. Just log onto *www.usps.com*, set up an account with an authorized vendor and you will be able to print postage on envelopes, labels or plain paper at your desktop.

- ***Find creative and affordable ways to delegate***

Even if only occasionally, find ways to delegate as many chores or errands as possible; have the newspaper, groceries or dry cleaning delivered, order stamps by mail, share running local errands with a neighbor or hire someone to clean your house if you can afford it.

Paper

- *Set up a good filing system*

Most people waste time trying to find a particular paper or a bill that must be paid. Having similar items grouped together in a specific spot saves the time of having to search through endless stacks of paper for what you need. By creating and maintaining a good filing system you will be able to find what you are looking for in a short amount of time.

- *Set up model letters or forms*

To avoid duplicating what you have already done, keep a copy of letters and forms you have created and may need again on your computer. Instead of spending time re-inventing the wheel, use what you have already done as a model for what you now need to create.

- *Never create a miscellaneous file*

If you create a file labeled *"miscellaneous"* you will be tempted to place too much into it. When it comes to paper: read it, sort it, decide on filing it or throw it out as soon as it touches your hands.

- *Sort bills by the date they are due*

If you pay your bills by mail, sort bills by the date they are due and print the date they are due on the envelope to alleviate having to look through all of your bills to see which ones need to be paid first. Think about online bill payment or auto-payment by credit card.

Daily Activities

- *Have a plan set up and ready to follow*

Whether it is merely a daily schedule or a well thought out financial plan, having one ready for you to follow allows you to go right into action. You save time by not having to figure everything out from scratch.

- *Do not allow things to pile up*

Whether it is paper or clothes or bills, the worse thing you can do is let them pile up. Not only will the pile keeping growing larger but it will also become a monumental task for you to sort through. Being organized allows you to control *"build up"*.

- **Do what you say you will do**

You are not really following your schedule if you postpone and procrastinate on a regular basis. It is your responsibility to commit yourself to actually perform the tasks you have planned for yourself. Keep your word and be on time so others do not have to wait for you. If you say you will do something, actually do it.

- **Make use of the Internet to save time**

For example, you can browse on your public library's website. You can determine if the book, CD, video or DVD that you are interested in is currently in the library (and worth the trip to pick it up) or you can reserve it.

In the Car

- **Use your time to digest some good books**

If you have a long commute or deal with lots of traffic during your morning and evening commute it can get boring. Listening to books on tape that you either buy or borrow from your local library will fill up the time enjoyably and wisely.

- **Use a hands-free headset to make calls**

If it is legal in your state, use a hands-free headset and keep your concentration on the road. You can use your commuting time to make some work-related or personal telephone calls.

- **Keep a tape recorder in your car**

Use a tape recorder to remember things you forget and cannot jot down. If you pass an item for sale on the road or a house for sale that you are interested in, record the phone number of the real estate agent or seller and later call to check the price.

- **Get a GPS in your car**

The use of a global positioning system in your car will assure that you will never get lost. GPS is a satellite navigation system that gives directions to drivers on display screens and through synthesized voice instructions. Once you set a destination it plans a precise route to get you there, thus, saving you time. *OnStar* is the most popular system. It comes standard in some car models and can be activated on any new or pre-owned vehicle. There are also PDAs that have GPS capabilities and do not incur a monthly fee.

It's Your Twenty-Four Hours

Everyone has the same twenty-four hours to spend each day. People who fill it by organizing projects logically and managing their schedule are very satisfied by the end of the day. They have set goals and made sure that they are kept in sight. Each day the actions they make take them closer to their objectives. These people are usually highly motivated and eager to rise the next morning to face the next day's challenges. Learning how to master or increase your time management and scheduling skills will allow you to make each moment count. Even if you find another person who can do the job well and you decide to delegate the task, you need a plan to put at least some of the time you save into more profitable activities.

Putting Balance in Your Life

Deciding to be organized will fill your life with all that is valuable and important to you. Everyday you will be doing all you can to meet your goals. You will constantly be on the look out for ways to save time. Practicing better control over your work and home life with simple techniques will free you up to focus on the things you consider important. Understanding the value of your time and what it is worth to you will motivate you to prioritize, plan and schedule. Organizing projects and learning how to manage your time and schedule effectively will relieve stress. It will allow you to simplify and streamline your life while overcoming everyday obstacles. Organizing will give your life the balance to spend your time as you see fit. You will decide what you want out of life and you can now go for it!

CHAPTER 2

YOUR LIFE IS YOUR BUSINESS

"Whenever you see a successful business,
someone has made a courageous decision."
Peter Drucker (1909 -   )

L ike me, most of my friends work in a corporate environment. When I discuss their dream job with them almost everyone says they would want to be able to own and run their own business. In today's world, being a business owner gives one a sense of independence, control, involvement, challenge, freedom and a high degree of personal satisfaction. Unless you are a part of senior management these feelings are absent in the corporate workplace. I point out to my friends that in actuality they are each a small business entrepreneur running their own company. Each one of them is in control of running their own life, for when it comes to your life, you are in charge. You are the main decision maker, planner, manager, scheduler and one who turns your desires into actions. You bring it all together and make sure that everything is running smoothly and accordingly to plan. Even if you decide to delegate several tasks you alone must orchestrate your daily life and head yourself in the right direction into your future. A healthy corporate culture is one that is led by a vision of what they want for the future, and your future should be directed towards your personal vision.

What Makes Up a Business

A business works by combining the talents, experience and knowledge of many individuals. Each person's job is important and each person has the power to make a positive difference. A business can contain many separate departments and divisions to handle the various functions it needs to operate. A business is a combination of many different processes. It is an entity that when broken into individual parts would not exist or be operable. Working together each segment of the business adds to the life of the business. Each part contributes what it is good at and works with other segments towards a common goal. A business is comprised of many functional units of operation such as management, marketing, production, purchasing, sales and finance. Anything that affects one unit affects them all and each unit and division contributes to the success or failure of the business. Management holds the structure of all the units together. A management team, with a strong leader at the helm, using successful business strategies, can lead a company into its future.

Organization in Business

The essence of business is to maintain a high level of organization. Being organized is the process of bringing together or combining for a common objective. It is the arrangement and the cohesive order that distinguishes an organization. Without organization there would be chaos and no clear direction. No viable work would be produced which would result in lack of profits and eventually the collapse of the business structure. A cohesive organization is a business that produces, sets goals, defines priorities and profits by working together for a common goal. This is all done by the development and implementation of a plan of action. Businesses are constantly examining, researching, analyzing and testing new techniques and strategies to apply to their organizational models in the hope of discovering the *"best practices"* within their industry.

How to Begin

- *Agree on an objective to make a profit*
- *Plan how to progress towards this goal*
- *Develop an organization to carry out the plan*
- *Maintain constant control and periodically re-evaluate*
- *Administrate the plan (actual operation of the business)*

Your personal life, like a business, has objectives. A business strives to make a profit, increase capital, grow and prosper. You strive to earn money to enjoy or even to raise your standard of living and save for the future. A business progresses towards their goals with a plan. You set goals and lay out plans on how to attain them. A business develops a management system to carry out the plan and to maintain and control current operations. You are the head of your own business as you plan, control and maintain your everyday life. To maintain a high level of standard, business management is constantly performing reviews, projections and research. You are constantly evaluating your goals and reviewing your plans to ensure that you are on track and can reach the targets you have set for yourself.

Business Planning

A business must plan to survive. A business owner and its management must have their finger on the pulse of their business. They need to plan where it is to be headed in the next few years. Planning is a system of investigation and of checks and balances to achieve a purpose. Business planning whether short range or long range must consider not only the resources of the business, current operational units and financial needs but also the changes and needs that can affect the business now and in the future. Many business pieces must be fitted together in the right way to improve the operation and expand the enterprise. By understanding the mechanics of how a business operates and the interrelationships of the various operational units it can help you determine the many jobs, tasks and multitude of operations that you perform in your everyday life.

Company Staffing

Business needs dictate what work each person connected with the company is expected to perform. Management must inform employees of exactly what is expected of them. In a large company various tasks are divided among many people. The total of all the separate efforts are far greater than what could be achieved by an entrepreneur alone. Management trusts their associates to use their skills and experience intelligently for the good of the business. The staffing department prepares job standards and qualifications for the different positions within the company. Each person is assigned a specific responsibility and must be accountable. Their job title and description lay out their responsibilities. It is of utmost importance to select the right person for the right job. When business people accept the fact that they do not know everything, they either employ or work with people outside the company who know what they do not know.

Personal Staffing

Think about your daily life in terms of a business.
How many paid professionals would you need to employ to run your life?

1. *Accountant* - keeps records of all your financial books and tax issues.
2. *Babysitter* - watches your kids during the day, evenings or on weekends.

3. **Bookkeeper** - performs systematic recording of your transactions.
4. **Caterer** - provides the food services for special functions.
5. **Chef** - head cook who plans and cooks all the meals.
6. **Cleaning Crew** - maintains the cleanliness of your home and belongings.
7. **Decorator** - furnishes and embellishes the interior of your home.
8. **Dispatcher** - makes sure people and items get to their destination on time.
9. **Financial Planner** - plans and controls your financial assets.
10. **Housekeeper** - manages the various domestic affairs in your home.
11. **Landscaper** - plans and maintains arrangement of outdoor features.
12. **Manager** - directs and controls the entire operation.
13. **Party Planner** - plans and makes all the arrangements for gatherings.
14. **Personal Assistant** - schedules your time and appointments.
15. **Receptionist** - receives your visitors and guests.
16. **Researcher** - researches and investigates new projects.
17. **Secretary** - handles all correspondence and clerical duties.
18. **Shopping and Errand Service** - buys and delivers what is needed.
19. **Taxi Driver** - transportation at a moment's notice.
20. **Travel Agent** - plans and schedules vacation and travel itineraries.

Even if you decide to hire, outsource or delegate others to take on some of these jobs, someone must still manage it all. The responsibility of seeing that things are completed and done the right way usually falls on one person. That person is you. So whether or not you actually perform the above tasks, you must still manage and coordinate each one.

Delegating

Delegating is a skill to learn in order to implement all your plans successfully. It is the process of assigning tasks to others in order to balance your time. It is not true that only you can do a job right. You may not always be the best resource to solve a problem or perform a particular task. If you stop doing everything by yourself you will have more time. An important technique for delegating tasks is to develop a network of people you can trust and rely on. Make sure that you select someone who is capable of what you ask of them. Be clear with your instructions and check on them regularly. Whether it is on the job or in your personal life, find areas or tasks that you can assign to others. Either, tasks you do not enjoying doing or ones that you cannot perform well.

> **Hint:** *Delegating and hiring someone else to do a job may not cost as much as you think and you can buy yourself the best gift of all - the gift of time.*

Business vs. You

There are many things that a business and an individual have in common. Both need to plan ahead, create schedules and stick to them. They need to maintain operations at current levels while improving their productivity. They need to make money and pay bills. They aim to increase their worth and make a profit while looking for ways to reduce costs. They constantly educate and research to develop new products or avenues of revenue. They must both meet the challenges of increased costs, higher taxes, new technology, governmental laws and regulations. By breaking down the various goals of major departments within a business, you can compare the similarities of your own personal actions.

	BUSINESS	PERSONAL
Research -	Design products	Develop personal goals
	Improve products	Refine personal goals
	Apply new technology	Use new technological products
	Seek better or cheaper material	Look for sales and areas to upgrade
	Design better production tools	Improve personal skills
Production-	Production schedules	Schedule your time
	Make purchases	Buy groceries, clothes and supplies

	Hire and train	Delegate and give instruction
	Maintain plant	Keep up your home
	Add or replace equipment	New purchases for your home
Financial -	Obtain money to run business	Salary, interest, dividends, etc.
	Pay creditors	Pay mortgage, utility, etc.
	Maintain accounts	Keep track of your spending
	Pay business taxes	Pay personal taxes
	Put money back in the business	Invest in yourself & your future
Marketing -	Price services	Prioritize your goals
	Advertise	Personal resume
	Product packaging	Personal appearance
	Transport	Get places
	New markets	New friends and associates

Business Research

Planning requires periodic review and analysis by studying the changes occurring both inside and outside the company. A business must constantly plan to hold the ground it has already won and hopefully expand. Smart companies don't stop once they have introduced a product. They continually strive to stay ahead to meet the changing needs of consumers. Researching and developing of new goods and services must be ongoing. You should also plan your goals, your challenges and your expectations. Schedules should be set up to meet specific milestones. You should constantly review your plans and adapt them to new external situations or obstacles that move into your path. Just as business uses market research indicators to make sound business judgments or investments, you too should do your homework and research projects prior to setting goals, priorities and making plans.

Change in Business

Changes are constantly going on inside and outside a business and they must be dealt with effectively. A business must plan alternate routes to meet their needs and have plans in readiness to meet changing market conditions. There are no secrets in business for success. To be successful you are required to have an informed and responsive management. A business must fulfill its obligations. Management must develop the required skills, techniques and understanding to respond to change effectively. If they develop the right skills people can learn to identify changes and needs, define their effects on the business and adjust operations to restore good balance. Controls must be instituted to ensure stable and profitable operations over the long term. Just as a business must respond intelligently to change, you too must get accurate facts and data, analyze them, define alternative actions, evaluate resources, select a course of action and quickly implement new solutions.

> **Hint:** *A business whose management is best prepared has the greatest chance for survival and success.*

Updating Skills

With all the new technology being developed, there is bound to be a new software package or a new business process that your company decides to provide education and training. The main reason to train employees is to get everyone up to speed and have all workers function at their maximum efficiency using the same standards and the latest methods. That's the same reason you may decide to take educational courses, to increase your knowledge on a subject. Even if the education is only for a hobby, it may be to learn a new technique or work with an expert in the field. At the conclusion of the course you will be educated in the specific technology or subject that in turn makes you more of an expert. Whether it is through your job or on your own, learning can be exciting. Expanding your knowledge of a skill you are already adept at can give you more confidence or a new one can add to your skill set.

Personal Image

There are times in your life that you may feel you just have to change something about your self. You may be tired of the way you look or feel or you just want to try contact lenses or a new hairdo. A dynamic business is always aware of the image that they project to their consumers. It is that special jingle, product name, commercial or advertisement that uniquely identifies them and makes you remember their product or service. Your personal qualities uniquely identifies you to others. People remember your hair, the way you dress, your make-up, your smile, your personality or your posture. Changing your appearance can give you a new outlook and can change the way people react towards you. Companies do this all the time to stay ahead, be competitive, generate positive energy, enhance the company image with their customers and keep up with the latest trends.

> **Hint:** *For a quick and inexpensive change consider professional advice from a wardrobe consultant or a personal color analyst.*

Increasing Productivity

In business each minute of time is translated into money. If something essential to the operation of a business can be done well in less time then it will ultimately cost less. The more work that can be done in a given amount of time results in the greatest productivity and lowers the cost. Cost saving and time saving both translate into higher profits. To increase time and profit use the following suggestions to increase your personal productivity:

- *Build in flexibility* - have an alternate plan readily available.
- *Increase development* - spend more time making your plans.
- *Improve consistency* - aim to obtain a high result every time.
- *Reduce rework* - do it right the first time and do not do it again.
- *Minimize risk* - use techniques and methods you have tested out.
- *Increase response time* - perform the same task in less and less time.
- *Increase quality* - limit the number of errors or mistakes you produce.
- *Simplify work streams* - breakdown tasks and complicated units of work.
- *Minimize complex interfaces* - simplify tasks and work through them smoothly.
- *Reuse what already exists* - design what you need from something already there.

Revenue and Costs

There is a constant tug of war between revenues and costs, profits and expenses, income and spending. If revenues outpace costs, you have a profitable business. On the other hand if costs exceed revenues you have an organization that is in trouble and out of control. A business must have the proper balance between costs and revenues to insure profitability. The purchasing department breaks down all of its needs in order to operate and meet scheduled goals. Every purchased item must be identified and noted: tools, equipment, facilities, supplies, labor and professional services. Every component of a product or service is broken down and priced to determine how it contributes to the total cost. Information covering all business activities needs to be readily available. You need to be aware of what you pay out and what profit is taken in. Each time a bill, a check at a restaurant, a toll on the road is paid, a newspaper is purchased or you give money to a needy person you need to know how it effects your finances. It is important to keep track and itemize how you spend money. If you are not aware of your spending patterns you can easily get into trouble by spending beyond your means. Just being aware of your personal outgoing costs can increase your profitability.

Quality and Respect

Selling is a matter of having a product or service a customer wants at a fair price and being able to deliver everything you promise. Customers want uniform quality as they rely on products having the same workmanship and produce the same performance results each time they are used. Business people like to feel respected by their customers, their associates, their workers and the people in their community. This desire for a respected place in the community is an important control mechanism on business practices. People prefer to do business with ethical individuals and companies that they can trust and with whom they believe will treat them fairly. The quality of a product is what distinguishes it from others of its type. It is the degree of excellence that separates a product into grades. The quality of an individual can be measured by their character and morality. Our criteria for judging people is based on the small moments that define their character and reputation, that tell people whether someone can be trusted or not and that attracts friends and allies. It is these little defining moments that accumulate over time and shape people's opinions of us. It is the inner personality and essential character of a person that represents their quality and gains the respect of others.

> **Hint:** *It is important when dealing with others to be honest and clear of your purpose in order to build long lasting relationships that endure.*

Financial Decisions

Another strong similarity between business and your life lies in the financial area. Financial decisions can affect both with the same magnitude. Not being able to pay the month's rent or mortgage on your home is the same as not being able to pay the monthly payments on a corporate complex. Not having enough money to pay the bills, spending too much and not doing a good job of saving can result in hardship for both. The key to good finances is good planning, performed early enough before the actual needs arise. Both businesses and individuals need to maintain a set of books to record financial transactions. They must each develop a specific way of accounting for all the money that goes in and goes out as well as a financial plan for how things should be run and how money should be managed.

Financial Statements

The profit and loss statements of a business are the road maps that management uses to steer sound courses and directions for the business operations. They tell management where the business is now, where it can go, how fast it can grow and what is the best way to get there. Your personal monthly budget and cash flow gives the same picture. Your financial statements can be used to project and calculate how much you will need for the future. They show you the details of what you own and its rate of growth. Analyzing these figures can help you plan future savings, make sound investment decisions and decide on areas of diversification. You should know how to organize files, bills, receipts and how to record and handle your savings and expenditures. You should always know what you own and how much you are worth. When a company gets into financial difficulties it is a precursor to layoffs, bankruptcy or going out of business. When you don't pay attention to your personal finances you can be on the road to a crisis when your income is stretched to the absolute limit.

> **Hint:** *To prevent personal difficulties become money savvy and make financial housekeeping one of your priorities.*

Future Needs

The potential for success in business is measured by the ability of a business to respond to changes and needs both internally and externally. Those businesses that respond to future needs tend to succeed. Those which cannot or do not respond tend to decline and fail. Don't get locked in by day-to-day pressures and demands. Take the time to monitor changes and needs in your own life, study their effects and plan measures to deal with them. Don't wait for trouble to develop to first become aware, as often it is too late and any remedy is costly. It is important for you to frequently step back, take a look at things, review your current plans and think with the future in mind.

> **Hint:** *Try to think of your life as a new start-up company, betting on yourself and taking a risk because you believe in the concept.*

Market Expansion

When a company needs to expand their base of operation they add new territories. Upon expansion of their sphere of influence they can attain incredible growth in both numbers of their workforce and capital. When a business decides to locate in a new area they first scope it out. They learn all they can about the people, the land, their tastes and their values. With this information an informed decision can be made as to whether or not they can successfully do business in that location. Once a business takes the plunge and opens up an office in a new city they must quickly assimilate to the culture in order to succeed. To expand your personal horizons, you may decide to embark on a new adventure or do some traveling. You probably have more ideas than the time and resources to implement them. You cannot do everything at once. You will need to make choices. Decide how you wish to expand your sphere of knowledge, learn about different cultures or visit new places. Do your research and educate yourself about the location, then make your plans, set your schedule, create an itinerary and you're off!

Measuring Success

Business has it easy. In order to determine how well the actual operation compares with the planned operation they can measure in quantitative ways - profit, loss, production rates and a score of other numerical statistics. You can measure and track your progress by reaching each step towards your goal but measurement is mostly subjective. Besides counting your assets and debits, you will have personal feelings of satisfaction and accomplishment. The responsibility to reach the objectives, both in business and your personal life is up to top management. Top management creates the organization to carry out the plan. In business, management involves the handling of employees, capital and materials to accomplish the objectives of the firm. In your personal life, management involves the handling of family members, friends, money and goods to accomplish the goals you have set out to achieve.

Good Business Practices

Economic success comes to businesses that practice good business ethics, honesty, accountability, reliability and uphold a good reputation. Practices that protect or make more efficient use of assets are called internal controls. They are the kind of things you may already do because they are generally good practices or policies to follow. This system of controls provides reasonable assurance that risks are being avoided. They involve a wide range of activities. We tend to follow many of the same good practices both in and out of business and our personal lives. As you read through the list of internal controls think how you practice and integrate them into your daily affairs.

Take a look at the following types of controls:

Accounting - Make copies of forms for your records
Compare records to verify transaction details
Keep an inventory of goods, supplies, equipment, etc.

Disaster -   Have emergency escape routes
Make plans for unseen disasters and emergencies
Prioritize processes to be maintained and how to maintain them

Quality -   Insist on reliability
Establish standards for quality
Check for consistent performance

Preventative-Perform credit checks
Get required authorizations
Conduct reference checks and verify information

Security -   Keep cash and valuables out of sight
Protect computer files with passwords
Make sure that doors are locked all the time

Tracking -   Maintain a file of receipts
Document costs and expenses
Track accrued vacation days and sick time

Days-Off Spreadsheet

To maintain control and account for my time off from work I use a spreadsheet to track my vacation, discretionary holidays, personal and sick days. A quick glance shows me the remaining vacation days that I have for the calendar year. *(See page 46)*

VACATION CALENDAR FOR YEAR 2005

DATE	VACATION	D. HOLIDAY	PERSONAL	ILL	DESCRIPTION
1/23			1		Snow Day
3/5–3/12	6				Virginia Trip
4/20	1				House Closing
5/17	1				Home for Delivery
5/21	1				Day in NYC
6/7–6/18	10				Montreal Trip
7/8–7/9				2	Sick Day
9/16–9/17		2			Religious Holiday
10/27	1				Day Off
11/19				1	Dental Work
12/16			1		My Birthday
TOTAL	20	2	2	3	27

Good Operating Principles

Whether you are managing a big operation or your own life, the following principles offer great rules to live by:

- Stay on schedule.

- Start and end on time.

- Make and meet deadlines.

- Be personally accountable for achieving results.

- Set appropriate expectations, goals and target dates.

- When you meet your goals, raise the bar slightly higher.

- Learn and improve from your decisions, both good and bad ones.

- Reward and recognize your accomplishments quickly and visibly.

- Make decisions based on facts, not speculation, guesswork or inaccurate data.

- Ideas are the seeds of innovation; get ideas from anybody or anywhere; every idea deserves consideration.

- Once a decision is made, a decision stands unless new facts are presented that were not previously considered.

- All decisions must support your goals, be consistent with your vision and values and meet your objectives.

Life Components

When I think of my life as a business I assign a separate folder in my mind to each component. I have a separate one for my schedule, personal finances, relationships, work, family, health, hobbies, entertainment and travel. My life is full. Sorting it all out could each fill a drawer or a file cabinet. And that is how I think. I learned to centralize my efforts and integrate my abilities. A well-run business has a special division to handle all the important matters and one or two people to run the whole company. If the head of the company needs advice or information from an operational unit, the data that is requested can be obtained instantly. If you need to make a split second decision you need to rely on data, prior observations and feelings in order to function and move ahead. Combining all your personal resources and strengths will help you function at your maximum efficiency.

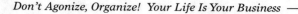

CHAPTER 3

SETTING GOALS AND MAKING PLANS

"Plan for the future, because that's where you
are going to spend the rest of your life."
Mark Twain (1835 - 1910)

For a business to be called a success it must meet or exceed its business goals. Determining what the goal of a business is can greatly differ from one company to another. If the business goal is to make money, financial growth means success. If the business goal is to be socially responsible, helping people in the community means success. If the business goal is to get a judicial decision, winning means success. And if the business goal is to be environmentally productive, saving land and resources means success. Each business must be clear about the goal they wish to meet, as does each individual. Goal setting is an important part of the organization process. In order to come up with a plan you need structure to work towards a goal. Setting goals separates what is important from what is irrelevant. Developing goals is part of the process for gaining insight into what matters or does not matter to you. Having goals helps you decide what is important for you to achieve. They reflect your deepest values, your unique talents, your sense of mission and they grow out of your chosen roles in life.

Goal Setting

Goal setting is the formal process for personal planning. By setting goals on a routine basis you decide what you want to achieve and then move step by step towards the achievement of these goals. The process of setting goals and targets allows you to choose where you want to go in life. Goal setting is one of the most powerful ways to create the life you truly want. People with goals succeed because they know where they are going - they have direction in their life. By knowing precisely what you want to achieve you know what you need to concentrate on to do it and what your distractions are. Goal setting is a standard technique used by top-level athletes, successful business people and achievers in all fields. It provides long-term vision and short-term motivation. It focuses your acquisition of knowledge and helps organize your resources to achieve a specific set of tasks to meet your goal.

Hint: *First you have to clearly define your goal, because you can't hit a target you cannot see.*

Individual Goals

Most successful businesses have a *"mission statement"* - this is essentially a snapshot of their goals. To be most effective goals need to be individualized. Goals need to be suited specifically to you. They need to be honed to represent an optimal challenge. When goals are too easy you are likely to be bored and unmotivated. When goals are too difficult you are likely to be anxious and inefficient. Goals are important for purposes of planning but they are equally important for helping to maintain your motivation. Human behavior is purposive, which means that behavior is directed towards a function or useful outcome. Concentrating on an activity centered on a goal provides fulfillment, and maybe even excitement, as you work to reach your objective. You are motivated when you expect that you can attain your goals. By aiming for goals you will remain on track and be able to assess whether you are making progress.

Benefits of Setting Goals

- *Allows you to accomplish more.*
- *Gives you enthusiasm and motivation.*
- *Helps you focus on what is important to you.*
- *Allows you to work at your maximum potential.*
- *Helps to make full use of your mind and your talents.*
- *Gives you direction and promotes concentration of effort.*

Various Goal Levels

Goals can be set on a number of different levels. Looking at it from an overview you first decide what you want to do with your life and what large-scale goals you want to achieve. Discovering what you want to achieve in your lifetime gives you an overall perspective that shapes all other aspects of your decision-making. Second, you break down the large-scale goals into smaller and smaller targets. Set small manageable personal goals and set a level that you wish to achieve upon their completion. Finally, once you have your plan you start working towards achieving it. You can use daily to-do lists, schedules or agendas to keep you on track and help you measure your success.

Lifetime Goals

Lifetime goals cover broad important areas in your life. Try to set goals in several of the following categories to balance your life. When you begin to seriously think about what you wish to obtain or achieve in your lifetime, it will help to answer the following questions. This will assist in limiting the scope of areas that you wish to concentrate on.

Artistic - Have you explored your creative instincts?
Do you want to draw, dance, write, play music, sing, etc.?

Attitude - Do you maintain a positive attitude?
Is any negative mindset holding you back?

Behavior - Does some of your behavior upset you?
Is there something you wish to change about yourself?

Career - What level do you want to reach in your career?
As a child what did you want to be when you grew up?

Education - Do you need a degree for your perfect job?
Is there any knowledge you wish to acquire?

Family - Are you or will you be a good parent?
Do you want to be a parent or have another child?

Financial - How well do you manage or relate to money?
How much do you want to earn in various stages in your life?

Physical - What steps do you need to take achieve good health?
Do you wish to alter your diet, exercise or nutrition habits?

Pleasure - How do you enjoy yourself?
Can you ensure that some enjoyment is in your life?

Romance - Do you wish to enter into a loving relationship?
Do you want to add more spice to an existing relationship?

Service -   Do you get satisfaction when you help others?
                  Can do something to make the world a better place?

Social -   Are you happy with your friends?
                  Do you wish to meet more people with similar
                  interests?

Spiritual -   Do you wish to devote more time to religious matters?
                  Is your relationship with a higher power all you would
                  like?

List the goals you wish to accomplish. Review the goals and prioritize your list until you are satisfied that your goals reflect the shape of the life that you want to lead. Make sure that the goals that you have set are the goals that you want to achieve - not what your parents, spouse, family, friends or employers want them to be.

What to Focus On

An important part of goal setting is working out where your focus should be directed. Many people work very hard all their lives doing jobs that do little to enhance the quality of their life. It takes time to clarify what you enjoy and what you wish to achieve. However, it is important for your quality of life that you enjoy your job, your family, your friends and yourself. If you already know what you like and dislike you will be more able to set your goals towards doing things that you enjoy and wish to achieve. You are much more likely to accomplish a goal and do a task effectively if you love it and are passionate about it. When you feel passionate about something you tend to create a way to make it happen. However, every job has tedious or unpleasant elements to it. It is important that these elements are minimal. As you begin to understand what your strengths and weaknesses are you will also discover your talents. You will learn to play upon your strengths and minimize your weaknesses to move in the right direction. When choosing your goals try to concentrate on what you actually enjoy rather than what you think you should do. Clarify each task and concentrate on doing it well.

Here are some tips to help you decide what to focus on:

- Learn to listen to yourself.
- Discover and follow your path.
- Find goals that feel right to you in your heart.
- Experience more to make your self-discovery easier.
- Observe yourself to discover what makes you feel good.
- Acknowledge your passions so you can be more successful.
- Be active, not passive and try to find out what you really want.

Hint: *The goals you decide to work towards today will affect your future.*

Setting Goals Effectively

An effective goal is one that focuses on results. For a goal to be effective, it must be realistic and achievable within a given amount of time. You should state a goal as a positive statement and explicitly express what you wish the outcome to be. You should set a precise goal; using dates and times to measure your achievements. If you set goals like this you will know exactly when you have reached the goal and can take complete satisfaction from having achieved it. When you have several goals, give each a priority. This helps avoid feeling overwhelmed by too many goals and directs your attention to the most important ones. Write goals down to crystallize them and give them more force. Set realistic goals, ones you can achieve. You may not see the obstacles along the way or understand quite how many skills you must master to achieve a particular level of performance. Do not set goals too low. People tend to set low goals when they are afraid of failure or when they lack self-confidence. Set goals which are slightly out of your immediate grasp but not so far that there is no hope of achieving them. If your goal involves a behavioral change, such as dieting, smoking or anger management, reach out to those you trust who can be helpful and supportive. Having a good support system can often play a key role in your success.

Break Down Goals

In order to reach your lifetime plan, you need to set small goals. Break down a goal into steps. Keep goals small and achievable. You will feel that you are not making progress towards your goal if it seems too large. Small goals give more opportunities for rewards. You need to separate and then prioritize all the tasks that you need to complete if you are to reach your lifetime goals. These tasks should be listed sequentially, as most often; the completion of one must be done before another can begin. Create a to-do list of things that you need to do today and in the future to work towards your lifetime goals. At an early stage some of your tasks may be to read books and gather information on the achievement of your goals. Research and education will help you to improve the quality and realism of your goal setting. Once you have broken down large tasks into smaller components review your plans and make sure that they fit the way in which you want to live your life. Once you have decided on your first set of plans, keep the process going by reviewing and updating your to-do list on a daily basis.

> **Hint:** *Periodically review long-term plans and modify them to reflect your changing priorities and experience.*

Whose Priorities Are They?

Priorities by definition are the goals, dreams and concepts that we deem important. The terrible truth about priorities is that they exert far more control over us than we do over them. Other people may have the power or authority (like our superiors at work) to tell us what they think our priorities should be, but we still have the choice and the will to decide whether or not we accept these priorities as our own. If there is a conflict, you can walk away. Unfortunately, very few people are actually clear on their priorities. The options range from the obvious appeal of fame and fortune to the simpler pleasures of spending more time with your family, finishing a project that is important to you or saving for the future. Clearly spell out in your mind which of these options is number one in your life. However, even when you have your priorities straight in your mind it is often hard to keep them in order.

How to Prioritize Your Goals

Once you have a list of goals you would like to accomplish and have broken them down into sizable tasks, it is time to decide which ones need to be performed first. No one can do everything at once and some tasks depend upon the completion of other tasks. It is time to rank one against the other in order of importance. If you have broken down your tasks in the right manner this should be easy to do. Think logically as you make the decision about what must be done before any others. Sure, you can do everything out of order but being organized is making a decision about what comes first, what must be done next and what is dependent upon something else. Fight the pressure to make split second judgments and leave time to sleep on it for a day or two. Review all the steps in your mind in the order of importance to see if you agree with the priority and rating you have assigned to each task.

Decide to Decide

Making a decision is making a choice. Life is a series of choices that we make about how we will or will not act. All of our choices can have positive or negative influences later on in life. Choice is choosing from alternatives and almost every alternative is better than doing nothing. Reduce your stress level by streamlining your decision-making. This will ultimately increase the time you have for yourself. Maintain your resolve when setting goals and prioritizing them. Once you have made a decision, do not go back on it, even if you have second thoughts. Get past the decision stage and start on the doing stage. Move yourself closer to finding more time for yourself, to spend that time however you choose and be closer to your goals.

Here are some points to keep in mind:

- Do it now!
- Be proactive.
- Remove doubts.
- Be clear and definite
- Write everything down.
- Crystallize your thoughts.
- Eliminate procrastination.
- Maintain a positive attitude.
- Do not make excuses for yourself.
- Give yourself credit for your successes.

Be Proactive

Setting a goal unifies your efforts and energy. It gives meaning and purpose to all you do. When you are proactive you make things happen each day that will enable you to meet your goal. You perform activities that keep you moving forward. Highly proactive people recognize responsibility. They do not blame circumstances or conditions on anyone else. They believe they are solely responsible for all their actions and decisions. Proactive people keep commitments made to themselves and others, take the initiative, think positive and work towards achieving their goals. Having the power to make and keep commitments is the essence of effectiveness.

Achieving Goals

By setting sharp clearly defined goals you can measure and take pride in your achievements. You can see progress in what might previously have seemed a long pointless road. As you obtain each goal you will also raise your self-confidence as you recognize your ability and competence. The process of achieving goals and seeing this achievement gives you confidence that you will be able to achieve higher and more difficult goals. When you have achieved a goal, take the time to enjoy the satisfaction of having done so. Absorb the implications of each goal's achievement and observe the process you have made towards other goals.

Reward Yourself

Reward yourself for completing all or part of a task. The reward is the inducement you offer yourself for work done well. It is a part of an end result that you can look forward to. If you work two or three hours each day on a big project, reward yourself at the end of each work period with something that you enjoy that is relaxing or pleasant.

Some of my favorite rewards are to:

- Watch TV
- Take a nap
- Take a walk
- Read a book

- Listen to music
- Take a relaxing bath
- Have a piece of cake
- Have a cup of coffee
- Enjoy a glass of wine
- Telephone a good friend

Give yourself an even bigger reward for having completed a particularly difficult or dreaded task:

- Get a haircut
- Get a massage
- Buy a new outfit
- Go to a theatre play
- Buy a gift for yourself
- Meet a friend for lunch
- Spend a morning in bed
- Go to an afternoon movie
- Spend the day/weekend at a spa
- Have dinner at a great restaurant

Incorporate your reward system in your daily or weekly routine. It should be a part of the day that you look forward to. Remember to reward yourself often, as it is a way to feel good about an achievement.

Perfectionism

If you believe that only you can get it right and always strive for perfect results you are probably a perfectionist. The dictionary defines perfectionism as *"the practice of setting exceedingly high goals or standards for oneself or for others"*. Perfectionists find all sorts of ways to waste time while striving for exceptional results every day. Perfectionists fear making a mistake, always try to do a superior job and constantly worry about what others think of them. They tend to repeat things over and over until they feel they have finally gotten it exactly right. They are afraid to let anyone else do anything for them because they believe the other person will not be able to do it as perfectly as they can. They are rarely satisfied with how something gets done, even if they did it themselves. People who are perfectionists have developed unique habits to deal with things and use them as an excuse to avoid doing something. They tend to confuse excellent with perfect.

Letting Go of Perfectionism

Excellence is less than perfect but is still *"the best"* and *"first-rate"*. Try to rid yourself of perfectionism by retraining yourself to expect excellent rather than perfect results. Try to lower your expectations and standards of yourself by understanding that being average should be *"being just good"* and you are still doing very well. Don't let making a mistake devastate you. Mistakes are to be expected and should not be considered unconstructive. Mistakes are opportunities to learn something new or to try another method. Learn to delegate by giving away parts or all of task. As long as someone else does it well, you don't have to worry about doing it perfectly. To teach yourself to stop giving in to perfectionism, let at least one imperfect thing happen to you everyday. Intentionally forget to wear your wristwatch, be a bit late for an appointment or wear a pair of shoes that do not perfectly match the rest of your outfit.

Not Meeting Your Goals

There is no better indicator of the health of a project then steady activity. If, on the other hand, time goes by and nothing positive has happened to keep you moving forward then this may be a sign that your goal needs to be re-evaluated. It is important to remember that when your performance falls short to view the situation as a problem to be solved - not as a basis for self-criticism. If you meet an unanticipated obstacle, failed to meet your goal or did not have enough time, do not be too hard on yourself. If too many things hinder you from reaching your goal, don't abandon it - just change your direction to get there. If you have learned from it, it really does not matter. It is better to think about how this can be improved next time to produce more positive results rather than being critically evaluative. What you need to do is integrate the lessons learned back into your goal-setting program. If your goal is set too high then now is a good time to be more realistic and break it down into smaller pieces or give yourself more time to complete it. Make sure your goals are well defined so that you know exactly what steps you need to do or perform to get it done. Your goals may change a bit as you work your way through the tasks. Your goals will also change as you mature and gain more experience. Review your long-term goals and adjust them regularly to reflect this growth. If a goal no longer holds any attraction, then let it go. Goal setting is your servant, not your master. It should bring you real pleasure, satisfaction and a sense of achievement.

> **Hint:** *Goals should help you plan to live your life your way.*

Motivation

Motivation must come from within. It comes from deciding you are ready to take responsibility for managing yourself. When people are really ready to change for their own personal reasons and they are willing to face and cope with a multitude of feelings - anxiety, inadequacy, rage, terror, or loneliness - that trigger their behavior, then they will have the motivation for change. A deep personal desire for change must come first. Then you can take steps to plan and set goals. Having long-range goals helps you to deal with short-term failures. The satisfaction of meeting your goal will most often be your biggest reward. If you are not really ready to work hard towards your goal, reconsider if this goal is really what you desire at this moment in your life.

> **Hint:** *Completing a task and being able to reach a small step towards your goal will give you inner satisfaction and a feeling of accomplishment.*

Meeting Your Goals

Each time you achieve a goal you are building confidence in your own talents and abilities. You can be certain that each step you take closer to your goal will give you the assurance that you will take it to completion. Each goal that you set for yourself should be small enough so that you can complete it within the time you have allotted for it. For instance, if you are trying to loss weight, setting a goal of 5 pounds is better than setting a goal of 50 pounds. If a goal is set too high or is too large to be manageable, it becomes overwhelming. Before you set your goals make sure that you are willing to make any necessary sacrifices before committing to them. Again, if your goal is to lose weight and get fit you must be willing to change habits, attitudes and discipline yourself. You will need to learn and practice eating differently and increase the amount of exercise you do. If your goals are small enough and planned out properly over time it will not feel like a sacrifice. But if you are spending time on a project you dislike, is not going anywhere or is not teaching you anything, simply let it go. A decision to pursue a goal may have been wrong to begin with or may have turned unpleasant in the course of executing it. You don't need a lot of good reasons to kill a bad decision - you just need one.

Action Plans

An action plan is a list of tasks that you have to carry out to achieve an objective. Although it may seem to be the same thing, it differs from a to-do list in that it focuses on the achievement of a single goal. A to-do list can include a combination of tasks encompassing several goals, or just a list of things you need to get done, with no specific goal in mind. Whenever you want to achieve a specific purpose, draw up a plan of action. This allows you to concentrate on the stages of a specific achievement and monitor your progress.

Example of an Action Plan

Here is the action plan I created when I began to write this book. It is an example of one you can create for yourself - using one of your goals.

Objective: Write a Non-Fiction Book

1. Select the topic I wish to write about
2. Have a specific idea in mind that I want the book to convey
3. Think about what sections of the reader market to address
4. Decide what to write about
5. Prepare chapter headings
6. Jot down ideas and topics to discuss in each chapter
7. Do research on specific topics
8. Start writing one chapter at a time
9. Re-read chapters and make each concise
10. Create charts or spreadsheets
11. Write an introduction
12. Prepare a glossary and index

13. Prepare website information
14. Put it all together
15. Have others review the book for ideas and comments
16. Decide to incorporate suggested new concepts or ideas
17. Proofread manuscript
18. Develop a book proposal
19. Find a book agent or publisher
20. Congratulate myself

To draw up an action plan list the tasks that you need to carry out to achieve your goal. This may seem simple but it is very useful. Use it to carry out each task on the list. When you are done, move on to your next objective.

Taking a Risk

Sometimes you just need to take a risk to be successful or move towards your goal. Taking risks challenges your comfort zone and requires some initial feelings of discomfort. You need to find out what is right for you. Sometimes you may regret that you did not take a risk. It may bring out your vulnerable side. You fear that things won't work out. When thinking about taking a risk, think about the worst thing that can happen and how you will be able to deal with it. The maximum risk is being successful. Then evaluate how important it is to you. Risks are relative and have different levels of responsibility. They can change over time and take on a different importance in your life. You may be unaware that you have taken risks in your life; when you move to a different city, start a new job or school, buy a home or investment, attempt something new or begin a relationship.

Measuring Success

There are no scoreboards, rules, officials or referees who will tell you if you have done something right or wrong. Most often you have to rely on your feelings. A feeling of competence results when you take on and meet the challenge or complete the task. The need to feel competent and successful is an important energizer. The feeling of being effective occurs spontaneously only when you have worked hard. To feel competent you only need to take on a meaningful personal challenge and give it your best. Evaluating your performance is always done against some explicit or implicit standard. You do well or poorly only with respect to some set of expectations about how you may be able to do at that time and place. If goals have been properly set they can represent the standard against which performance is used to evaluate. If you participate in setting your goal you can also participate in evaluating your own performance.

> **Hint:** *You will feel successful when you enjoy the benefits of reaching the goal.*

Strategies for Success

- **Always give each goal a deadline** -
  A deadline helps you measure success and gives you something to shoot towards.

- **Avoid setting too many goals at once** -
  Too many goals will not allow you to focus on the most important ones.

- **Be true to yourself and set goals that fit your personality** -
  Do not let others influence you or set your goals for you.

- **Be positive and enthusiastic** -
  Projecting a good feeling about the outcome will affect your eagerness and zeal.

- **Be proactive and stop wasting time doing too much *"over thinking"*** -
  Concentrate on and support activities that get things done.

- **Be specific about your goals** -
  Pinpointing exactly what you wish to achieve will clearly define your objectives.

- **Divide and conquer; break goals into small pieces** -
  Completing small goals & tasks makes you feel that you have accomplished a lot.

- **Don't fight change** -
  Go with the flow or you will be left behind if you stand in the same spot in our rapidly changing world.

- **Don't agonize over minor decisions** -
  Small issues do not make a big difference in the big picture.

- **Don't let other people wear you down** -
  Be confident in your abilities and avoid critical people.

- **Give your goals top priority** -
  Remember, you are the most important person in your life.

- **Have long-range goals as well as short-range goals** -
  A well-balanced life includes lifetime goals in addition to day-to-day goals.

- **Know when to stop: avoid too much information or over analyzing** -
  Sometimes you just have to bite the bullet and begin.

- **Never lose sight of your overall objective** -
  Always have a clear vision of your goal in mind.

- **Overcome indecision** -
  Ignore feelings of insecurity about your decisions.

- **Understand the rewards of risk taking** -
  Taking a risk can make the result much more satisfying.

- **Use a tally sheet for pros and cons** -
  In times of indecision try summing up all the positives and negatives.

- **Visualize success and keep your eyes on your goal** -
  Form a mental image of the result of your achievements.

- **Watch out for roadblocks and obstacles** -
  Always be on the lookout for people and situations that hold up your progress.

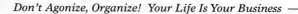

CHAPTER 4

TIME MANAGEMENT SKILLS

"If you want to make good use of time you've
got to know what's most important..."
Lee Iacocca (1924 -   )

Time is the unlimited duration in which things are considered as happening in the past, present and future. It is every moment there has ever been or ever will be. Time can never be replaced; once spent it is gone forever. It can be a valuable commodity. In business you often hear "time is money". Time and money are inter-connected in the business world. In manufacturing, the loss of production time means loss of profit. You can miss out on a great deal by just not being at the right place at the right time. A minute or two of trading on the stock market affects the economics of countries worldwide. Your time is also related to money. The time you spend working to earn a living ultimately buys what you need and enjoy. The sooner you start saving and investing for college and retirement, the more money you will have when the time comes. Time is precious and there is just so much of it. By saving time doing things you do not like doing or must do you can spend that time doing things that bring you pleasure. Learning how to organize your life and managing your time will afford you more free time to spend as you wish.

Control Your Life

Managing your time is a way of bringing control into your life. Without a schedule you are not in control. Circumstances that just pop up tend to dictate your actions. By managing your time you can arrange and administer all your affairs when you wish to deal with them. With careful management of your time you can get a jump on big projects so they do not overwhelm you. You can schedule free time whenever you wish. You can instantaneously juggle and revise your schedule to your heart's content. You are the skillful master of your life. What you decide to include in or take out of your schedule is all under your control.

The Art of Time Management

Time management is a very important concept to learn and practice. Time can be kept, killed, longed for, lost, saved, spent or wasted. At its most basic time management can be defined as the art of being able to divide your time into sizable durations giving you the ability to control and plan what is happening inside of each timeframe. However, only through trial and error will you begin to master it. You first need to learn how to go about organizing your time.

Next, you must become proficient at arranging your schedule. Then you must learn by application. Every new schedule and every new application of it will increase your comfort level. As with any other art or skill you need to take the time to carefully fine tune it and make adjustments until it works best for you. Once you have become expert at it, it will no longer be a chore. Eventually it should become a part of your regular daily routine and you will come to rely on it.

Time Management Misconceptions

• *Efficiency and effectiveness are the same* - being efficient is doing things quickly and properly but efficiency is not time management. To get results you have to be effective, knowing what your priorities are and doing the right things at the right time to achieve your objectives. Effectiveness is doing the right things and good time management will enable you to do things right.

• *To do a job properly, do it yourself* - the ability and willingness to delegate tasks is essential to good time management. Conversely, the inability or unwillingness to delegate is one of the primary reasons for not managing time efficiently. By not delegating tasks that are not relevant to your objectives, you cannot focus on the things that will make a difference to your results.

• *There's only one right way to do a job* - it is always worth spending some time thinking about how a particular time consuming task could be done more efficiently. Don't allow yourself to get into a rut - ask yourself questions like: What is the required outcome of something? What do I wish to accomplish?

• *Time management is a waste of time* - a good time manager spends some time each day thinking and planning activities that are vital to long-term success. Having properly planned and scheduled your tasks for the day will increase your effectiveness and you will be less troubled by the pressure of time.

• *A good time manager lacks creativity* - good time management techniques are there to be used when and how you choose. They are designed to remove unwanted crisis management and panic from your working day and to allow more time for creativity. You can also get very creative with the time management techniques you tailor to yourself.

Identify Time Wasters

Surprisingly, most of us do not have an accurate picture of how we spend our time. To learn to manage your time better, see how you currently spend it. Just as auditors overlook a business by auditing the books checking for accurate record keeping, auditing your time can be useful. We may think that we know how long we spend on each task but these impressions usually turn out to be inaccurate when compared to a detailed time log. In order to truly evaluate time wasters you need to keep track of how you currently spend your time. Time logs show time we forget about - time spent opening and reading junk mail, talking to a friend on the phone, making morning coffee, eating lunch out, comparison shopping, etc.

Interruptions

An interruption is an unanticipated event that disturbs you either in person or electronically, via telephone, fax, e-mail, beeper or pager. With each interruption your distraction tends to increase and the potential for getting things done decreases. It is best to keep interruptions to a minimum. Here are a few suggestions to do just that:

Telephone Interruptions
- Turn off the ringer and send calls directly to voicemail.
- Use an answering machine or screen your telephone calls.
- Do not assume that each time the phone rings it is important.
- Tell the caller you are busy and ask them politely to call another time.
- If you must have a phone conversation politely ask to get right to the point.

Room Interruptions
- Do not make eye contact.
- You can walk out of the room.
- Frequently look at your watch to give a hint about the time.
- Close the door so no one can walk into the room without knocking.

- Do not have any extra chairs around to sit down and get comfortable.

Child Interruptions
- Prepare activities for your children.
- Use rewards for not being interrupted.
- Prepare snacks for your children to get for themselves.
- Schedule serious work when your children are not at home.
- Explain to your children the importance of not interrupting you.

Keeping a Log

Keeping a time or activity log for several days helps you to understand when you perform best during the day. You may also be unaware that your energy level changes at different times of the day. You may be more alert and active in the morning. You may possess heightened awareness or have a stronger attention span in the late afternoon. You can easily see how you use your time by keeping a log or journal that details what tasks you did, when and how long you spent doing each. It is similar to making a photo album as you take small snapshots of time and record them in your album. Plan a normal day and do not alter your usual behavior. Each time you change your activity, note it and jot down the time of day. Biologically everyone has his or her best time of the day. Note how you feel at certain times of the day - are you tired, depressed, energetic, alert, moody, etc. Recording in a log should not take more than ten minutes a day and you can analyze the results. Looking carefully you will see minutes spent on time wasters that could be put to more profitable use. Ask yourself: *"If I had planned ahead would I do things differently?"*

As you look back at your time log entries ask yourself some of these questions:

- Do you need more free time?
- Did you take too many breaks?
- Could you have combined some errands?
- Have you made the best use of your time?
- Did you include everything you need to do?
- Did you spend too much time doing nothing?

:d for the most important tasks first?
: for an appointment or with time to spare?
back and make adjustments to your

gh time allotted to the items that must get

ted your tasks evenly among the days in the

e for traveling in-between appointments,

mple tool you can use to record how your time s you to make adjustments and take corrective nized and increase your productivity.

make to organize and control time has gone
history. We attempt to comprehend the past,
edict the future. We are a culture who lives
he beginning of our lives we are always made
count the days, weeks, months and years to
t of the sun, moon and stars. We try to cap-
mall squares that spread out like a network.
up of small boxes that contain everything
nd no more. With thousands of little squares
gical lifetime. Calendar time has a past, a
When that day is over you cannot return to
l.

age your time, you must develop a schedule.
imes by creating an inventory of actions. To
: a list of all the activities you must do, need
fter writing each of them down, categorize
ies that you must get done; you absolutely
be a daily chore or a job or just housework.
nal things that you need to do depending on
ght be tasks like dropping a coat off at the

cleaners or starting to write a business report a bit early. Last are the activities that you just want to do. For instance, visiting the art museum to see a new exhibit, going shopping, planning a vacation or enjoying a new movie.

To-Do List

A to-do list is a list of all the tasks and activities you need to carry out. Try looking at a to-do list as a roadmap of what you have to do and what you want to do over the next twenty-four hours to maximize your efficiency. Having only one list consolidates all the jobs that you must do. These lists are very simple to devise and are extremely powerful tools. A glance at your list acts as a method of organization to reduce stress. Depend on your to-do list as a way to relieve everyday pressure. There are enough situations that are beyond one's control that create tension. Why should you create additional stress for yourself when it can so easily be avoided? When there are many demands being made upon you, look at your list or jot something down. If you are burdened by a problem, use your list as way to record things to think about or research at a later time. If you have made too many commitments use it as way to get back on track, back on schedule. It helps give you a feeling of control over your life.

> **Hint:** *You may have to periodically revise your to-do list in response to changing schedules and priorities. At the same time, be prepared to renegotiate deadlines with yourself.*

Make a List

The first list you create should be composed of anything and everything. Write down whatever you need to accomplish and complete. Some of the tasks will just pop into your mind and others you will have to actively think about. Try to recollect any items you have been thinking about. Look a week or two ahead and anticipate anything coming up. One example would be to make an appointment for your car inspection a few weeks before it is due or to purchase a gift for an upcoming birthday. Try to break large tasks down and list them as several smaller components. After you have written all the various items on paper they should no longer be taking up any space in your mind and you may even feel relieved. You will feel a sense of comfort and satisfaction by having created your first list and you can now proceed to the next step.

SAMPLE LIST FOR STEP 1

MAKE A LIST
JOT DOWN WHATEVER TASKS YOU THINK OF

1. *Estimated quarterly taxes due next Friday*
2. *Look into plans for a vacation*
3. *Pick up tickets for concert*
4. *Buy office supplies*
5. *Return books and DVDs to library - due 2/15*
6. *Arrange to meet with Becky to coordinate treasurer notes*
7. *Call Fred - Re: new roof*
8. *Update resume*
9. *Make dentist appointment*
10. *Research adult education course*
11. *Renew driver's license*
12. *Write letter to Claude in Paris*
13. *Buy new cartridge for printer*
14. *Give dog a bath*
15. *Buy gift for Adam's wedding*

Categorize Your List

Hopefully, the prior example will give you an idea of how to go about creating your own list and what types of items you should be listing. The next step is to review each item on the list to decide if the task is one that you:

*1 - Absolutely need to get done and **have** to do before many of the others on the list.*

*2 - Just want to complete because these are items you feel you **need** to do for yourself or others.*

*3 - Only **want** to do and there is no urgency attached to when they need to be done.*

First ask yourself if you can perform the task i
ner or if it can be delegated to someone else
think about an item, the level of anxiety and a
feel about it can help determine how you sep
particular category. Only you are aware of the
the tasks you have listed. For items that you h
plete before all others your stress level wil
urgency of their completion. As the deadline
the significance of the task will increase and
ciated with the task may also rise. By placi
gories you are beginning to organize your pri

Hint: *It is always best to complete tasks bef*
gets out of hand and you begin to feel helpless

SAMPLE LIST FOR STEP 2

SEPARATE EACH TASK INTO ONE OF TH

A - THINGS YOU <u>HAVE</u> TO DO
Estimated quarterly taxes due next Frida
Return books and DVDs to library - due 2
Arrange to meet with Becky to coordinat
Renew driver's license
Buy new cartridge for printer

B - THINGS YOU <u>NEED</u> TO DO
Pick up tickets for concert
Buy office supplies
Make dentist appointment
Give dog a bath
Buy gift for Adam's wedding

C - THINGS YOU <u>WANT</u> TO DO
Look into plans for a vacation
Call Fred - Re: new roof
Update resume
Research adult education course
Write letter to Claude in Paris

Prioritize Your List

After you have made the list and separated each item into one of the three categories, you're ready for the next step. Prioritize each entry as to its relationship and importance to the others in the same category. This will enable you to tackle your tasks in the order of their importance. To accomplish your main tasks you will often need to place equally desirable but less important ones at a lower priority. Remember to balance any commitments and responsibilities to others with tasks that only concern you. You will need to estimate the amount of time it will take you to complete each of the tasks on your list. Take time to compare them to each other and evaluate which has a higher priority. Then write down a number, with one being the highest priority, next to each item. Prioritize each in relation to the others in terms of the importance of completion. Separate the important jobs from the many time-consuming trivial jobs.

Hint: Try hard to perform the task you dread the most, first. By doing this one thing everything else you do afterwards will be a breeze.

Estimating Time

Figuring how much time it will take you to complete tasks may seem to be the hardest part. However, you probably already know how much time to allot for attending a movie or a play. You know how much time it will take you to get dressed and ready for a night out on the town. You know how long it will take you to go to the cleaners and back again. You might even decide to combine a task with other errands that are in the same neighborhood or in the near vicinity. As a matter of fact, this would be good planning. Sometimes you will have to estimate how long a task will take you to complete. This is especially true for a new assignment or traveling to someplace unfamiliar. Try to build in a little padding, in terms of the time, as you may have to deal with some unexpected situations such as traffic, interruptions, running into a friend or just getting lost.

SAMPLE LIST FOR STEP 3

PRIORITIZE ALL THE ENTRIES WITHIN E
WRITE DOWN HOW MUCH TIME TO COMI

A - THINGS YOU HAVE TO DO

1. *Renew driver's license*
2. *Return books and DVDs to library - du*
3. *Arrange to meet with Becky to coordin treasurer notes*
4. *Estimated quarterly taxes due next Fr*
5. *Buy new cartridge for printer*

B - THINGS YOU NEED TO DO

1. *Buy gift for Adam's wedding*
2. *Pick up tickets for concert*
3. *Give dog a bath*
4. *Buy office supplies*
5. *Make dentist appointment*

C- THINGS YOU WANT TO DO

1. *Look into plans for a vacation*
2. *Update resume*
3. *Research adult education course*
4. *Call Fred - Re: new roof*
5. *Write letter to Claude in Paris*

Accurate Estimating

Once you build your experience for c;
mates they will become more accurate and
vastly underestimate the amount of time
task. This is particularly true when they
task to be carried out. They forget to take
or unscheduled events. People often fail
plexity involved with a task. To accuratel
understand what you need to achieve. T!
task in detail so that there are no unknow
the task is to list all of the components in !
broken down the task into the smallest r
best guess at how long each task will take

> **Hint:** *Accurate time estimation is essential to good time management as it drives the setting of deadlines and target dates.*

Be Selective

Think about how much reward will result from the investment of the time that it will take to perform a task. If the time spent outweighs the reward, decide not to include it on your list. Your everyday decisions of how you use your time (e.g., traveling, phone conversations, lunch with a work associate, meeting new people, searching for something specific on the Internet, attending a lecture, etc.) should be weighed against the reward you expect to receive. You can be selective and say no to an opportunity or task where the time to result ratio is not in balance. Being able to assess and reject dead end tasks is an effective control in the management of your personal time.

How to Use Your List

People use to-do lists in different ways for many situations. I like to have one for each day to keep on track. I keep a separate to-do list for all the tasks that I have not yet scheduled to work on. Following a list is like following roadmap directions, which are a lot easier to do than following a map or creating a path. Once you start at the beginning of your list, after completing one task, you know exactly what to do next. You do not have to think, decide or prioritize, only read what is next. You can use it to plan your day and schedule what tasks can be easily grouped together (running several errands in the same area or shopping for a few gifts at the same store), what tasks are the most important to get done, what order to best perform them and what can wait for later. Once your list is ready you can use it to format a schedule for yourself.

Design a Schedule

Now you are ready to compose a weekly schedule for yourself. Go to a stationary store and shop for a daily diary or calendar that is divided into hourly increments. Find one that is big enough for you to read but small enough to be able to carry with you, or consider a Palm Pilot or some type of electronic PDA (personal digital assis-

tant). Sit down in a quiet space and take o
categorized list of things to do. Start your da
tant items on your agenda. It spares you from
about them the rest of the day. That worr
whether you realize it or not, slows you down.
ing person" perform the tasks that require th
are most alert. Fill in all the blocks of time
job or activity you must do and cross out that
down all the things you need to do. Remem
ty you have assigned to each. List each task
ority within the category. You are not expec
one day. Lastly, fill in what you want do to
Do not forget to leave some free time to jus
fun. Now that you have completed your tim
you must be exhausted. So take a rest befor

*Hint: The real trick is sticking to your sched
changes along the way and still getting it a*

10 Simple Scheduling Tips

1. *Don't rush*
2. *Be on time*
3. *Get up early*
4. *Put things near the door*
5. *Don't stay up past your bedtime*
6. *Get a good alarm clock and battery ba*
7. *Set your alarm clock correctly (AM vs*
8. *Think ahead and always ask what cou*
9. *Prepare your clothes, briefcase, etc. th*
10. *Make signs to remind you - take lunch*

Overload

No matter how organized you are you   ien
you feel so overloaded your stress level   You
feel as though you are overrun by a sen   ess-
ness, no longer in control. I get into th   lays
after multi-tasking at work, talking on th   ails
and handling crisis after crisis - then coming home to face a whole

new set of obligations and situations concerning family, friends, relatives and finances. Stress can be a killer. Feeling like you have to handle all the issues at once you have to face the fact that this can't be done. The only way to stop the overload is to meet it head on. Sit down and try to relax, close your eyes for a moment, concentrate on your breathing and take your mind somewhere else. You have to cut into the seriousness of the overload and handle one issue at a time. Accept the fact that even though you are capable of multi-tasking you are only humanly able to perform one action within each second of time. Prioritize and deal with the one most pressing situation. You may not get to handle all your issues that day but at least you will get some squared away and by using good time management skills you will have the opportunity to tackle the rest tomorrow.

Crisis Management

Time management is the essence of organization. Without it you may not pick up your suit from the cleaners before your big meeting, you may have to pay additional interest charges on all your unpaid bills, you may arrive at the library after it has closed and you may not be left with any free time. Learning good time management techniques teaches how to complete all your work and still have time to breathe. It allows you to check your progress on a project to determine if you are still on schedule. It avoids a crisis. Crisis management is what results when a deadline has arrived and you are now a slave to the clock instead of being in control of your time. All your packing prior to a trip should be completed so you do not have to stay up the night before thinking of what you forgot to pack. Ideally, your taxes should be completed a few days before they need to be submitted. When your computer printer runs out of ink you will have time to get a new cartridge before your business report is due. You will be able to relax the night before the big party you are giving. Your stress level will be normal.

Hint: If you are able to learn and practice good time management techniques, your life will be easier.

Do It Now!

The most powerful technique used in time management is to make an instant decision or to immediately perform a task when you first hear about it, first think about it or remember that you must do it. Instead of putting something off into the future you can get it out of the way, right now. You get instant results because of your quick action and enjoy a rousing sense of accomplishment. Getting things resolved as soon as you can eliminates something to add to your to-do list. Too many tasks left undone will create an overwhelming list that keeps on growing. Eventually the length of the to-do list can prevent you from acting on it. Your best defense against crisis management and overload is to start that report, make that telephone call, set up that appointment, buy that gift, join that gym, begin that diet, visit your relative or pay that bill as soon as you possibly can.

Make Decisions

Decision-making is an important aspect of time management for classifying activities by urgency and importance. Do not agonize over each and every activity. Focus on the main reasons or arguments to pursue a task. Do not spend too much time analyzing the pros and cons - it can paralyze you. Having already decided how important each task is, progress through the tasks quickly and efficiently. If you want to improve your decision making you will need to identify a job you put off and the reasons and excuses you give yourself. Admit to the real reason for putting off a task and change the way you feel about the task. Putting off jobs we dislike is a common trait. Putting off jobs has another disadvantage in that it tends to lead to an increasing number of tasks that remain outstanding. This growing list becomes increasingly daunting and it then becomes more and more difficult to start on any of them. The best way to apply time management is simply to begin. Taking the first step is often the hardest thing to do.

Reasons Why People Procrastinate

There are many reasons why people procrastinate. Aside from wasting time in the present it can become a personal frustration. A life of indecision does not help you to accomplish your goals or give your life fulfillment. It is important to sit down and think about why you procrastinate. Your reasons may frustrate you because they seem so easy to correct and control. Once you understand the reason and face the problem you can take the first step to overcome it.

Here are a few common reasons people procrastinate and why this behavior can occur:

1. **Do not know how to begin** - Feeling of helplessness, do not know where or how to start the project.

2. **Task seems too time consuming or overwhelming** - Your goal is set too high, it seems too difficult or complex.

3. **Procrastination is a regular habit** - You have done it for so long, it seems normal.

4. **Task is tedious and boring** - Your image of the task is not exciting and may not be realistic.

5. **Fearful of change and new situations** - Change can seem intimidating and not changing keeps you feeling comfortable.

6. **Worry about being judged on your efforts and work** - You worry how others look at you and you seek the approval of others.

7. **There is no deadline so there is no rush to get started** - No time limits can lead to a cycle of endless procrastination.

8. **Feel unworthy of your accomplishments and successes** - Feel you do not deserve all the good things and recognition that comes your way.

9. **Like to do things at the last minute** - Find last minute scrambling exciting but also exhausting.

10. **Rather be doing something else** - Activity holds no draw or value for you and probably not connected to a goal.

11. **Someone else will do it if you postpone it long enough** - Not taking responsibility or being dependable and accountable.

12. **Fear the end results** - Believe that you will accomplish all that you set out to but still won't be happy or content once you reach your goal.

How to Overcome Procrastination

You can postpone and delay so long that often the time for action has passed by the time you do act. Sometimes you have to combat the negative feelings you have and move forward.

To help you take action here are some suggestions:

- Attack one problem at a time
- Accept the challenge

- Be decisive

- Concentrate, keep your mind clear
- Decide to delegate or dump it
- Do not allow distractions
- Do the most important stuff first

- Get it off your plate
- Get organized

- Get motivated
- 1-2-3 Begin

- Have a positive attitude
- Just start even if it is a *"baby step"*
- Make a bold decision to change
- Make deadlines
- Plan ahead
- Reward yourself
- Set a definite amount of time
- Set priorities
- Keep the task small and *"doable"*
- Take a risk
- Just go for it!

Hint: *Don't start what you can't finish and finish what you start.*

Be Accountable

Like it or not, you are accountable for your own actions. No matter how hard you try, you cannot blame someone else. The more accountability you accept, the better your odds are for success, the more you are in control. You are not at the mercy of other people's schedules or objectives. The things you decide to do, or not to do, or put off until the last moment, are up to you. If you ignore a task - it will not get done and it will not go away. If you feel exasperated about all the tasks you choose to tackle, you may do one or two and drop the rest. The goal for time management is getting tangible results. Complete all the things you have to do and do not wait until the last minute to do them. Prioritize them, take ownership of them and do them. Taking ownership is doing the things you say you will do and not blaming others if things do not get done in time. Seeing yourself complete your tasks in a timely fashion and maybe even ahead of schedule can give you the confidence to accomplish even more. Deadlines will not concern you as much if you are totally prepared and ready before they arrive. Being punctual will become a habit - and a good one to have. Your life will not be in crisis mode all the time.

Small Ways to Save Time

1. *Multi-task* - do two things at once
2. *Keep a reminder list* - of important tasks
3. *Use TV commercial time* - to get little things done
4. *Limit TV time* - decide beforehand what you want to watch
5. *Use the phone or Internet* - to locate what you want or to shop
6. *Leave a complete message* - so you may not require a call back
7. *Telecommute or carpool* - or move closer to work or work closer to home
8. *Call rather than write* - state what you want and eliminate extra conversation
9. *Speed dial* - set up your work & home phones with frequently used numbers
10. *Listen to traffic reports in the car ahead of time* - be aware of alternate routes

End of the Day

You can tell a lot about your time management skills by how you end your day. You can have a daily plan or agenda but you must also schedule a time to stop working each day and stick to it. If you work over that time you probably haven't been able to concentrate your full attention on all that you wished to get done. You may have lots of crucial items left unfinished or not yet tackled. You need to review your day - see what interruptions prevented you from working, determine what you need to eliminate or where to make harder choices. To get a balance between your personal and professional life you need to close your files, snap your briefcase shut, turn of the computer and call it a day.

Successful Time Management

Once you see the positive outcome of your time management skills, you will be rewarded with a new awareness. You will be able to apply all that you have learned to every new circumstance or problem that arises. You will be able to sit down and carefully evaluate each situation calmly and in an orderly manner. You will be able to break a big job into manageable sized pieces and get it all done in time. You may learn to enjoy tasks that you used to dislike. You will be filled by a sense of accomplishment and fulfillment. Your peers will respect you for all you are able to accomplish and you will impress others by your sense of timeliness. You will have learned to skillfully manage your time to best suit you.

Chapter 5

SCHEDULING AND GETTING THINGS DONE

"Never leave that till tomorrow,
which you can do today."
Benjamin Franklin (1706 - 1790)

Good businesses run on a schedule. A good schedule is a plan detailing what work is to be done, specifying deadlines along the way. It provides a program of forthcoming events or appointments that everyone can follow. It keeps business going, moving towards the future, using a documented program worked out beforehand. With a project or goal in mind, a schedule is the blueprint for getting things accomplished. Using a schedule a project is placed on the calendar giving everyone a date by which the objective will be met. This systematic arrangement of details is a necessity for the running of a successful business. Individuals also need personal schedules to make the best use of their time in an organized, productive manner. Weekly organizing gives you the freedom and flexibility to handle unanticipated events, shift appointments if you need to, enjoy relationships and interactions with others and have spontaneous experiences knowing that you have organized your week to accomplish key goals in every area of your life. Daily planning and taking a few minutes each morning to review your schedule puts you in touch with the decisions you made as you organized the week as well as unanticipated factors that may have come up.

Why Schedule?

Scheduling is the process by which you look at the time available to you and plan how you will use it to achieve the goals or tasks you have identified. By using a schedule properly, you can really see what you can realistically achieve with your time. Scheduling is *"working smart"* the practice of using your time to achieve maximum results. Learning good organization skills and using computer software to manage your files and finances, finding information on the Internet and waking up on schedule all raise your level of productivity. Scheduling allows you to plan and make the best use of the time you have available. Be sure to have enough time for things you absolutely must do and then save some time in your schedule for the unexpected.

Hint: A well-planned schedule will minimize stress and avoid over committing yourself.

Schedule Early

Beginning a task can seem very daunting. Imagine you are a writer facing a blank sheet of paper - not knowing where to begin, not knowing how to start and with no notion in your head as to how to get a great idea. The thought of beginning your task may be so intimidating that you put it off until the last possible second. Of course, you can research, investigate, make an instant decision or complete a task at the last minute but the pace and pressure would be horrendous. Starting your task when you have the least amount of time puts extra stress on you. Putting off starting your task will hurt you in the long run as you will not be able to afford the time needed to do your best or take the best approach. To avoid last minute decisions and shoddy work start planning and scheduling your tasks early.

Hint: Arrange to get your schedule in order, select your clothing and prepare things you wish to take along with you (like lunch) - the night before.

Scheduling Tools

There are many good scheduling tools available -

- Weekly or Monthly Calendars
- Free-Form or Time-Lined Diaries
- Paper-Based Organizers
- PDAs - Personal Digital Assistants
- Cell Phones
- Organizing Software

The tool that you decide on will depend on your budget, your taste and your situation. Carrying a large calendar book or daily planner is not necessarily practical and may be better suited for a briefcase or a desktop. Posting a big monthly calendar on a kitchen wall is great for family planning so that every member of the family will know where to find you and so you can plan your personal schedule around pre-scheduled events. If you love gadgets, a PDA may be for you. Whatever tool you select, you should be able to refer to it at all times and it should be easy for you to use. No matter which type of planner or scheduling tool you choose, spend some time customizing it by deciding exactly where you are going to record different types of information.

> **Hint:** *Your planner should record your schedule in the detail and by the timeframe slots you use for your appointments.*

PDAs vs. Paper

Both the PDA and the paper based appointment planners offer several time management features. Both contain a place for addresses, phone numbers, appointments, to-do lists and extra notes. They are both small and portable and keep track of your life. What you use is a matter of personal preference but if you are considering a switch here are some pros and cons of each medium.

PDA	PAPER
WRITING EASE	
Use of a stylus	Use of pen or pencil
Must hit correct key or selection	Write anywhere on the page
Use of on-screen menus or keyboard	Write in any size font you like
DURABILITY	
Recharge battery	Self maintained
May break if dropped	No damage if dropped
Can back up data on computer	No backup unless photocopied
READABILITY	
Eye Strain	No scratched screen
Limited to screen size	Buy any size you like
Hard in low light situations	Easily read in daylight
COST	
Getting less expensive	Cheaper than a PDA
Larger storage capacity	No cost for batteries
May require software upgrades	Cheap expansion capabilities

SPEED OF USE

Set up time and effort	Instant on
Must navigate through several menus	Can flip though pages
Learn various commands to locate info	Go immediately to a marked page

UNIQUENESS

Downloads from Internet	Putting pen to paper
Alarm to remind you of an event	Writing helps you remember
Can synch up with your computer	Guaranteed access to information

BlackBerry for Individuals

Technology can be credited with breaking many communication barriers and producing innovative products. The latest product out on the market is BlackBerry, a new type of PDA (personal digital assistant). It offers you an integrated wireless email solution. You get the functionality of your mobile phone along with email and Internet capabilities. With its browser functions you can easily access information on the web. You can make phone calls and send and receive email messages. Like other PDAs, it comes as small as a pager with an integrated address book and calendar. But, unlike a regular PDA you are not required to write messages with a stylus; instead, you are provided a small keyboard. This small package gives you all you need to be organized while *"on the go"*.

Cell Phone Technology

Another innovative product that keeps getting more advanced and sophisticated is the cell phone. When cell phones were first introduced they were only capable of telephone communication. You basically used them to keep track of your kids, to find the book you forgot at the restaurant you just left or to tell your boss you were stuck in traffic and would be late for work. Today's cell phone technology provides you with an excellent tool for organization. You get a built-in calendar, clock, camera, calculator, work pad and to-do list to help you plan, schedule or easily re-schedule appointments, plans and tasks. Not only can you input reminders on a calendar but you can set an alarm to be alerted at the exact time you need to be reminded. For an extra monthly charge you can have the benefit of the Internet to access news, weather, stock quotes or send a photograph, all in an instant. These pocket-size handheld cell phones are an all-in-one organizing tool, loaded with great features and they keep getting better.

Hint: As cell phone companies engage in price competition consumers reap the benefit of lower costs for more services.

Scheduling Tips

• Write your schedule in pencil so you can make adjustments if you need to.

• Always carry along paper and pen, a PDA or a small tape recorder so you can record thoughts or tasks you think of that you can later write in your schedule.

• Avoid being too general in your schedule. Instead of scheduling *"study time"* commit yourself more definitely to *"study history"* or *"study chemistry"*.

• Keep a list of unscheduled tasks handy so you can perform them when you encounter bad weather or a cancelled appointment prevents you from carrying out your intended plans.

• If you perform some of the same tasks on the same day every week, start a new weekly schedule with these chores already on it. An example would be food shopping every Friday afternoon or an exercise class each Monday morning.

My Schedule

Get into the habit of devising a schedule on a regular basis. I usually plan my schedule each Sunday for the upcoming week. When I open my planner to the current week it usually contains a few dates and appointments I had previously marked. I like to plan ahead. I try to schedule appointments ahead of time. I call for a doctor or other appointment a few weeks prior to my preferred date to get my first choice. I would rather schedule appointments at my convenience than at someone else's. In the time I have left open, I schedule tasks I absolutely must do. I then schedule in what I would like to accomplish. I estimate from prior experience how much time each task should reasonably take and slot it in my schedule accordingly. If I am invited to an event, a party, a gallery opening, or have made a medical or personal appointment, I write it down as soon as I schedule it.

> **Hint:** *As you have a limited amount of time, that can fit only so much, do not overbook your schedule.*

Making Appointments

You can make an appointment when you remember, or at the last minute. You can make a reservation or you can wait for hours before a table opens up at your favorite restaurant. It's your choice and it's your time. Making appointments ahead of time affords you the luxury of scheduling your time the way you want it, the way it works best for you.

Here are some helpful suggestions:

1. Carry your appointment book with you.
2. Call a day ahead to confirm your time and appointment.
3. Carry a cell phone and give the number to the other party.
4. Do not over commit your schedule - leave time for traffic and delays.
5. Take directions and a map with you if you are traveling to a new location.
6. Always keep something with you to do while you wait: use your waiting time wisely.
7. Be prepared with insurance cards or forms when you go to a medical or dental appointment.
8. When you make an appointment ask for the first appointment of the day, when the office is not running late.
9. If you must change your appointment, do not cancel - reschedule for another date and time of your choice.
10. Always include the phone number of your appointment in your date book so you can call if you expect to be late.
11. Call right before your appointment to see if the office is backed up and your appointment will be delayed - gives you more time to get there.

12. Add a *"tickler"* to your computer calendar, send yourself an email, write a note or set your pager to remind you of the time for your appointment.

Allow Free Time

Most of us have been taught to work hard. But you need balance in your life between work, family, time for yourself and fun. As you plan your schedule leave in some free time to do the things you enjoy and give you pleasure. Also allow for *"just in case time"* - if something special arises or you are faced with a major interruption. If you do not have any free time think about delegating some tasks, putting some off to next week or doing them in an abbreviated fashion. Do not invest your time on tasks that have no payoff or reward for you. Try to use some type of technology, a software program or spreadsheet to automate a task and save time. Bundle similar tasks together and share available resources.

Forget a Date?

Imagine that the date is January 10th and you just realized you have forgotten your co-worker's birthday today. You usually exchange a gift and a card but today you have nothing. You feel so bad; you invite her to lunch but she knows you have forgotten and she feels it is only a gesture you have made as an afterthought. How could you have remembered? You forgot last year too and had marked it down in your date book. You had vowed to yourself never to forget again. You can be sure that you will remember by following a simple process of going through your past year's calendar looking for all the important dates, events, birthdays, anniversaries, etc. After you make the decision to celebrate the occasion in the future, you need to mark that date on your calendar for the next year. Also, add it to your computer calendar and have it prompt you a week before.

Next Year's Calendar

By reviewing your old calendar in December you will be ready when January 1st rolls around. You will be able to start off the new-year in an organized fashion. In December, prior to buying my calendar for the next year, I have tons of *"post-its"* flopping around in my date book as a reminder for a date or an appointment to schedule for the next year. After having spent the time transferring all the important dates from my prior year calendar to my new one I then fill in all my new appointments. Then I get to discard all those sticky notes that seem to tag along and nag me. One year I could not find the type of calendar book I prefer and decided to start the year without one. Big mistake, as I rely on my date book for everything I do; I was quite lost. I had to break down and buy a different brand just to continue my life, make appointments and maintain my schedule.

Ways to Remember

Memory controls the flow of information within the human mind and we utilize different ways to remember things: recall, recognition, paired associates and reproductive memory. According to neurologists, who investigate how the brain works, the most popular kind of memory is recall. It is a recollection of a telephone number you have just heard, a list of items you are to purchase at the store or a list of dates you just learned. Items are remembered in sequence. Recognition is easier than recall. You need to simply indicate which of several events were experienced, such as identifying a familiar face in a crowd. Paired-associates is remembering an article of clothing someone else was wearing, the color of a car and the name of a person whom you know. Here you are associating one item to another. In reproductive memory you recall some experience and you produce a replica or close copy of the original situation. Examples of this type of memory are drawing a picture of something you have just seen and impersonating or mimicking someone else.

Memory Techniques

As I said, without my daily calendar I am lost. Whenever I need to remember to do something I take the time to write it in my date book. Usually, if I do not write it as an item on my calendar, it doesn't get done or I just do not remember it. I think of the strangest things I need to do, at the oddest of times. Sometimes it is impossible for me to write anything. If I am driving my car or on a crowded train it is pretty difficult to whip out my date book and record an entry. So what I do is think of a short word or acronym capturing the first letter of what I need to remember. Sometimes I have to stick a vowel in there to make it a real word. So instead of having to remember three things I only need to remember one. When I have that extra minute, I take out my date book and recall my word. I retrieve from memory what each letter in my made up word stands for. After total recollection I can write each item down and get it out of my head. Knowing that I no longer have to remember anything I can then rest at ease.

Forgotten Details

Let me give you an example of what I mean. I am on a crowded subway in New York City in rush hour, going home from work. I remember that in my haste to leave the office I forgot some last minute details for tomorrow's presentation. I forgot to include a note about the new production region and to make extra copies of the handouts for the two new associates in the department. I also forgot to return the key to the supply cabinet to its proper place. I just know that I will never be able to remember these things and if I do not keep repeating them in my head over and over again I will truly forget them. So I associate each code or task with an alphabetic letter to remember it by.

P = Production = Note about the new production region or

R = Region

C = Copies   = Extra copies of the handouts

K = Key   = Return key to proper place

I think about the letters P - R - C- K and I immediately think of the word *"rack"* or *"pack"*. I figure that *"pack"* is better because the word *"production"* will tip me off better than the word *"region"* when I need to recall what each letter stands for. As we pull into the station everyone is jamming against each other trying to be the first one off the train and all I keep thinking about is *"pack"*. After climbing a set of stairs and changing train platforms I finally find a moment to recall what each letter of *"pack"* is associated with and scribble each of the tasks in my notebook while waiting for the next train. And for the next few minutes I have the relief of only clear thoughts swimming around in my head.

Mnemonics

What I just described above was mnemonics, a system of principles and formulas designed to assist or improve your memory (when you are unable to write things down). I created an acronym by taking the initial letters of each word. If your goal is to be organized it can be helpful to learn many of these mental tools. They are techniques that are particularly good when you need to remember detailed or structured information. They also help make remembering people's names and a list of things much easier. The three fundamental principles underlying the use of mnemonics are imagination, association and location. Once you understand how each one works you can use them together to generate your own system.

• *Imagination* - is what you use to create an association. The stronger you can imagine and can visualize a situation or task, the quicker it will stick in your mind for later recall. Your imagery can be violent, vivid or sensual as long as it helps you to remember. As an example, imagine scuba diving off a tropical island surrounded by colorful fish as a way for remembering to stop at the fish market on your way home from work.

• *Association* - is the method by which you link a thing to be remembered to a way of remembering it. You can create an association by merging images together, placing things on top of each other, linking them by using the same color, shape or feeling. In my case, I selected the alphabet to identify the beginning letter of each task.

• *Location* - is how to set the environment. It allows you to place information so that it hangs together and is a method of separating each mnemonic from another. In my case, each letter separated each task I needed to remember. There was no need to specify an order as each task in my example was independent of the others.

Creating Associations

By coding language and numbers as images you can both code and structure information so you can easily remember them later. Making associations between items on a list and linking them either by a word, an image or a story will give you the cues for retrieval.

To make the mnemonics more memorable you can:

- Exaggerate the importance or size of the image.
- Use simple images instead of symbols that hold hidden meanings.
- Use colorful images, as they are easier to remember than drab ones.
- Use positive and pleasant images as the brain tries to block out unpleasant ones.
- Use images or words that denote three dimensions and movement to make it more vivid.
- Use humor or a peculiar word or image, as funny things are easier to remember than normal ones.

What's In My Date Book?

Use your date book or planner to record all the things you need to get done and remember for the day. I use it to record and help me keep on track of:

1. *Telephone calls I need to make*
2. *Appointments I have for the day*
3. *Tasks I need to do on a particular day*
4. *Meetings I have scheduled for the day*
5. *Major bills I need to pay on a special date*
6. *Birthdays, anniversaries and other special occasions*

The night before I usually read through all the entries I have written in my date book for the next day and order each by time. I simply place a number prior to each entry as to the time sequence I will try to get each item done. It is important not to number each task by its importance but rather by the time of day it can be best performed. I need to write a letter before stopping at the mailbox to post it. I need to create a grocery list before I do my weekly food shopping. I must first think about whom I wish to invite to a party before I write out the invitations. By glancing at the number you have assigned each item you can easily determine what to do next.

> **Hint:** *In the back of my date book I keep an address and phone directory so I can easily locate people, places or businesses I frequently have contact with. Many people program their cell phone with these numbers and synch up with their computer.*

Family Business

Not only do you have your own life to plan, but most mothers and fathers must plan activities that the whole family does together. Whether it is attending a school play, a religious service, a baseball game, going to a cousin's birthday party or on a vacation - someone must plan it and make sure that everyone makes room for the date on their personal schedules. There may also be gifts to be bought for an event, clothes shopping for a special occasion, lunch to be prepared, tickets to be ordered or various other tasks that must not be forgotten and scheduled. Time may also need to be allotted just to get your family together to co-ordinate the logistics of the event or the travel arrangements.

Planning Family Time

We let so many wonderful opportunities to be with our family slip by because we simply do not take the time to make them happen. With everyone so busy with their regular routines and responsibilities, getting the family together in one place at one time may be a big chore in itself. Planning to spend the dinner hour together for quality family time is a great idea, guaranteeing you seven hours of quality time per week. Dinner should always be held at the same time every day to give consistency to every member's personal schedule. There should be no interruptions, no television or radio turned on and let the answering machine record any telephone calls. Dinner should be a time to discuss the day's events and share your feelings and opinions with the entire family. It is also a time to ask questions that provoke family discussions and make family decisions.

> **Hint:** *If you are traveling or on a business trip you can electronically be at the dinner table with your family by turning your laptop, cell phone or PDA into a long-distance parenting tool.*

Create a Family Pinwheel Task Chart

In a typical household there are many tasks that must be done every day.

Here is a fun way to organize simple tasks as a family.

1. Create an Inner Circle - with every member's name in the household.

2. Create an Outer Circle - with list of tasks or jobs to do for a day.

3. Leave some spots open on the outer circle marked "FREE".

4. Cut out two circles.

5. Place the Inner Circle on top of the Outer Circle.

6. Place on a wall or bulletin board and attach thumbtack to middle of both circles.

7. Spin wheel to determine the day's tasks.

8. Rotate in the same direction for the following day's tasks.

Extra Hints to Make It More Fun

1. Use cardboard to make it sturdy.

2. Make each section a different color.

3. Allow kids to swap tasks with each other.

4. Periodically modify (add or delete) tasks.

5. Have everyone in the family take part in creating the pinwheel.

FAMILY PINWHEEL TASK CHART

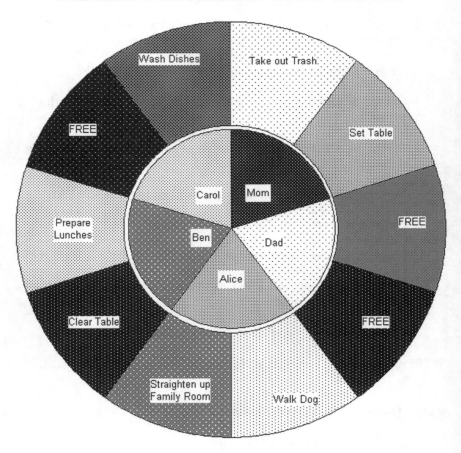

Keeping Track of Your Children

When your children are young you know where they are at all times and whom they are with. You organize their schedules, play dates and after-school activities and often accompany them. As they grow older and gain their independence they learn to plan their own schedules. They make new friends whom you do not know. They always seem to be busy outside the home. As a parent you are still responsible for them. You need to have a way to keep track of them or be able to contact them. Although technology has given us pagers, the cell phone and the Internet to assist parents in this task there is no substitute for a simple list. Have your teenager or young adult compile a list of their friend's names, addresses, home and cell phone numbers. In an emergency you can have one quick list to reference.

Create a Job Chart for Your Child

WHAT'S MY JOB?							
	MON	TUES	WED	THURS	FRI	SAT	SUN
1. FEED THE CAT							
2. GATHER RE-CYCLING							
3. CLEAN UP ROOM							
4. EMPTY ROOM GARBAGE							
5. DO HOMEWORK							
6. SET THE TABLE							
7. BRUSH TEETH							
8. GET CLOTHES READY							
9. GET BACKPACK READY							
10. TAKE A BATH							
PERCENT FOR THE DAY	100	100	100	100	100	100	100
EXTRA JOBS = EXTRA AWARDS							

Organizing Your Children

No child is too young to learn about organization. Cleaning up toys in a room is probably the first thing we would like to teach them. The more organizing tasks your children do, the easier it is for the parents. Assign daily and weekly chores when kids get older. Most kids love checklists (because they love checking things off), so create a checklist for each child - Monday through Sunday and list age-appropriate tasks: make bed, put clothes and toys away (for younger children), etc. Have them get ready for the next day the night before by preparing their books and clothes. As they grow older, add on more complex tasks such as washing dishes, setting the dinner table, doing laundry, taking the dog out for a walk or caring for a family pet. It makes children feel good to contribute to the household plus it teaches them good habits and lightens your load of responsibilities. If you use a job chart, at the end of each day calculate a percentage of completed tasks so they can see what they have accomplished. You can add an extra row onto the job chart to note when your child does extra special tasks by themselves, without even being asked.

Cards and Gifts

Being organized is remembering special occasions. Finding the perfect gift for someone you care about at the last minute can be impossible. It's even tough to find one when you know what you are shopping for. Throughout the year whenever I see a gift that would be perfect for someone I buy it on the spot and put it away in a special drawer especially meant for gifts (so I can find it when the time is right). Besides marking the date in my date book I keep a list of birthdays, anniversaries and other special occasions for every person that I will send a card to or give a gift. When I see that the occasion is about to arrive I go to my list and see if I have already bought a gift for them, then all I need to do is decide how to wrap it. I go into my card box, where I have stockpiled cards for almost every occasion and select one appropriate for the person and occasion. Since I already have a card and a gift that is perfect I am able to save time by not having to go shopping just for this purpose.

Gift Recycling

When I receive a gift that I just know I will never use I either place it in my thrift shop bag or add it to my gift list. At times it is kinder to accept a gift you are not crazy about than hurting someone's feelings. I keep a special box where I place new, unopened gift items. It may even be an item I had bought myself and in between the time I purchased it and brought it home realized I did not really need or want it. Besides placing these items in a specific spot I write each on my gift list from whom or where I received it. To make it easier to remember I try to describe the item in as much detail as I can. When I need to give a quick gift or a token of appreciation to someone special I can go directly to my gift list and look there first.

> **Hint:** *Perusing through my gift box has saved me both time and money.*

GIFTS TO GIVE   LAST UPDATED 10-28-2005

1. JEWELRY GIFTS:

ZEBRA PIN
SILVER PENGUIN PIN
CHINESE PANDA EARRINGS
SILVER KEY AND LOCK PIN
BRASS FEATHER EARRINGS

2. STATIONARY GIFTS:

BRASS LEAF BOOKMARK
STATIONARY IN FLAT PACK (FROM VERA) VERY DELICATE
REMEMBRANCE CALENDAR – ART IN BLOOM (FROM TOMMIE)
ART NOTE-CARDS AND ENVELOPES (MUSEUM OF MODERN ART)

3. TOILETRY GIFTS:

LAVENDER BATH SET
BLUE TOILETRY TRAVEL BAG

BOX OF SOAPS (LAVENDER AND LILAC)
ALMOND SOAPS AND LOTION (FROM NOREEN)

4. HOUSE GIFTS:

GLASS BOWL (FROM AMY)
CERAMIC COW MILK CREAMER
FLOWER VASE (FROM SUZY AND STEVE)
APRON WITH COFFEE CUPS ON POCKETS

5. MISCELLANEOUS:

BABY CALENDAR
BABY GROWTH CHART
LE SPORTS SAC ZIPPERED BAG

SPECIFIC PEOPLE PRESENTS/BIRTHDAYS IN 2005:

1. ALICE - MAKE-UP AND COSMETIC ACCESSORY CASE – FEB 12
2. GEORGIE - SILVER EARRINGS WITH PARROT – FEB 23
3. SANDY - TWO 14K GOLD EARRINGS – MAR 31
4. HEIDI - MONET WATER LILIES CUBE NOTEPAD – MAY 18
5. MURIEL - SET OF 3 BLACK/FUCHSIA COSMETIC BAGS – MAY 23
6. KAREN - 50th BIRTHDAY STUFF – JUNE 17
7. HELEN - SILK SCARF – OCT 5

Holiday Cards

I have a lot of friends and at holiday time I need to organize in order to send out cards, buy gifts and not go crazy. I do in multiple what I usually prepare for one birthday. First I do my holiday cards and then I attack my gift list. Every year I make a list of people to whom I send a holiday card. I have two lists because I know people who celebrate Christmas and Hanukkah. When I receive a card back I mark it on my card list with a small red star next to their name. The next year I write out my holiday cards I add any new friends, acquaintances or co-workers to the list. I also type up a holiday letter describing the big events my family experienced the past year including any new family news. I then get my supplies ready: address book, stamps, *"white-out"* (for mistakes) and a comfortable writing pen. I have holiday cards on hand as I tend to buy them in prior years after holiday sales. I personalize each of the cards, address and stamp each envelope then stuff the correct card into the correct envelope with a holiday letter and seal each one.

> **Hint:** *Maintaining a computer database for your mailing list and computerized labels can save you even more time.*

Holiday Gifts

After I have my card list ready, I start on my gift list. As I said, I have a lot of friends so I create a spreadsheet and in the first column list each gift recipient's name. (I really start with last year's list and just add or delete a name.) Then I decide what gift I wish to give them and list it next to their name. Following the gift, I create three more columns. Column one is checked when I purchase the gift. Column two is checked after I have wrapped the gift and column three is checked after I have delivered or given them the gift. This all works out pretty well. As I previously mentioned, picking up items on sale throughout the year when you see them will give you a boxful of gifts to begin with. In the long run, this should make your holiday shopping less costly and shorten your holiday shopping expeditions.

Year End Cleaning

Many people who live up North believe that January is the worst month of the year. It is dreary and depressing with nothing to do, nothing to prepare for and nowhere to go in the extreme cold (at least where I live). What a contrast to December, a month that is full of life, bright lights and good cheer for the upcoming holidays. For organizers, January is the best month of the year because you have all this free time and are indoors most of the time. Without many plans and a pretty empty social schedule, this is the best time of year to clean. I call it my year-end cleaning. I schedule this month and into February to go through files, folders, closets, drawers, clothing, the kitchen and the rest of the house and belongings to get rid of paper, clothing and things I no longer need or want.

Completion

The best part about accomplishing a task is being able to cross it out or check it off your list. The thing to remember is that you are not Superman or Superwoman. Just because you did a great job and compiled a giant list of things to get done don't get down on yourself if you do not get to them all. That is what tomorrow is for. Try to get as much done as you had planned to do but if you don't - do not forget about them or cross them off. Move the tasks you did not get to. Transfer them to another day, a day in the future when you possibly can fit it in. Some people think that if they write something down, the task will get done. But if you do not do it, it will not be done. If you do not write it down on another date, it will most probably not get done and just be forgotten.

Chapter 6

INCOMING & OUTGOING

"I find the great thing in this world is not so much where
we stand, as in what direction we are moving."
Oliver Wendell Holmes (1809 - 1894)

Paper is everywhere. Even though we are in the electronic age you cannot escape from it. There are newspapers, catalogs, trade journals, bills, faxes, letters, reports, incoming mail, bulletins, correspondence, financial statements, advertisements, coupons, newsletters, printed e-mails, magazines, documents, junk mail and forms. From the mailroom, packing and shipping departments to the filing department companies maintain entire sections or floors devoted to just incoming and outgoing materials. Don't forget all the electronic correspondence, computer security, data entry and the order department. We handle many papers in our personal lives, from the bills in our mailbox to the tax returns and copies of transaction receipts we walk away with after every monetary operation. Getting some control over the paper flow will help organize your life. Sorting, filing, reading, prioritizing and getting rid of paper are major issues when it comes to all the incoming and outgoing correspondence that crosses your path in the course of a day.

Avoid Paper Clutter

Paper clutter often represents unmade decisions. Cutting down on the amount of paper in your home or office is very important because too much of it leads to clutter and eventually chaos. By the time you develop that feeling of chaos it is usually too late to be calm and to make the right decisions. You are usually under pressure to find something in a hurry or locate an item that has been missing for too long. Your memory cannot cope and instead of helping, you are overcome by a feeling of helplessness. Everyone's paper issues are specific to their particular life style so the system you develop needs to be tailored to fit your situation. Once you practice good organizational skills on a daily basis they will become part of your routine and paper will no longer be a problem.

Paper Accumulation

What tends to occur is that paper accumulates faster than you can go through it. Make an *"on the spot"* decision and do not waiver from it. Practice the *"one touch"* rule for paper. Handle it only once - read it, file it or throw it out. Do not let a day go by without making the time to go through all the incoming paper that comes across your desk. When reading a newspaper or magazine, anything you wish to keep - cut it out or tab the corner of the page. After you are finished reading the publication go back and mentally review if you really need to hang onto that information. If any of the answers to the below questions are *"Yes"* then clip it out.

Ask yourself -

1. Is this information unique?
2. Will this serve as a reminder for me?
3. Can I find this information anywhere else?
4. Do I wish to give this to someone else to read?
5. Will this information be current a month from now?

How to Control Paper

- Develop a filing system.
- Keep papers where you need them.
- Place a paper where you can find it.
- Use computers to cut down on paper.
- Stop the amount of paper that comes in.
- Pass paper on to the garbage or someone else.
- Immediately discard envelopes and junk mail.
- Make instant decisions about a piece of paper.
- Try to handle a paper the least amount of times, only once.
- Do not keep too many copies. One copy is enough if you know where it is.

Garbage is Your Friend

Garbage is thought of as a negative word. It is often associated with dirty, unwanted and worthless items. When it comes to paper, garbage is your friend. The disposal of it provides a method of getting rid of waste and unnecessary things. Garbage helps you eliminate what you do not need. Elimination is more than a process of removal; it's a solution to the problems created by excess. Garbage can help you trim your files, locate an old report card, cut down the amount of paper you look through, see your desktop and allow you to find what is important at the moment. By getting rid of useless paper you are a step closer to living an organized life. As it is, we are used to having so much paper in our lives that an overflow and excess of it almost seems normal. Try to use garbage in a positive way and look at it as your helpful friend.

Hint: *Think of garbage as an aid to help avoid clutter and assist in organizing your paperwork.*

How to Reduce Paper

You need to organize paper every day. Being vigilant and paying careful attention to detail will help you avoid clutter. After eliminating all the paper that you can get rid of, you will need to organize what is left.

Try some of these suggestions:

- Do not ask for information you do not need.
- Do not take handouts you have no interest in.
- Do not let paper stack up; sort and file regularly.
- Learn to let go of paper by throwing things away.
- Keep sample letters and correspondence on your computer.
- Prioritize everything immediately and route it to the proper place.
- Make it a practice to open your mail everyday as soon as you can.
- Be selective of what you copy and remember that one copy is enough.
- Go through your in-box and email at least once a day to prevent pile-ups.
- Be realistic about your time and do not accumulate too many papers to read.

File Cleaning

I use the year's end as an excuse to carefully weed through all my files. I look through files that are filled to the brim with individual papers. I first shred and then discard individual bills and monthly statements if the provider of service has sent a cumulative statement that shows all the transactions that have taken place in the prior calendar year. I scan each paper in a folder and make an instant decision as to whether or not it should be kept or thrown away. I can then start the year with a thinner folder. Use staples to attach papers together, instead of paper clips. Paper clips often get caught on other papers and take up more space. Discard old notices and bulletins that may be out of date. Throughout the year, whenever I receive a new policy change or service agreement I pay attention to the date. When I file a new bulletin I look for a match in my folder and discard the older notice. Check with your CPA, attorney or order *Publication 552: Record Keeping for Individuals* from the IRS to find out how long you need to hold onto records and documents.

> **Hint:** *By keeping your papers up to date, you can avoid confusion; you can be sure that you are reading the most current version of any important document.*

News Clippings

When you are done reading your mail, newspaper or magazine you should be ready to dispose of it. Some people like to hang on to a week's worth of newspapers or the last several issues of a magazine. That is alright but only if you get rid of the old ones. If you decide to hold onto the last 12 issues of a monthly magazine, when that 13th issue is added to the pile, make sure you dispose of the first issue that is now over a year old. Remember, when it comes to paper, garbage is your best friend. It can save your home from looking like a library or warehouse. After you have finished reading you may have a bunch of newspaper clippings or magazine articles lying in different spots around your home. You need to find a central spot to place them. Once you have collected about ten pieces it is time to file them away. If you plan to get organized a filing system is the way to go. In order to find any paper again you must store them in an arrangement that allows for quick reference. What is the use of saving information if you are not able to get at it when it is most needed?

> **Hint:** *If you decide to save newspapers or magazine clippings correctly file them to gain maximum use of their information.*

Paper Sorting

You must sort before you file. Faced with piles of paper, gather them all in one spot and file away the important ones. Keeping and filing papers that are not needed clog up files and take away room for the important ones. Basic sorting involves placing the sheet of paper on the correct pile. Begin with five piles for simplicity.

PILE	**WHAT TO PLACE IN IT**
1. To Do	What must be taken care of immediately.
2. Bills to Pay	Separate bills from all other papers.
3. To Read Later	For the future when you have time to spare.
4. To File	What needs to be saved and later retrieved.
5. Garbage	Anything you don't really need - be ruthless!

Filing System

Everyone believes that they alone have the perfect filing system but there is no one perfect system. A filing system must be right for the individual. The best system is one created that allows for easy retrieval of papers that you require. To file correctly you need a permanent place to go and a system by which you use to sort. Use a file cabinet, a drawer, a box or any suitable container to house your files. In case you have lots of paper you may need more than one receptacle. Most people sort by using an alphabetical system. I find it best to sort by topics. I have arranged my files in 3 levels. The most important level concerns my everyday affairs, current bills and financial statements.

My First Level Categories

Mortgage	Bank Statements
Electric	Telephone
Home Fuel	Garbage
Property Taxes	Medical Statements
Investment Company # 1	Credit Card # 1
Investment Company # 2	Credit Card # 2

The second level concerns my interests and hobbies. Whenever I come across an article that will benefit me, I clip it out and sort it in the correct file. When I need to research a particular topic I will browse through the file. I quickly find the result of my search. If you own a computer scanner, for even quicker retrieval, scan your papers and save them on your computer.

My Second Level Categories

Personal Awards	Photography
Travel	Personal Finance
Retirement	Education
Investing	Jewelry Making
Organizing Articles	Health Articles

The third and last level is just for keeping. There are many papers that I never look at once I have filed them. However, because of personal liability and responsibility I need to hold onto them. Falling under this heading are tax returns and lots of papers dealing with the purchase of my home, car and mortgage. Even though the originals are located in my safe deposit box I keep copies of deeds and titles in my files for easy reference.

My Third Level Categories

Mortgage Closing Papers	Property Records
Old Tax Returns	Home Inspection Report
Cancelled Checks	Insurance Policies
Motor Vehicle History	Prior Year Tax Returns
Medical Records	Vaccination Records

How to Be a Successful Filer

Following these easy steps to set up your filing system can save you time, money and effort. You can look forward to years of efficient and cost-effective filing.

1. Decide What You Will Be Filing

- What are the sizes of your documents?
- What is the volume of material to be contained in each folder?
- Where your system will be stored (new or existing shelves or drawers)?
- Will there be other material in the files that is smaller or larger than standard documents?

2. Choose the Proper File Folder Type

- Top Tab folders have a smaller area for identification, located on the uppermost vertical area of the folder. These are stored in traditional drawer style filing cabinets.
- End Tab folders have identification on the side of the folder. These are stored on open shelves.
- Pocket Folders are primarily end-tab. They provide secure storage for smaller loose documents and materials.
- Divider Folders have a larger capacity than standard folders and include built-in dividers that separate areas of the file.

3. Select a File Labeling System

- A labeling system is a series of labels that are consistent in size, shape and color. This promotes efficient folder retrieval and replacement.
- Uniform labeling also allows identification of misfiled folders.
- Popular labeling systems include single-color labels or color-coded labels.
- Color-coding file folders is the single biggest step you can take to enhance filing efficiency.
- Utilizing labeling software reduces the cost and storage concerns associated with purchasing individual labeling components.

4. Storage For Your Files

- Selecting a filing storage unit is the last step.
- When choosing your unit have the maximum floor area dimensions available.
- Filing drawers and cabinets are most useful for Top Tab folders.
- Open shelf systems are needed for End Tab folders.
- There are stationary, moveable and modular storage systems.
- Consider floor strength when deciding where to locate your storage unit.
- Do not block ductwork, outlets or electrical breaker panels with permanent storage units.
- Decide on how many shelves or tiers you need.
- Take into consideration any growth over the next 3-5 years when determining needed file storage capacity.

File Cabinets

Despite the increase of electronic documents, file cabinets remain a fixture in most homes. Choosing one involves more than simply selecting the number of drawers. Subtle differences can affect whether you wind up with a neatly organized filing system or mounds of paper stacked on top of a desk. Factors you will want to consider include: space, the sizes and types of documents you store and the quality of construction.

Vertical File Cabinets - are the traditional type of cabinets. These have from two to five drawers per cabinet. Letter or legal sized files are stored facing the front of the drawers.

Lateral Filing Cabinets - these are much wider than standard designs, allowing files to be stored front to back or side to side in the drawers. They are not as deep as vertical cabinets allowing them to serve as wall partitions or credenzas.

Safety and Quality - examine the suspension system that holds the drawers. Even when filled with weighty files, well-built cabinet drawers should open and close smoothly. To keep the cabinet from tipping over high quality units use counter weighed drawers and internal locking devices that allow only one drawer to open at a time.

Open Shelving - is another option. They are sets of shelves placed side by side and on top of one another. With open fronts all files are easily accessible. It is simple and inexpensive to add shelves as your filing need expands.

Pricing - depends on the material used, the number of drawers, the dimensions and the lock. A lateral file will generally cost more than the least expensive vertical file. Fire and impact resistance can add more to the cabinet price. You can save by buying used cabinets from dealers or at auctions. Since older units are typically made with high quality materials they can be a good bargain.

Incoming Mail

Did you know that incoming mail is a daily test of organization? If you keep all the mail that you receive you would not have enough space to move around in your home. You most probably do a pretty good job of sorting out your mail. First of all you have a lot of practice; you do it at least once a day. Secondly, you can quickly recognize junk mail and distinguish it from real mail. Toss out all the extra advertising that comes with your bills. When looking through the mail, first sort out mail for each member in the household. I start four piles; one pile for my husband, one for my daughter, one for myself and lastly, one for the garbage. Here again, garbage is my friend. The bigger the garbage pile, the less paper I have left to decide what to do with.

> **Hint:** *The least amount of paper you are left with will ultimately produce the least amount of clutter.*

Family Mail

Once I have sorted out the incoming mail I place mail for the other family members in a specific spot. To avoid clutter in your home find a central spot. Most often the kitchen is a room that everyone seems to past through in the course of the day. Set aside a specific place to keep the mail. If you have a large family, it's a good idea to buy a simple accordion envelope containing several sections. Place the name of each family member on a section tab. This allows each person to easily identify where his or her incoming mail can be found.

Here are some suggestions for family mail:

- Don't let a new paper pile begin.
- Respond to invitations as soon as they arrive.
- Make sure family members pick up their daily mail.
- Mark any dates for family events on a calendar for all to see.
- Keep a wastepaper basket nearby to quickly dispose of empty envelopes and junk mail.

Billing Statements

Bills are unavoidable and consistently flow into our lives. Just living in your home incurs expenses that you must pay for in a timely manner. When billing statements arrive in your daily mail, file them separately. Check each bill for accuracy and write the total money amount and date you plan to pay the bill on the envelope. Place each bill so you can clearly see the payment date. I usually review and pay my bills once a month. I find that it rarely takes me more than half an hour as most of my bills are automatically paid through my bank checking or credit card accounts. I add an entry for each of the automatic payments and debits to keep my checkbook in synch. If you do not already have an electronic bill paying system you may want to consider one, as it will save you lots of time. You can set it up through your bank account, credit card or an independent bill paying service. After you have paid a bill, file it away immediately so you do not have to handle it again (handle paper once).

My Style of Reading Magazines

I have noticed that everyone has their own personal preference when it comes to magazines. I prefer to subscribe to my very favorite ones even though I can visit my local library to browse through current issues of magazines. As I read through each magazine I think whether or not this information will be important to me in the future or just reading it once is enough. If I decide to save it, I place a small fold or tick mark on the top corner of the page. I may also tick the corner to help me remember to do a follow-up on something I've read. An example would be going to a website mentioned in the article for more detailed information on the topic. I may decide to tick the corner because I wish to give this article to someone else to read. At the conclusion of my reading I clip out all the ticked pages, throw out the magazine and review each clipped page to see if I still want to hang onto it. Then I sort - I make an instant decision to file the page away in the appropriate folder, stick it in my important pile, give it to a friend or jot down a website address in my date book (to look at when I have an extra moment).

> **Hint:** *You can arrange to re-circulate publications and magazines among friends or co-workers.*

My Friend's Style of Reading Magazines

My friend has a different approach. She takes more time reading magazines and is usually in the middle of two or three at a time. When she is done with them she stacks them in a pile and there they remain. Sometimes she moves the pile to another section of the room or places one pile on top of another. When company comes, the piles disappear and when the company leaves, the piles reappear. There exists a constant growth process. When she has the desire to find an article she is in the middle of reading, or for future reference, it entails a one-to-two hour process. First she must sift through the piles to locate the magazine she believes the article is in. Then she locates the table of contents to see what the issue contains. She repeats the process until she finds what she is looking for. Depending upon the mood she is in, she either gives up without finding it or spends a few days on the hunt.

Catalogs

The worst clutter is caused by catalogs, especially around holiday time. I love to look through catalogs. It feels like you have the whole world at your fingertips. Of course, most items look better in the catalog than in person. Photographing an item in the right light and at the right angle can create an intense desire for it. Many times I have ordered and received an item that did not look the same as it appeared in the catalog. Did you ever notice that companies bombard you with the same catalog and a different cover causing catalog clutter? Check it out - you may receive the exact same inner pages as your last catalog except for the front cover. Many companies offer one main catalog and lots of specialized catalogs. Their main catalog may contain a section for men, women, children, luggage and bedding. They also send specialized catalogs: one for men, another for women, and one just for children, etc. It is important to identify these right away and throw out old catalogs. You are mailed a new catalog for each season because inventory changes and new products are being adding. It is important to discard old ones. In case you need to save a few pages of your old catalog - just rip them out, place them inside your new catalog and throw the old one away.

> *Hint: Keep one separate spot in your home to store catalogs.*

Copy Papers in Your Wallet

Keep an extra copy of all credit cards, bank ATM cards, medical cards and papers that you carry in your wallet. Keep one copy at home and one locked in your desk drawer at work. If your wallet is accidentally lost or stolen you will be less stressed if you can immediately account for what you have lost. When you make a copy of your cards include the backside if the contact telephone number is included there. Contact all the credit card companies and your bank as soon as you notice your wallet is lost. Having the contact telephone numbers and your account numbers handy can save you unneeded stress and hours of hunting for them.

> *Hint: In case there is a fire in your home, keep copies of all your important documents in a safety deposit box. A fireproof box is also a consideration.*

Shopping

There are many reasons why people shop and many emotions attached to shopping. Shopping can be a joy or a chore. It is not enjoyable when you leave something to the last moment and stress out trying to find the perfect item within a minimal amount of time. However, it can be a joy when you leisurely stroll around a store and just happen to spot an item you have been looking for everywhere. Whether you like or dislike shopping, once you have purchased a new item you bring it home and add to your collection. Shopping usually brings new items into your household. Most Americans have too much of everything. Whenever I bring home a new piece of clothing I get rid of an old piece. I have just so much drawer space. My drawers and closet are at their limit. I must make hard choices. When I wish to buy a new item I decide prior to purchasing it that I like it more than others (of its type) that I already own. On arriving home I decide what to get rid of, what the new item is to replace. That is how I keep from moving to a bigger house.

Thrift Shops

I hate throwing things in the garbage when they are almost new or never used. So I keep a bag handy - to go to my local thrift shop. Besides being a tax write-off, contributing or donating items to a charity produces a feeling of benevolence and good will. Everyone in the family knows the location of this bag and generously fills it whenever they discard an item. Someone else may be able to use this item that has been so carefully kept, is new, hardly worn, kept only for sentimental reasons or been stored in the back of a closet for the past seven years. However, no one wants a very old, dirty, broken or shabby item, so throw that item out. Once a month I go through the bag and discard items that are not in desirable condition. After washing the clothes and cleaning off appliances and books, I drop the bag at my local thrift shop, come home and place a new empty bag in the same spot.

Make Money from Your Trash

If you are getting rid of things that have some value you can hold a garage sale. It is a quick and easy way to get money for your unwanted stuff. You can advertise the sale around your neighborhood, place it on *www.craigslist.org* (an advertisement search engine in major cities) or send in an announcement with your sale date and address to your local newspaper. You can also find out if your local resale shop will take any items to sell for you. Antiques, collectible, jewelry, paintings, china, silverware and very fine things can be taken to an auctioneer in the hope that they can sell it for you. Be reasonable and do not set your financial expectations too high. At least you can have people pay you to haul away the stuff you do not want anymore. Another alternative is selling items on *eBay*. This Internet site acts as a go-between for buyers and the sellers. Here you can find new and older items and purchase them directly from the seller. All you need to do is set up an *eBay* account. If you own or have access to a digital camera you can take and scan in photographs of your sale items.

Recycle Useful Items

When you are stuck with something that is too nice to throw away or you were unable to sell, go onto *www.freecycle.org*. It's an online matchmaking service for givers and takers where you can give things away or acquire something for yourself. It is an innovative way to use the power of email to connect people with things they want to get rid of with others who would like to have those things. The Freecycle Network is made up of individual regions around the globe. It began as a grass-roots movement by people who wanted to reduce waste and help keep usable items out of landfills. Membership is free and the one rule is that every item posted must be free. To sign up, first find your city on the website. If you cannot find your city you can start your own group by following the instructions. You can post your item or if you see something of interest you can respond to a posting. It will be up to the giver to set up a pick-up time for passing on the item. By keeping this website in mind you can empty your closets knowing your unwanted items will be getting a new loving home.

Why We Keep Things

Throughout the years we have given lots of excuses. We somehow need to justify to ourselves, why we keep things. Instead of taking the time to decide what is important and what we no longer need, we feel it is easier to give an excuse. Because we save so much stuff we do not realize that it will take more time and effort to find what we need, when we need it. Look through these excuses to see if you have used one of them lately:

1. **If I get rid of it today I just know I will need it tomorrow -**
   Even if you really did need it tomorrow go out and buy your self a new one.

2. **It has sentimental value -**
   You keep good memories in your head, not in your closets.

3. **I'm saving it for my children -**
   Most probably your children will not want it and just take it to be polite.

4. It's really old -

If it is an antique and worth real money sell it on eBay or to an antique dealer.

5. It's still in good condition -

If you never use it, it does not matter what condition it is in.

6. It was on sale -

Once you own it the thrill of a good buy is over.

7. Someone gave it to me -

Just because someone gave it to you, if you have no use for it, you don't need it.

8. I inherited it -

We feel inheriting comes with special value but only if it's valuable to begin with.

9. It will be worth money one day -

If it is not worth money now, it probably will never be.

10. I paid good money for that -

It's hard to get rid of an expensive item, but may be more expensive to store it.

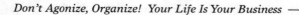

Chapter 7

WHERE IS IT? FINDING & STORING YOUR THINGS

"Order marches with weighty and measured strides.
Disorder is always in a hurry."
Napoleon Bonaparte (1769 - 1821)

Businesses use intelligent and computerized tracking systems to store and instantly retrieve papers, documents, photographs, reports, folders and data at a moment's notice. They would not be able to operate efficiently if they did not. They are constantly making efforts to decrease the amount of paper and replace them with computer files. Setting up a good computer or filing system can make a big difference in the rate of efficiency and data retrieval. Because people think differently than one another retrieval of data can be accomplished by many different methods. Businesses must standardize the preferred retrieval system throughout their organization. By doing this every department will be able to access and retrieve previously filed data without any problems. All the things we own tends to expand to fill the space allotted to it. Unless you wish to live in a warehouse you must store all your belongings efficiently by providing a permanent place of deposit for things that you have a need for in the future. As it is, it is hard enough to keep up with the clutter of incoming mail, new purchases and gifts. You need to find an organized method that you feel comfortable with to store your things.

Organized Storage

I currently live in a house but I used to live in an apartment. I know the value of free space. I was never fortunate enough to have a walk-in closet or one large enough to be organized into proper shelving components. I have learned to organize all my things in small ways, by keeping similar items together, in an orderly manner. The hardest task was learning how to discard clothes, papers and items I no longer wore or needed. As my taste seems to change every so often, so do the contents of my drawers. They reflect the *"me"* I show the world in terms of the clothes I wear, how I present my home and what I value. I wish to portray the person I am and I am constantly changing; so do my tastes and preferences. If I tried to keep everything I ever owned I would need to rent that warehouse.

Hint: *Don't wait for a catastrophe to happen before you are forced to throw away accumulated junk and wanted things.*

Planning For Storage

When planning for storage think about what functions you will perform in the room and store items related to that function. For an example, if you are a reader who likes to read while in bed consider a shelf for books and magazines over the bed. Think of the function and identify how you will access the item. Analyze, prioritize, downsize, categorize and examine what you have. Start with something as simple as cleaning off your desk and storing what you decide to keep in a proper place. Then move up to organizing a single room. Before planning storage areas look through architecture and decorating magazines. Clip out interesting storage ideas and start a file. Then take a walking tour of your home, room by room, and try to visualize changes to get more storage space. Think about utilizing a room in a way in which it is not currently being used. For an example, visualize your guest room as a computer, sewing room or library. When you plan for storage don't be afraid to move things around.

Hint: Start with the room that offers the greatest storage challenge and break down the probable storage areas into units.

Location, Location, Location

You need to place items in your home where you can find them and where you will need them. If you need a hammer to hang up a picture or a screwdriver to tighten a screw on your can opener, you need to have them handy. Keeping a small tool drawer in your kitchen is better than keeping everything in your garage or keeping your tool kit in the back of your hall closet. Assign a spot in one of your kitchen drawers to store several tools that are needed on a frequent basis. Continue to keep your main storage of tools in your garage or in the back of your hall closet for the times when you do major repairs or renovations. Another example may be travel books. You may store all your books in your den, bedroom or basement. However, if you enjoy reading about new places to travel, keep some of your travel books in your living room or wherever you like to read. This way you do not have to waste time finding them and can browse through them whenever the whim strikes you.

Place of No Return

As simple as it sounds, having a convenient place to stash those frequently used items in your daily routine is a great stress reducer. The important thing about keeping things organized is returning them to the same place you originally found them. If you do not return an item to its proper place, you defeat the purpose of keeping things organized. You need to feel that you know where to go to find a certain article or implement. Easy access to your stuff gives you the power of organization. It lets you feel at ease, even in times of crisis, because you are in control and know where to locate things. If you do not return an item to its specific spot you eventually lose this power. You will no longer be able to depend on it being there, when you need it.

> **Hint:** *One of the basic rules of organizing is that everything has its place.*

Disposal

If an item has served its purpose and been good to you, unless you really believe that you will use it in the near future, you should dispose of it. Ask yourself if you will really miss it or if a new one, when the time warrants, will bring you more satisfaction. Things wear out, appliances get better and more sophisticated (VCRs have been replaced by DVDs; CD players by iPods and MP3 players), software is updated and items need repair. Nowadays, it may be cheaper to buy a new one than replace an old one. Consumers are constantly being offered the same wares, with more options, at lower prices. If your closets are bursting with stuff, ask yourself:

- Do I use this?
- Can I let it go?
- Is it a duplicate?
- Is it broken or beyond repair?
- Has it worn out its usefulness?
- How much will it cost to store?
- How much will it cost to clean?
- Do I already have one just like this?
- Why have them take up valuable space?
- Why keep things around just to store them?

Maximum Hangers

Even if you use thin hangers the storage of clothing, coats, shoes and accessories is usually a problem. We tend to have more than we need and we buy more than we discard. Many of us buy things just on impulse. I for one cannot resist a sale and must control myself when I really do not need it. I am attracted to it at the store, it looks good on the hanger and it looks great when I try it on. Unless I can use, need it to compliment something I already own or love it more than an item I already have, I know it will only take up space in my closet. What I do is count the number of tops, sweaters, dresses, skirts, etc. that I own. That's the number that my closet can comfortably handle without cramming more hangers on the rail or being able to close my dresser drawers. When I wish to buy new clothing I remember that I must get rid of something. So I ask myself:

- Do I really need it or just want it?
- Am I buying it just because it is on sale?
- Do I love this new item more than any of the others I now own?
- Do I wish to replace this new item with one that is similar and old?
- Can I justify buying this item if I have one similar that I love to wear?

Clothing Disposal Tips

When looking through your clothes trying to decide whether or not to hold onto an article of clothing, ask yourself these questions:

- Is this comfortable?
- Does this flatter me?
- Does this fit me now?
- How long ago did I wear this?
- Does this go with anything else I own?
- How many items like this do I already own?

And remember these tips to help you thin your closet:

- Stay on top of your system.
- Clothes tend not to improve with age.
- Only keep clothing that fits your current figure.

- Set aside things not worn that season and give them away.
- Keep it moving - once organized, a clothing system is a circulating system, new things in, old things out.

Color Coding

Most people store clothing in their bedroom because it is a convenient place to plan what to wear. Organized people usually store pants, sweaters, underwear, etc. in separate drawers. I get very little direct sunlight in my bedroom and after washing the laundry and placing my clean clothes back in the drawer I need a bright light to separate my black pants from my blue ones. I store them separately so when I am in a rush or do not have enough sunlight coming into the room it is easier to detect the color of a pile than one by itself. By keeping all my sweaters or pants of the same color together I can easily see which ones I like to wear and which ones I seldom wear. Color coding makes it easier to match an outfit when you already have the pants you want to wear and just need to find a matching top. You can limit your selection to one or two matching color sets. Then when I open my clothes closet and see the rainbow of color, it just makes me smile. It also makes the task of finding or discarding a particular one easier.

Seasonal Storage

I love my house but my closets are much too small. Every six months I face the task of bringing my summer clothes up from my basement closet and bringing my winter clothes downstairs. It's an inconvenience but it does allow me the time to go through my wardrobe. I get to discard items I no longer fit into, wear, wish to wear again, are uncomfortable or just don't like the way I look in them anymore. At the end of winter I review my spring/summer wardrobe and at the end of summer I alternately review my autumn/winter wardrobe as I hang them in my bedroom closet and place them in my dresser drawers. This way I only review an item once a year. After I discard an item I subtract it from my maximum amount for the item and look forward to shopping - to fill up my hanger quota again. By doing this chore twice a year I am effortlessly able to clean, organize, simplify and update my entire wardrobe.

Closets and Drawers

You may be the type of person who keeps everything in order. You may have your color-coded shirts hanging neatly in the closet, each one facing the same direction and your shoes lined up in a row. You may be the type of person who throws everything in a pile and lets the piles creep closer to one another. No matter what type you are, taking the time to sort out what you really need and wear will make your life easier. Lots of time you look longingly at an old sweater. You see that the color of it has faded and it does not have the zing it had when you first started wearing it. You see a thread pull and a small stain you can never get out. You also see the night you met your true love, while wearing that sweater. It has become a memoir more than a piece of wearable clothing. You now need to psychologically separate your memories from this article of fabric. It is taking up usable space. You never really wear it any more. You just look at it now and then to remember the good old days. Be strong and get rid of it.

Closet and Drawer Suggestions

1. Organize one drawer at a time.
2. Face items in the same direction.
3. Clean clothes before storing them.
4. Arrange your drawers by categories.
5. Divide your junk drawer into sections.
6. Use a cleared counter to sort your things.
7. Decide what you want to store in the closet.
8. Place all empty hangers in their own section.
9. Arrange items hanging in your closet by length.
10. Don't place things in a closet that do not belong there.

Bedroom Storage Suggestions

A bedroom is a room that is reserved for peacefulness and relaxation. Maintaining an organized room will set a calm mood so you can unwind.

1. Store shoes by color, season and heel length.
2. Use under bed storage for out of season clothes.

3. Spend time on well-designed closets and drawers.
4. Keep jewelry you wear often in a divided container in a drawer.
5. Organize pocketbooks by color and stuff them to keep their shape.
6. Hang belts and a multi-compartment bag on the back of a closet door.
7. Store socks by color and weight, then fold in 1/2 or roll both up into a ball.
8. Use hangers that accommodate your closets - jacket, shirt, pants, belt combos.
9. Arrange clothing by season, sections (blouses, plants), dark to light then prints.
10. Furnish a child's room with modular pieces that have storage and room to grow.

Kitchen Clutter

Kitchen clutter is like a magnet. There is no other room in a house that gets as much clutter as a kitchen. The kitchen is usually the room that forms the center of family life. It is the place to come to for meals, to talk over the day's events, the world events and what matters to you most. The kitchen is usually the hub of activity in a busy household. When I enter my home, the first room I lay down all my packages, briefcase and bags is my kitchen. After I hang up my coat I attempt to tidy up the hurricane of papers and packages I have brought in for the day. Sometimes I do not always succeed and I leave behind an additional item or paper in the kitchen. Plus, my husband and I love to collect kitchenware. You know the kind - they are advertised as making your life easier, a new, easy-to-read while standing measuring cup and a chopper for garlic with the comfortable squeezable handle. Its okay to buy new things but it is better to replace these new kitchen aids and throw out your old measuring cup or garlic peeler. Now it's time to go through it all and throw out what is no longer used, too old or no longer liked.

Kitchen Storage Suggestions

Because of all the daily tasks performed in this room the kitchen requires greater organization and efficiency than any other room in the house.

1. Arrange glasses by size and frequency of use.
2. Keep spices alphabetically ordered on a swivel plate.
3. Hang wraps and foils on a storage rack on the back of a door.
4. Place items not used frequently in cabinets over the refrigerator.
5. Face all labels forward. It's easier to find things. Plus it looks better.
6. Arrange storage containers by size, lids underneath and one inside another.
7. Store frequently used items and kid's items on lower easy-to-reach shelves.
8. Store the same items together. It makes it easier to see how many you have.
9. Place similar size things in same cabinet (cereal boxes and packaged mixes).
10. When counter space is limited use underneath cabinet appliances like can openers.

Hall Closet Suggestions

The hall closet is one that usually all family members make use of. It accumulates everyone's favorite stuff very fast. Monitor the contents and return personal belongings to their rightful rooms.

1. Arrange coats by person.
2. Use containers to store similar items.
3. Arrange coats by long and short lengths.
4. Devise underneath storage for short coats.
5. Use the back of the door for more storage.
6. Use matching hangers all facing same way.
7. For maximum closet space use thin hangers.
8. Place unused or infrequently used items on the top shelf.
9. Place separate baskets in the closet for gloves, mittens and hats.
10. Children's coats should be on closet hangers at their own reach.

Bathroom Storage Suggestions

1. Use the back of door for extra storage.
2. Be creative with storage bins in this room.

3. Check expiration dates on prescription drugs.
4. Store make-up, face and hair products together.
5. Set up a small make-up area with a mirror and all your cosmetics.
6. Arrange medicine cabinet by categories (nose & cough, pain & headache).

Linen Closet Storage Suggestions

1. Store linens by room and by person.
2. Fold and lay towels facing all the same way.
3. Hang iron and ironing board on back of the door.
4. Keep vacuum, hamper or bulky items on linen closet floor.
5. Arrange towels by size, bath, hand, wash clothes and dishtowels.
6. Sheet sets - place pillowcases to top, then top sheets, then bottom sheets.

Space Savers

Living in an apartment taught me lots of storage tricks that I still apply in my house. The best storage I own is my bed. My husband and I share a captain's bed. This type of bed is built with drawers underneath a platform providing easy access and lots of storage space. In case you own a traditional bed do not overlook the storage room under the bed frame. You can buy containers or drawers on wheels that slide and provide extra storage. Give your bed headboard some depth and make it functional. Buy or design a storage space that is at least 12 inches in depth to fill with extra linen, pillows, blankets, etc. We designed one with a shelf for our alarm clock, tissue box, clip on reading lights and other items. If you design it, do not forget to include a front panel that opens to insert stuff. For a child's room it is a great space to store toys or stuffed animals. To save even more space my husband built a vertical bike rack in our apartment. Instead of having our bicycles sitting side-by-side on the floor they hung one on top of the other.

Hint: When you use your creativity and imagination you can come up with unique ways to store objects.

Storage Suggestions

1. Use plastic containers to sort mail.
2. Arrange items in an easy to see fashion.
3. Label and date items you place in the freezer.
4. Display and rotate china and pottery collections, etc.
5. Keep all appliance manuals in a folder in a kitchen drawer.
6. Keep one lost sock in a plastic bag until you find the other one.
7. Schedule time for organizing and maintenance of storage areas.
8. Store items as close as possible to the place where they will be used.
9. Use shelf dividers to separate different groups of items for easy access.
10. Create sets of similar objects and store items with a similar function together.
11. Stow away once-a-year decorations (Xmas, Halloween) in unfrequented areas.
12. Make a travel box - alarm clock, sewing kit, mirror, passport case, packing list.
13. Make a gift-wrap box - scissor, cards, ribbons, boxes, wrapping paper, tissue paper.
14. Store old tax records, out of season clothes, bridal gowns and sporting goods in out-of-the-way areas.
15. Organize the inside of your refrigerator with "Lazy-Susan's" to easily see everything and avoid spoilage.

Space Savers Suggestions

1. Mount bicycles on a wall.
2. Use a bookcase as a room divider.
3. Use luggage and nice old boxes for storage.
4. Turn a closet into a library and store books in it.
5. Store baking sheets and muffin pans in your oven.
6. Use a bench with a seat that opens for hidden storage.
7. Expand or modify closet space for shelving or hanging items.
8. Hang various serving pieces around kitchen as attractive decorations.
9. Take advantage of diagonal dead space underneath a staircase for bookcases.

10. Create a mini office area near the phone (paper, pens, address book or rolodex).
11. Use a bulletin board for emergency numbers, artwork, calendars, schedules, lists.
12. Use suspended racks for hanging pots and pans or store toys in a suspended sack.
13. Remove newly purchased items from the boxes or packaging they come in to take up less space.
14. Take advantage of what you have and find ways of using space you have not thought of yet.
15. Use plastic zippered bags for woolen blankets and delicate clothes to keep them safe from moths and moisture.

Book Storage

Books are a storage problem. I love books and I need to be surrounded by them. You can find them in almost every room of my home. They are organized by subject and category. In my kitchen are cookbooks. In my bedroom are my favorite old classics that I love to re-read. In my living room are my art and photography books and in my basement are all the rest. I love to go to flea markets or thrift stores and find a good buy. Every time I bring a new book into my home, my rule is, I must discard one. Books are dust collectors and if I do not open one then my only contact is through my dust cloth. One day I realized that the public library is filled with an extensive number of books and very highly organized. Instead of holding onto the old classics I re-read every five years I discarded most of them and now visit my library more often. Figuring that I pay local taxes for the storage and organization of books in the library, I just keep my favorites in my home.

Hint: Why would you take up space in your home when you have easy access to a larger variety of books, CDs, videos and DVDs in the library?

Magazine Storage

If you collect magazines you need a plan, you need to organize and you need a system. You also need lots of room because older issues can add up fast, especially if you save various magazines titles. Decide if you wish to keep a certain number of current issues and cap it to that number. You may decide to only hold onto recent issues published in the past year to two. If you plan to keep several years worth you need to plan for magazine storage. Find a place where they can reside in your home. As the pile grows you will need a sturdy box, magazine case or bookcase in which to store them. Make sure you arrange them in order by type of magazine and issue date. Have them all face the same direction and dust the top ones once in awhile.

Labeling

If you are a saver (and almost everyone saves something) you need to label your collection. How worthwhile is a collection of coins if they are all jumbled up in a jar? Like many other collections, coins can be sorted by country, date or denomination. You need to decide how you wish to sort or categorize your collection. Is it easier for you to label them by country, date or denomination? If you share this hobby, or belong to a club, ask others their sorting method. It may give you a new way of looking at it or can confirm your own method of organization. You can also decide to sort chronically by the age of the item or when the item came into your possession, in size order, by monetary value or by an author or artist's name. However you decide to organize your collection you need to label each item so it can be identified and located in a short amount of time. What good is a collection if half of it is scattered in a box at the bottom of your drawer? The best part of keeping a collection is sharing its unique contents with others and gaining a peek at their collections.

Types of Collections That Can Be Sorted and Labeled

Magazines	Postcards	Jewelry	Cassettes
Coins	Baseball Cards	Stamps	LP Records
Pictures	Slides	Fabric	Paintings
Photos on CDs	Music CDs	Pottery	Buttons

Labeling and Sorting Example

The next two pages contain the label and sorting system I created for all the travel and personal color slides I have collected. After

I receive the developed package of slides I closely review each one over a light box to decide if I wish to keep or discard it. For those slides that I decide to keep I label each with the subject of the photograph. Each category of slides is differentiated by a unique two digit alphabetic code (relating to the subject matter). If I do not have an existing category to place the slide, I assign a new two digit alphabetic code for the category. I print the two-digit category code and sequentially number each new slide in the category. I number the slides in chronological order. Several categories contain pictures from several trips to the same location. For new categories I add it to both the Major Slide Category List and Slide Box List. Then, whenever I wish to locate a particular category I can quickly check my list and physically find the slides I wish to view.

Hint: Use a label maker for neatly labeling your collections.

MAJOR SLIDE CATEGORIES IN PLASTIC BOXES:

AE (6)   AROUND EUROPE (WINE COUNTRY) 1982
AM (4)   AMISH
AF (4)   AUTUMN FOLIAGE AT CABIN 1983 thru 1992

BE (2)   BERMUDA
BL (4)   BLOOPERS OF ME
BA (4)   BALLOON FESTIVALS

CA (4)   CABIN
CC (2)   CROSS COUNTRY 1980
CM (5)   CAPE MAY 1996

EW (7)   ENGLAND & WALES 1974
FL (3)   FLORIDA & DISNEY 1989 & 1991
FR (7)   FRANCE 1976

FW (4)   FIREWORKS
GB (7)   GREAT BRITAIN 1976
HA (8)   HALLOWEEN

IT (1)   ITALY (2003)
KU (4)   KUTZTOWN FAIR 1977 & 1993

MO (9)   MOROCCO 1978
MQ (3)   MONTREAL & QUEBEC CITY 1988, 2004
MV (5)   MARTHA'S VINEYARD 1975, 1979, 1981, etc.
NE (3)   NEW ENGLAND 1981

NP (5)   NEWPORT, RHODE ISLAND 1986
NS (3)   NOVA SCOTIA 1973
NY (4)   NEW YORK CITY

OP (3)   OP SAIL   1976
PR (6)   PRAGUE   2004
PE (2)   PEOPLE

RE (4)   RENDEZVOUS
RF (8)   RENAISSANCE FAIR
RU (8)   RUSSIA

SO (6)   USA SOUTH TO NEW ORLEANS 1977
SP (9)   SPAIN 1978
SW (6)   SOUTHWEST 1999

VA (5)   VIRGINIA
VT (3)   VERMONT 1990
WA (2)   WASHINGTON D.C.
WS (5)   WILLIAMSBURG, VA. 1979

MAJOR SLIDE CATEGORIES PER BOX:

BOX # 1:   IT   ITALY 2003

BOX # 2:   BE   BERMUDA
                CC   CROSS COUNTRY 1980
                PE   PEOPLE
                WA   WASHINGTON D.C.

BOX # 3:   FL   FLORIDA & DISNEY 1989 & 1991
                MQ   MONTREAL & QUEBEC CITY   1988, 2004
                NE   NEW ENGLAND 1981
                NS   NOVA SCOTIA 1973
                OP   OP SAIL 1976
                VT   VERMONT 1990

BOX # 4:
AM	AMISH
AF	AUTUMN FOLIAGE AT CABIN 1983 - 1992
BL	BLOOPERS OF ME
BA	BALLOON FESTIVALS
CA	CABIN
FW	FIREWORKS
KU	KUTZTOWN FAIR 1977 & 1993
NY	NEW YORK CITY
RE	RENDEZVOUS

BOX # 5:
CM	CAPE MAY 1996
MV	MARTHA'S VINEYARD 1975, 1979, 1981, etc.
NP	NEWPORT, RHODE ISLAND 1986
VA	VIRGINIA
WS	WILLIAMSBURG, VA. 1979

BOX # 6:
AE	AROUND EUROPE (WINE COUNTRY) 1982
PR	PRAGUE 2004
SO	USA SOUTH TO NEW ORLEANS 1977
SW	SOUTHWEST 1999

BOX # 7:
EW	ENGLAND & WALES 1974
FR	FRANCE 1976, 1996
GB	GREAT BRITAIN 1976

BOX # 8:
HA	HALLOWEEN
RF	RENAISSANCE FAIR
RU	RUSSIA

BOX # 9:
MO	MOROCCO 1978
SP	SPAIN 1978

Your collection may just require a simple list to keep track of what you own. This helps to eliminate purchasing duplicates and quickly shows you what you have already collected. Recording the last date you updated the list shows how current and reliable your listing is.

MY PEZ DISPENSER COLLECTION
Last Date Updated   9-18-2005

Batman
Bugs Bunny
Barney Rubble
Charlie Brown
Daffy Duck
Daisy Duck
Darth Vader
Donald Duck
Easter Bunny
Fozzie Bear
Fred Flintsone
Garfield
Glow in Dark Ghost
Gonzo
Goofy
Kermit the Frog
Lamb
Lucy
Mickey Mouse
Miss Piggy
Ninja Turtle - Donatello
Pink Panther
Pluto
Pumpkin
Skull
Snowman
Speedy Gonzalus
Star Wars Characters
Sylvester
Tazmanian Devil
Tweety Bird
Valentine's Heart
Whistle
Witch
Woodstock
Yosemite Sam

Hiding Clutter

Most probably you have rooms or spaces in rooms that act as a magnet for unwanted, un-needed items (especially in the basement, attic or even the garage). Storage areas are havens for unused materials, items you once picked up and thought that you would one day use. We store things in places that only we can see for one of two reasons. Either we really love the item and wish to save it or we are undecided and ambivalent. It is okay to hang onto an item that you wish to keep and do not have room for but it is not good practice to hang onto one that you just know you will no longer use. Many of these items have outlived their lifetime. Having a place to store these items only prolongs the saving of them and adds to clutter. You may have even believed that you had gotten rid of many of these items long ago. Remember, garbage is your friend and it is okay to rid yourself of an item that has worn out its usefulness, even if you are attached to it. Think of the saying "out of sight, out of mind". Hiding it in a box or drawer only delays the actual act of ridding yourself of the article. Most often you will forget you decided to save it. When you look through the box a year or two from when you first placed it, you will question why you decided to save the item. So, bite the bullet and spend the time sorting through these areas. You may even take the time to repair or revitalize an item of value.

Chapter 8

PERSONAL FINANCIAL PLANNING

"Money is better than poverty,
if only for financial reasons."
Woody Allen (1976 -   )

Most often the main goal of a business is to make a profit. To accomplish this they take definite actions and measures to gain income for the company. The income a business makes is balanced against their expenses as portrayed in a profit and loss statement. If they produce more income than expenses they make a profit. Conversely, if they have more expenses than income they owe money, do not make a profit and have unhappy creditors. The financial end of business is similar to the financial concepts that individuals grapple with everyday. We all do some type of work to produce an income. We balance the income we make against our bills and expenditures. If we have more income than expenses we can save or spend the rest. If our expenses outweigh our income we go into debt and owe money to our creditors. Both a business and an individual can save money, must decide how to invest money, can go bankrupt, must pay taxes, need a method to account for their money, should be covered by insurance and can become very successful financially.

Money in Our Lives

Money constitutes a very powerful force in our lives. It is many times a source that motivates our actions. You only need to look around to see how willing people are to engage in a wide range of activities for money. They drag themselves to work at jobs they hate to earn a steady salary. They get hooked on gambling, sometimes losing everything they own, because of the belief that they will hit the big one. They take on extra assignments at their jobs that unduly stress them, because of the extra money. They buy lottery and raffle tickets in the hope they will be the grand winner. They overextend themselves to maintain a higher standard of living than they can really afford. They engage in a wide variety of criminal activities that promise handsome rewards. As money motivates much of our behavior you need to realize how personal it is to you. How easy your life is with it and how hard your life can be without it.

Hint: By organizing the financial part of your life and learning how to set financial goals you can gain some very lucrative and effective results.

Personal Planning

The attainment of financial security requires organized plans and coordinated actions. We all need goals of one sort or another to give direction to our lives. Personal financial planning involves the setting of personal financial goals and the specific plans and financial arrangements that put those plans into action. One of the pay-offs of sound money management is an improved standard of living and one of the major benefits of financial planning is that it helps to more effectively organize and control your financial resources. It allows you to gain a greater level of enjoyment from your income. Planning how to spend your money wisely is another payoff of financial planning. Your plans give you a better idea of what you should do with the money you make. You can either spend it, or save and invest a portion of it for the future. Defining your current and future financial goals determines how you will spend your money.

Financial Planning in a Lifetime

- Early Childhood - getting allowance
- High school and College - paying for an education and incurring car expenses
- Family - covering insurance needs, health needs and for financial security
- Career - income, pension, tax and retirement planning
- Pre-Retirement - saving and investment plans, as well as estate planning
- Retirement - income stream and inflation

Financial Priorities in a Lifetime

- Living - paying monthly bills and expenses
- Pleasure - spending money on travel, entertainment and fun
- Children - future needs and college education
- Disability - protect against loss of income
- Reduce Taxes - tax saving techniques and estate planning
- Investing - accumulating assets
- Retirement - investing in the future
- Death - taking care of family

Financial Planning

Instead of attacking personal financial planning head on, let's break your whole money world into smaller pieces and see what each part entails. By exploring how each part of financial planning affects your life you can learn how to organize and control it.

1. **Income and Expenditures** - *a measurement of your financial performance*
2. **Budgeting** - *a summary of your income and expenditures for a given period*
3. **Financial Goals** - *mapping out your financial future, defining and setting goals*
4. **Coping with Taxes** - *documenting your income, deductions and tax planning*
5. **Savings and Investments** - *allocation developed for your risk tolerance*
6. **Assets and Acquisitions** - *home, boat, autos, mutual funds, stocks and bonds*
7. **Credit** - *retail charge cards, bank credit cards, loans and mortgages*
8. **Insurance** - *life, health, property, automobile, disability and long-term care*
9. **Planning for the Future** - *college planning, retirement goals and estate planning*

Income and Expenditures

Income is any money that comes into your household. It consists of wages, bonuses, commissions, tips, pensions, annuities, dividends, interest, rents, proceeds from a sale of assets, tax refunds or even, gambling winnings. The amount of your household income establishes your standard of living. Your standard of living indicates the presence or absence of certain material items, such as a home, cars, expensive jewelry or the wealth of an individual. Consumption is the using of goods or services to satisfy your wants. Expenditures for food, clothing, shelter, utilities, entertainment and insurance are considered expenses for current consumption. Expenditures for a retirement fund, a child's education, a vacation home or major acquisition such as a car or boat are considered expenses for future consumption. Balancing your income and expenditures are a big part of financial planning. The expenses you think you can control are usually the costs that get out of control. When people are given a chance to spend money what starts as a novel nice-to-have expenditure can quickly become a necessity.

> **Hint:** *Financial planning and money management provides the ability to gain a greater level of enjoyment from the money you make and improve your living standard.*

Budgeting

Creating a budget will show you how and where you spend money. It is a detailed list of all your daily, monthly and yearly expenses. It can be used to monitor and control your expenses, purchases, income and savings. A budget is a short-term planning device that you can design to help you achieve your financial goals. It can assist in controlling what you spend money on and can help reduce the amount of money you spend. A budget worksheet is easy to design. Look at the budget worksheet on the next page to begin.

- List all the items or categories that you spend money for. Use any categories listed plus others for which you spend a portion of your income.

- Write down the amount of money you pay for each item.

- Determine if the item is a monthly, semi-annual, or yearly expense.

- Multiply (by 12 for monthly or by 2 for semi-annual) to calculate the yearly cost.

- Total up the yearly cost of all your items to get a picture of your annual expenditures.

Periodically review your budget and update categories when they change or amounts when your costs increase. A balanced budget is one in which your total income for the year equals or exceeds your total expenditures. A budget deficit is a situation that occurs when your expenditures exceed the income in your cash budget. Once you know where your money is going, you can start making conscious choices about how to put it to work for you. Having this information allows you to be in command; however a budget that is elastic and ever changing should be questioned and treated with skepticism.

Hint: *Use your budget as a mechanism of isolating areas that need to be adjusted.*

2005 BUDGET
HOUSEHOLD AND FAMILY EXPENSES

ITEM	Per Cost	Occurs	Yearly
1. Mortgage / Rent	935	12	11,220
2. Property Tax	1,350	4	5,400
3. Home / Renters Insurance	400	1	400
4. Auto Insurance	1,000	2	2,000
5. Car Maintenance	225	4	900
6. Telephone	65	12	780
7. Cell Phone	40	12	480
8. Cable	55	12	660
9. Electric	85	12	1,020
10. Oil Heat	960	1	960
11. Internet	25	12	300
12. Garbage Removal	165	4	260
13. Water & Sewage	150	4	600
14. Lawn and Garden Supplies	200	4	800
15. Groceries	80	50	4,000
16. Clothing	300	4	1,200
17. Child Care	800	12	9,600
18. Personal Care	40	12	480
19. Savings	500	12	6,000
20. Vacations	1,500	2	3,000
21. Dining Out	50	12	1,800
22. Entertainment	200	12	2,400
23. Religious Contributions	550	3	1,650
24. Charitable Contributions	500	4	2,000
25. Magazine Subscriptions	35	4	140
26. Hobby Supplies	275	5	1,375
27. Gifts	250	2	500
28. Dues	75	1	75
TOTAL			$60,000.

Financial Goals

In an ideal world you wouldn't have to choose between saving for retirement, taking that once in a lifetime vacation or buying your dream car. But here in the real world, financial trade-offs are a fact of life. You need to use personal financial planning to achieve your financial goals. Knowing what you hope to accomplish financially and how you intend to do it gives you an edge over someone who reacts to financial events as they occur. Meeting and exceeding expenses and savings are dependent upon your spending habits and goals. You may wish to pay bills on time, create a budget, start an emergency fund, save for a home or car or child's education, get insurance, make a will, start your own business, control your living expenses, manage taxes effectively, establish a saving and investment program, pay back loans on time or address your retirement needs. Some financial goals can be defined rather generally while others should have a dollar value or a goal target date assigned to it. At different points in your life, different types of financial goals and plans become more important than others. Short-term goals set each year should be consistent with any established long-term goals. Long-term financial goals can have short and long-range results. Future financial goals can go into retirement and sometimes beyond.

Hint: Define short-term goals to achieve within one year, intermediate goals to achieve from one to five years and long-term goals to achieve over five years.

Tips for Setting Financial Goals

- Rank your financial goals in order of priority.
- Set financial goals in terms of the results you want to attain.
- Set financial goals that are realistically attainable, not a pipe dream.
- Set a target date or monetary amount when you are to meet your goal.
- Set your financial goals with a definite timeframe in mind - short or long term.

Psychology of Money

Your emotional response to money can be positive - love, happiness, security or downbeat - fear, greed or insecurity. For some people saving and accumulating money provides financial security and is a high priority. Others place greater emphasis on spending money on material goods in order to reduce anxiety and enhance feelings of self worth. Each individual is a unique personality and their emotional makeup determines the importance and role of money to his or her life. You need to assess the role of money in your life. This understanding is a prerequisite to the development of realistic and effective financial plans and goals. Your financial plans must not only consider your wants, needs and financial resources but also realistically reflect your personality and emotional reactions to money.

> *Hint: The key to effective personal financial planning is having a realistic understanding of the role of money and its use in your life.*

Coping with Taxes

The average American family pays about a third of its income in taxes. Income taxes are levied against your taxable income (the amount remaining after all adjustments, deductions, credits and exemptions are subtracted from your gross income). Learn to take advantage of every tax benefit, deduction and credit to minimize your personal income taxes.

Here are a few tax organization techniques that you can follow:

- To insure that you take every deduction into account put all tax related receipts and statements in one place. A simple folder or large envelope labeled *"Taxes"* will collect all your papers until you prepare to fill out your taxes.

- To eliminate the need of reconstructing sales transactions months later, record all security purchases and sales onto a copy of the Schedule D (capital gains and losses form) when they occur.

- Make a serious hobby into a side business and cash in on the many tax breaks entrepreneurs get for buying supplies, equipment, insurance and more.

- Every tax year check that you have the correct amount of with holdings allowances claimed, do not overpay withholding taxes.

- Keep a separate folder for all charitable contributions and receipts so you can easily add them up when tax time arrives.

- Place a checkmark next to any entry in your checkbook that can be considered deductible or is a taxable expense.

- If you pay estimated taxes do so every quarter.

Saving Money

Saving money for long-term goals or big acquisitions and purchases is essential for having enough to cover the cost. Accumulating money may be a first step to accomplishing some of your goals. Saving money may not be so easy as spending it but it can be painless. There are ways to save money that you do not even know you are doing it.

Here are some smart money savings suggestions:

1. Cut coupons.
2. Use up gift cards.
3. Save all your change.
4. Consolidate credit cards.
5. Buy no load mutual funds.
6. Be on the lookout for sales.
7. Save money by spending less.
8. Practice comparison shopping.
9. Keep credit cards to a minimum.
10. Start saving early in your lifetime.
11. Find items you need at garage sales.
12. Keep cash in interest bearing accounts.
13. If you are self-employed - start a Keogh plan.
14. Consolidate telephone services with one carrier.
15. Switch credit cards to ones with lower interest rates.
16. Be wary of inflation and do not forget to account for it.
17. Perform an annual review of your auto insurance for changes.
18. Be conscious of the yields, interest and dividends you receive.

19. Leave your nest egg alone and just use the interest or dividends.
20. Treat saving as a fixed expense like an automatic payment to yourself.
21. Shelter income from taxes in IRAs, Roth IRAs, 401K, 403(b) or 457 plans.
22. Choose a bank that is convenient, competitive and gives a high interest rate.
23. When you pay off a loan, continue to write checks for the same amount as the monthly payment but send them to your savings.
24. Practice dollar cost averaging - invest the same dollar amount each month to purchase stock or mutual fund shares at various prices to average your cost.

Investments

Just as businesses make investments for the future hope of making more money, so can you. Investments are assets that are acquired to make a profit rather than to provide a service. Investments are typically stocks, bonds, mutual funds and other types of securities held for the future benefit or profit they offer. Nowadays there are so many ways to invest your money: stocks, bonds, mutual funds, money markets, real estate, certificates of deposit, etc. There is also so much information available to you. Financial and investment firms vie to get your business and they provide a wealth of information. Consider consulting with a financial planner before making any major decisions. A financial planner looks at your whole financial picture and can help guide you to the right choices to meet your financial goals or particular situation. The type of investments you select should be in concert with your goals and your personality. You need to decide on your risk tolerance, the timing of your financial goals, the performance and rate of return of the particular type of security and your comfort zone.

Hint: Do not buy an investment that you are uncomfortable with or do not fully understand.

Financial Risk

There are uncertainties associated with every type of investment. The business you invest in may fail or the stock market may turn downward. The price of a security is always changing. Stock markets are so closely tied to everything that happens in the world and can react in an extremely volatile manner. There are no guarantees that you will get back what you put in. You take a risk - most often, the greater the risk the higher the return. How big a risk are you willing to take? A lot may depend upon your time horizon and when you will actually need the money. The longer your timeframe, the more aggressive you can be. You cannot control the future but the present is in your hands. One way to lessen your risk is to make good choices. Do your research and compare performance by looking at prospectuses and annual reports.

Diversification and Asset Allocation

To be a successful investor, you need a plan. You should spread your money over a broad spectrum of stocks and bonds and consider the growth, value and international sectors. Diversification is choosing securities that have various risk-return characteristics to create a balanced portfolio that will provide an acceptable level of return while giving you an acceptable exposure to risk. Such diversification will protect you against sharp swings in the market, help you stay the course in rocky times and can improve your long-term returns. An investor's most important decision is selecting the mix of assets to be held in their portfolio. Asset allocation involves how you divide your assets among stocks, bonds and cash investments, as well as within those asset classes.

Hint: *Watch out for additional charges and management fees as these can eat away at your principal.*

Assets and Acquisitions

For the most part, it is your assets that determines how wealthy or well off you are. An asset is a useful or valuable item you own and an acquisition is an item you have purchased and now own. The accumulation of various assets and acquisitions total your worth or determine how wealthy you are. Assets and acquisitions can consist of a home, automobile, boat, mutual funds, stocks, bonds, jewelry, collectible, antiques, silverware or a valued work of art. The key here is the word *"valued"*. To be considered an asset the item must have value to someone, besides yourself. You can usually exchange an asset for a price or dollar value. The goal of many people is to accumulate as many assets as possible thus increasing their wealth. A measure of a person's wealth is called their *"net worth"*. Adding up all your assets and subtracting all your liabilities will give you this figure. Everyone should be aware of his or her net worth. The two worksheets essential for organizing your financial life is a budget, which is the basis of any good financial plan and a worksheet detailing your net worth.

Create a New Worth Worksheet

NET WORTH = ASSETS – LIABILITIES

1. Create a list of all your **ASSETS.**	2. Create a list of all your **LIABILITIES.**
Cash	Credit Card Balances
Checking Accounts	Credit Card Debt
Saving Accounts	Car Loans
Money Market Accounts	Car Leases
Certificate of Deposits	Student Loans
Treasury Bills	Loans against Investments
Bonds	Loans against Insurance
Mutual Funds	First Mortgage Loan
Stocks	Second Mortgage Loan
Stock Options	Home Equity Line
Investment Real Estate	Personal Debts
Retirement Accounts	Taxes Due
Pensions	Other Liabilities
Value of Personal Residence	
Value of Automobiles	
Value of Life Insurance (Cash Surrender Value)	
Personal Belongings - Jewelry & Furnishings	

3. **Subtract your total liabilities from your total assets to get your net worth.**

- The key to increasing your net worth is to preserve more of your assets. Create an action plan to control expenses and increase investments.

- Keep the worksheet current with any financial changes you make in your life so you will always know your net worth.

The next pages detail a net asset worksheet for a working couple and a young child.

FAMILY TOTAL ASSET CHART
DICK'S PORTFOLIO

SECURITY NAME	INITIAL VALUE	CURRENT VALUE	TYPE
Retirement Funds			
401K Fund at Work	varies	143,000	401K
Clipper Fund	12,000	15,000	Roth IRA
Mutual Funds			
Fidelity Magellan	10,000	13,000	Growth
Vanguard Index 500	12,000	16,000	Growth
Securities			
Verizon	2,000	3,560	143 Shares
IBM	4,000	8,440	45 Shares
Dick's Retirement Accounts		158,000	
Total Mutual Funds		29,000	
Total Stock Value		12,000	
Total Stock Value		10,000	
DICK'S TOTAL ASSETS		199,000	

JANE'S PORTFOLIO

SECURITY NAME	INITIAL VALUE	CURRENT VALUE	TYPE
Retirement Funds			
401K Fund at Work	varies	113,000	401K
Vanguard Index 500	9,000	13,500	Roth IRA
Mutual Funds			
Fidelity Growth & Income	5,000	8,600	Blend
NJ Municipal Fund	10,000	12,400	Tax-Free

Securities

Coca-Cola	2,000	3,440	100 Shares
IBM	4,000	6,560	25 Shares

Jane's Retirement Accounts	**126,500**
Total Mutual Funds	**21,000**
JANE'S TOTAL ASSETS	**157,500**

SALLY'S PORTFOLIO

SECURITY NAME	INITIAL VALUE	CURRENT VALUE	TYPE
College Fund			
Education IRA	10,000	13,000	IRA
Securities			
CATS due 2010	500	2,000	Zero Coupon Bond
Sally's College Account		**13,000**	
Total CATS Value		**2,000**	
SALLY'S TOTAL ASSETS		**15,000**	

TOTALS FOR FAMILY

Dick's Portfolio	199,000
Jane's Portfolio	157,500
Sally's Portfolio	15,000
Totals of Portfolios	**371,500**

House	70,000	(300,000 - Mortgage 230,000)
2 Cars	24,000	
Jewelry	6,000	
Personal Property	25,000	

TOTAL ASSETS	*496,500*

LIABILITIES FOR FAMILY

Mortgage	230,000
Car Payment	13,000
Credit Card	500

TOTAL LIABILITIES	**243,500**

TOTAL ASSETS	**496,500**
– TOTAL LIABILITIES	**243,500**
NET WORTH	**= $253,000**

Credit

Credit is a debt that you owe. Retail charge cards, bank credit cards, loans and mortgages are forms of credit. Sometimes buying on credit is a good thing. Businesses rely on their credit all the time. It is a convenient and effective way to purchase a variety of goods and services. However, if it is not kept organized it can easily become unmanageable and get out of hand. How you manage your debt is just as important as how you manage your assets. Create a list of your creditors, how much you owe and when you need to make payments to keep on track. Paying your bills early and paying off your creditors is advantageous. You can benefit because it creates trust between you and your creditor, ensures excellent future service and builds a positive credit profile for you. Organize files to have a folder for each of your creditors. Look over incoming statements and file away paid ones. Hang onto statements in case a discrepancy occurs. Most credit companies provide a year-end statement listing all the transactions from the past year. If you have received a year-end statement, clean out your folder and discard all the individual monthly statements.

Preventing Identity Theft

Identity theft is an invasion of your privacy. It can be an expensive and timely ordeal, causing great emotional and financial distress. A thief only needs your social security or driver's license number, birth date, PIN (personal identification number) or one piece of personal information. Your best defense against identity theft is prevention. Keeping organized files plus being vigilant and alert should keep you out of trouble.

Here are some suggestions you can use to protect yourself:

1. Cancel inactive credit card accounts.
2. Never leave your wallet or purse unattended.
3. Refuse to give any caller personal information.
4. Never place a PIN on your card or in your wallet.
5. Monitor your credit card reports on a regular basis.
6. Never leave your wallet inside a coat that you hang in a public place.
7. Vary your passwords for financially sensitive accounts and online banking.
8. Call your card issuer if a new or reissued card does not arrive when expected.
9. Sign your credit and debit cards in permanent ink as soon as you receive them.
10. Check your statements frequently and carefully for all activity on your account.
11. Obtain a copy of your credit report once a year from the 3 national credit bureaus.
12. Shred papers and receipts that contain credit card, social security or PIN numbers.
13. Do not carry your social security card, birth certificate or passport unless it is necessary.
14. Place your work phone number on your personal checks instead of your home phone number.
15. Consider dropping your address from your phone book listing or getting an unlisted phone number.
16. File a police report if your wallet or purse was stolen as a first step in case an investigation takes place.
17. Keep a list of your credit and bank accounts so you can quickly contact the issuers to inform them about missing or stolen cards.
18. Do not write your credit card number on a check instead just write the last four numbers and the credit card company will know the rest.
19. Keep a watch on your mail and if your bills do not arrive when they usually do each month, someone could be tampering with your mail.

20. When ordering new checks omit your first name and only list your initials and last name. Then if someone takes your checkbook they will not know how you sign your checks (with just your initial or your first name) but your bank will know how you sign them.

If you feel you are victim of identity fraud:

- Notify all your bank accounts and credit card companies immediately.
- Call the three national credit reporting organizations to place a fraud alert on your name and social security number.

Equifax:	(800) 525-6285	www.equifax.com
Experian:	(888) 397-3742	www.experian.com
Trans Union:	(800) 680-7289	www.transunion.com

Insurance

Insurance provides a means of protecting both income and assets. A sound business practice is to purchase insurance to cover all aspects of the operation. One disaster or unexpected incident can incapacitate a business. One serious illness or accident can wipe out everything you have accumulated over the years. There is insurance for your home or apartment. You can get flood insurance or earthquake insurance. There is insurance to cover your life and your health - medical, dental and vision. There is insurance for your personal property and also liability (umbrella) insurance. There is disability insurance for when you are disabled and long-term care insurance for when you are elderly. Not everyone needs every type of insurance. You can easily over insure yourself. Defining your insurance needs and goals are part of financial planning. Once you have defined them, educate yourself on all your insurance options before you make any decisions.

Planning for the Future

In a carefully developed financial plan a portion of current income should be set aside for the future. You may want to put money aside to build up a retirement fund so you can maintain a certain standard of living in your elder years. Put money away for a child's college education, a large expense, a second home, a major acquisition or even a vacation. Many of the goals you set for yourself contain future objectives. Planning for your financial future and accumulating towards your financial goals will allow you to put your plans into action. The attainment of financial security requires organized plans and coordinated actions. The money you put aside for the future is placed into various saving and investment vehicles to generate a return over the time it is held. The portion of your current income that you save for the future will be a function of the amount of money you earn and your level of current spending. The more you earn and the less you devote to current consumption the more you can commit to your future needs. That is why practicing good saving habits are important to your future.

College Planning

If you are planning ahead you may consider saving for a college fund before the birth of your child. Your child's education is one of the major responsibilities you may face as a parent. It helps to begin saving as early as possible. College costs can be very expensive and consistently rise over time. The goal should be to earn as much interest, dividends or capital gains as you can and pay as little taxes as possible on it. The more money you have saved for college the less you will need to borrow. With the help of Education IRAs, State IRA plans, 529 College Savings plans, prepaid tuition plans, savings bonds or any combination of other investment tools you should plan to accumulate as much as you can. Of course, if you do not have enough saved there is always eligibility for financial aid or low-cost student or parent loans. Your child may even decide to contribute to their own college fund from a part-time job or from gifts they have received throughout the years. If they work diligently in high school and attain high grades they can look forward to possibly being offered college scholarships. The sooner you establish a college fund, the better are your chances for accumulating enough.

Retirement Planning

Money is a big concern in retirement, having enough money put aside to enjoy yourself, spending time on a favorite hobby or being able to travel when retirement actually rolls around. The sooner you begin thinking about your financial plans for retirement the better off you will be. Time is on your side. The longer you have to save and the larger the amounts you save, the more money you will have when you retire. The best person to decide how to build and invest your retirement monies is you. You first need to assess your current financial picture and anticipate how much money you will need in your retirement. You can then figure out how much you need to save with the amount of time you have until you begin your retirement. Depending upon your risk tolerance, the amount of assets you have amassed and your investment goals, you can adjust your investment plans. Besides, social security, the government has provided us with tax-deferred (401K, Keogh, IRA, 403(b), 457 plans) and tax-free (Roth IRA) investment vehicles. Learn what you need to, to start planning early and saving for your retirement so you can enjoy it to the fullest.

Hint: Your retirement investment savings should surpass or at least keep pace with inflation.

The Sandwich Generation

You may be one of the many baby boomers who have obligations towards their aging parents and their college-age or college-bound children. They are called the *"sandwich generation"*. Along with providing for the care of elderly parents and paying for the education of their own children they are often pulled in several other directions by the need to save for their own retirement, by career pursuits, pressure at work and by other family relationships. Keeping money matters organized should help to lessen the financial and emotional strains. If you find yourself in this situation have frank discussions with your parents and children. Plan to discuss the resources available and the financial planning issues that will affect the entire family. Get to know about and organize your parents' finances and make any adjustments you need to keep your own financial plans on track.

Estate Planning

Estate planning is developing plans and taking action during your lifetime to ensure that your wealth will be accumulated, preserved and upon your death distributed in your desired fashion. Even if you just have sentimental items that you wish to leave to certain people you should prepare a will. Estate planning requires knowledge of legal trusts, wills and taxes. It uses tax minimization tools and techniques to provide the greatest possible financial security of an individual and his or her heirs or beneficiaries. The overall objective of estate planning is to ensure the orderly transfer of as much of one's estate as possible. One challenge of effective retirement planning is to achieve a comfortable standard of living in retirement while preserving as much of your accumulated wealth as possible.

Computers Can Help You with Your Finances

Computers and technology have made dealing with your finances and bookkeeping easier. You no longer have to spend hours keeping track of your investments, evaluating various financial scenarios, deciding on the best diversification for your assets or paying someone else to do your taxes.

Here are some ways you can let computers help you:

1. Check writing and bill paying
2. Prepare and monitor a budget
3. Manage investment portfolios
4. Keep track of major purchases
5. Manage insurance coverage plans
6. Keep track of your retirement plans
7. Evaluate and control exposure to taxes
8. Evaluate insurance coverage and credit decisions
9. Try various financial scenarios with financial calculators
10. Do time consuming, mathematical computations and analytical work

Achieving Financial Goals

How will you achieve your financial goals? Once you have set and prioritized your financial goals they can be put into action through various types of financial strategies. There are a variety of different types of financial plans - insurance plans, savings plans, investment plans, tax plans, retirement plans, college plans and estate plans. Together these plans cover the most important financial decisions of your life, from the amount of debt you incur to how effectively you gain and dispose of your assets. There are calculators, planners, worksheets and interactive toots to assist you with all your unique financial planning needs. You can find them on the Internet, in books and through many financial institutions. Here is a general description how each type of plan helps you organize your financial life and how it can improve your financial situation.

Investment Planning

- *Portfolio Review* - Compiles a list of your assets and investments. Creates integrated investment strategies for your specific goals.

- *Investment Growth* - Tracks the growth of your current portfolio. Helps you see how different factors may affect the growth of your portfolio.

- *Asset Allocation* - Categorizes how your current assets are allocated. Helps you explore other investment options that match your objectives.

- *Fund Evaluator* - Identifies and compares mutual funds and individual stocks according to your own criteria.

- *Stock Analyzer* - Shows you charts, graphs, past performance and various financial data on your stock selection.

Insurance Planning

- *Life Insurance* - Determines how much life insurance is necessary for your family to maintain their current standard of living should the unexpected occur.

- *Medical Insurance* - Calculate what type of medical plan, traditional indemnity or managed care (HMO, PPO, high-deductible) plan will cover your family's needs.

- *Disability Insurance* - Even if you get disability from your job it may not be enough. Calculators can help figure out how much additional coverage is needed.

Tax Planning

- *Tax-Deferred* - Compares the future value on an investment under both taxable (subject to yearly income tax) and tax-deferred (taxed at time of withdrawal).

- *IRA Converter* - Helps you decide if you should convert your Traditional IRA to a Roth IRA and pay taxes now or keep your Traditional IRA and pay taxes later.

College Planning

- *College Planner* - Helps you estimate the cost of your child's college education and how much your savings will be worth when your child goes to college.

- *Education Savings* - Explains and compares the various options you have for saving for college education: State IRA plans, 529 College Savings Plans, etc.

Retirement Planning

- *Retirement Planner* - Assesses your expenses and income and projects how long your retirement savings will last.

- *Retirement Calculator* - Evaluates the amount of money you will need in your retirement and long-range savings strategies you can use to meet your goal.

- *IRA Evaluator* - Explains the different types of IRAs and helps you evaluate which type of IRA may be right for you.

- *MRD Calculator* - Minimum required distribution calculator. Tells you the minimum amount you need to withdraw from retirement accounts once you turn 70 $1/2$ years of age.

Estate Planning

- *Estate Tax* - Estimates the potential amount of your Federal Estate Tax liability so you can begin taking steps to preserve your wealth and protect your heirs.

- *Estate Planner* - Creates planning strategies based on your financial needs and goals. It encompasses your personal wishes, family's well being and charities.

Master Financial List

It is important to keep a list of personal financial information. This is necessary in case you or someone else in charge of your affairs (if an emergency situation occurs) needs a handy list of accurate financial information.

Compile a list of:

1. Social Security Numbers - for every member in the household.

2. Address of Primary (and Secondary) Residence.

3. Children's Name and Birth Dates.

4. Education for every member in the household.

5. Driver's license numbers for all family members.

6. Wedding Date and Dates of any Divorces.

7. Location of Documents - life, auto, disability, medical and dental insurance policy numbers, deeds, titles to cars and home properties, birth certificates, passports, military discharge papers, marriage certificates, death certificates or divorce papers.

8. Names of Consultants for Financial Planning - attorney, accountant, bank, insurance agent, security broker or mutual funds companies.

9. Assets - checking account, money market account, certificate of deposits, cash and security investments - include the location, balance, cost basis and date acquired of each asset listed.

10. Liabilities - list the original amount of the loan, interest rate, payment amount, how often paid and pay off date.

11. Credit cards - company, credit card number, annual fee, interest rate and maximum line of credit.

12. Will or Trust - where it can be found, plus the names and addresses of beneficiaries.

Chapter 9

LET THE GOOD TIMES ROLL

"Home is heaven and orgies are vile,
but you need an orgy once in awhile."
Ogden Nash (1902 - 1971)

Businesses look forward to celebrating their successes. They aim to promote team spirit and communication among employees and management. What better way to celebrate than to hold a party. Parties and celebrations are a major part of business social life. By reaching out to their customers and employees businesses can thank them for their hard work and a job done well. Holidays are often a common time for employees from different departments to socialize at parties. To handle all the arrangements for a successful party all the planning, preparing and invitations are done ahead of time.

Businesses also arrange for travel away from the office. Many executives, as well as employees, must travel between offices to meet with staff, take a class, oversee a business process or operation at a different location, attend a meeting, take part in a conference or temporarily work on an assignment. Even though business trips are not for pleasure they must still be planned and scheduled. Usually the travel department or the administrative assistants in each division of the company are responsible for making all the arrangements, creating an itinerary and obtaining the necessary tickets.

Party Planning

Everyone wants to have a wonderful party where every detail has been taken care of, no incidental items are missed, no one is left off the guest list, the weather is great, nothing terrible occurs at the last minute and everyone enjoys themselves. To accomplish all this, planning ahead is a must for holding a successful party, an event or just an intimate dinner party. There is a definite thought process that accompanies the organizing and scheduling of a party. All the petty details need to be decided upon and reviewed before the actual actions involved in getting the party together can begin.

Hint: Organizing a party usually involves being creative, flexible and innovative.

Defining Objectives

Once you have answered some preliminary questions and defined the purpose of the party you will be ready to begin planning. The first question you need to ask is - what is the goal of the party or event? Are you honoring a special birthday, an anniversary or celebrating an event in someone's life or a success? Once you are clear on your goal you need to think about whom you are reaching or rather who will be invited. Will it be friends, family, business associates, neighbors or any combination of the fore mentioned. You then need to think about the size of the party you are about to plan. Will it be a large gala, catered affair or an intimate party of close acquaintances? Think hard about the actual number of guests, who will be invited as this will drive many of the other decisions you will have to make along the road.

- Purpose of the event
- Number of guests
- Who will you be inviting

Hint: Checkout www.evite.com to create personalized invitations and manage your RSVPs online.

The Dinner Party

Just because you are only inviting another couple to your dinner party, instead of 100 people, does not mean it lets you off the hook. You still need to plan. You need to make sure that everyone you wish to invite is available at the specified time. If you wish to have a flawless affair (one where you too can enjoy yourself) you need to make prior preparations and make sure that everything is ready and timed appropriately. You must still decide what to serve, what ingredients to buy, flowers for the table, background music or other atmosphere. Aside from cleaning your home, you need to grocery shop and prepare your dinner. I always prepare a menu for any meal I make for guests. Many times in my excitement I forget to take out a food dish from the refrigerator and then I feel badly afterward. By making a menu and placing it on my refrigerator door I can easily glance at it throughout the evening. It keeps me on track and assures that I serve all that I had planned. The best part of having prepared as much as I can beforehand is that I can mingle with my guests and do not have to be away from the conversation for any long period. The point of entertainment is for the enjoyment of your guests and as greedy as I am, I want to enjoy them too.

Hint: To avoid seating confusion at the dinner table print name cards for each of your guests where you wish them to sit. This will provide an extra touch of style and set an elegant mood.

Preliminary Planning

Money is a major factor in party decisions. Ask how much are you willing to spend and what is the maximum you wish to pay? A party that appears effortless involves many small details, each attributing to the total cost. Next you need to think about how you will attract attention to the affair. Will you send out formal invitations with a RSVP, casually telephone the guests or advertise your event? You must decide on the site or location you wish to hold your event - in your home, someone else's house, a catering hall, a restaurant or in an outdoor setting? This factor is dependent upon the number of people you are planning to host at the event. Selecting an appropriate date and time of day for the event will depend on whether or not people need to travel to get to the event location, the type of event and the availability of the guests.

- Site selection
- Budgeting for the cost
- Appropriate date and time
- Promotion and attracting attention

Program Planning

What you plan for your guests to do during the course of the event is very important and must be planned in detail. The agenda will be dependent upon the type of event. You need to think about the ambiance and atmosphere you wish to create. If you decide on music, will you need the professional resources of a band, DJ, quartet or singer? Will you need an announcer, clown, comic or musical entertainer? Think about the type of music you wish - classical, contemporary, rock n' roll, R&B, jazz, etc. What type of audience participation are you expecting? Do you wish the guests to dance, sing or give speeches? Will you need the services of a professional photographer to photograph or video your guests? Are there materials that must be secured beforehand? Will you require a film or slide projector, a microphone, a recording device, musical instruments, audiovisual device or a special prop?

- Determine the agenda
- What type of audience participation
- What materials are needed to achieve it

Space Planning

The actual physical space that you wish to hold the event must accommodate everyone you wish to invite. If you plan on doing any extra activities you need to provide a space and the material for them. The room size and room capacity is dependent on how you wish to fill the space. To help you calculate the space you need to think about table arrangements and how many guests you plan to seat at each table. The food and beverages you wish to serve at the event must not only be ordered in advance but most often prepared and purchased in advance. Will you be providing everything or will it be catered? Do you need to plan for the services of a bartender or cocktail waitress? Do you plan on decorating the space or having flowers or balloons? How will your guests get to the event? Must you provide transportation or directions? Do you need to make hotel arrangements for guests coming from other locations?

- Decoration
- Transportation
- Food and beverages
- Room size or room capacity

Planning Checklist

The following pages contain a party-planning checklist of items that you should review while organizing your next event. Once you have made some decisions, write them down. You can always change them later, if you come up with more ideas, as it is only meant to be a guide. There may be some items that will not fit with your event on this checklist or you may need to add other items specific to your event. Use it as a guideline to make sure you cover all the necessary basics.

> ***Hint:*** *If all the planning seems to overwhelm you, consider hiring a party planner, if you can afford one.*

Objective/Purpose of Event _____

Theme of Event_____

Date of Event _____

Time of Event _____

Location of Event _____

Place or Location - Check Availability
Cost
Size
Dance Floor
Service charges

Transportation - Air
To / From Hotel
To / From Events
Other Transportation
Parking
Hotel Accommodations

Invitations - Theme
RSVP
Date
Guest List
Select Stock and Envelopes for Invitation
Create Message for Invitation
Print Invites
Mail Invites
Track Invites

Food and Catering - Determine Provider
Consider References
Consider Quality
Servers
Determine Menu
Determine Quantity
Consider Diets and Special Meals
Place Final Order

Rental Items - Arrange Delivery of Tables, Chairs, Linens
Tented or Outside Enclosure

Lighting
Weather Considerations - Heaters, Fans or
                            Canopies
China or Plastic Ware

Entertainment -   Appropriate Theme
                      Professional References
                      Timeline and Schedule all of the Events
                      Children's Activities - Select for Appeal, Safety,
                                Supervision
                      Adult Activities - Theme Appropriate and
                                References
                      Decorations - Samples and Quantity
                      Flowers or Centerpieces
                      Pictures or Video - References, Quantity and
                                Additional Charges
                      Photographer or Video
                      Lighting - Stage, Buffet, Bars, Décor, Selection
                                and Installation
                      Audio and Visuals - Sound, VCR or Overhead
                      Props or Staging - Built to Suit, Rental or
                                Installation
                      Giveaways - Door Prizes, Gift Per Guest

Miscellaneous -   Security
                      Liability Insurance - Banquet Hall or Home,
                                Vendor Insurance
                      Back Up Plans - Location, Entertainment, Food,
                                Sound
                      Medical Emergency
                      Place for Gifts
                      Thank You Notes

    Once you have reviewed the list you are ready to make some definite decisions. Create a to-do list for yourself. Remember to keep track of what you have arranged and what is still outstanding. Keep track of dates and date when each item is to be completed. If you change something major, review the entire list to determine if you have affected anything else. By the time the event rolls around everything should be taken care of and you can have fun at the party along with your guests.

Budget Worksheet

Everything has a price. Working within a budget or working with a maximum dollar amount will help you in planning and making all the decisions. If cost is a major factor you need to be concerned with the quality and getting good value for your money. Set a suggested or maximum target amount on the budget worksheet. Not all categories may apply to your event. You may need to go back and adjust the amounts allocated for each budget category. If there isn't enough money allocated in a category to cover known expenses you have the following three choices:

- Other categories need to be reduced.
- More total dollars need to become available.
- An alternative or less expensive choice needs to be made.

To Make a Budget Worksheet

1. Enter the total dollars available

2. Enter number of people attending

3. Check off all the categories which you need to budget for

4. Enter the budget amount for each category checked

5. Add up all the budget amounts to get the TOTAL AMOUNT

6. Calculate the percent of budget for each category checked

7. Compare the TOTAL AMOUNT to Total Dollars Available

8. Make adjustments

BUDGET WORKSHEET

Enter Total Dollars Available . . . .$_____

Enter Number of People Attending . . . . . ._____

Category	Budget Amount	% of Budget
Event Site Rental		
Per Person - Food		
Per Person - Beverages		
Entertainment		
Decorations		
Audio-Visuals		
Equipment Rental		
Printed Materials		
Invitations		
Transportation		
Lodging		
Gifts		
Flowers		
Miscellaneous & Tips		
Last Minute Expenses		
TOTAL AMOUNT		

Travel Planning

Travel has become a part of everyday life. Businesses are no longer centralized in one place. A business may be spread over many physical locations. They usually have one office to house their headquarters, plus buildings at several other satellite locations. These locations may be separated by function for electronic processing, marketing, telecommunications, customer service, research, legal, production, shipping, etc. Business travel is pretty much the norm nowadays. A large company or corporation will usually have a separate department that handles all their travel arrangements or have selected to outsource the function and use the services of an independent travel agent. Regardless of how the business operates, a central unit compiles all the airline, train, bus, car and hotel arrangements. After everything has been prearranged, the traveler is handed tickets and an itinerary for their scheduled trip.

Personal Travel

Travel is also more common for individuals as more and more families are spread around the country. Some husbands and wives must even commute to see each other as they are physically separated due to the different locations of their jobs. Business travelers have it easy as they can just place a call to the company's travel service. Individual travelers have it a bit more difficult as they must either do the legwork themselves or go through their own travel agent. Since the electronic and Internet age has arrived there are so many more resources to access and a boundless array of travel discount services. Information is readily available from state or government offices on tourism, personal travelogues, travel guidebooks, travel videos and travel agents. There is information available on weather forecasts, locations of ATM machines, interactive and detailed maps, hotel discounts, air flight discounts, rental cars, tours, etc. You can obtain information, price vacations or cruises, book trips and reserve tickets ahead of time all via the Internet.

Prearrangements

From the moment you step out your door to the moment you arrive at your destination you should know what to expect. The arrangements of getting there and back again should have been made beforehand. Your actual trip should be uncomplicated. Last minute and unplanned glitches all too often outweigh the glitter of travel and the experience gradually leaves more than can be desired. It is wise to plan ahead so you will spend less time with the fuss and aggravation that accompanies traveling. You save time and money by scheduling trips in advance. Avoiding peak travel times will increase your chances of being able to travel without being hit with unexpected delays that can cause havoc on your schedule. Part of your planning should be to pre-arrange a hotel or place to stay or to have arranged for someone to meet you upon your arrival. Being able to look forward to a final destination can give you peace of mind. However well you prepare you should always build some flexibility in your travel plans

Choose Your Destination

You are one step closer to planning your trip if you know your destination. You may need to schedule a visit to your parents, wish to attend a special seminar, take an educational course, ski in the European Alps, stroll around Paris, see the Grand Canyon, visit a relative, or travel to explore a new part of the world. If you do not have a definite destination in mind your choice of location becomes your first decision. You can get good ideas from travel magazines, travel Internet sites or the travel magazine section in the Sunday paper. When deciding where to go, consider your goals. Do you wish to rest and relax, want to experience nature, go on a cruise, take a road trip, perform a physical sport or activity, see historical sites, go camping, travel around in a recreation vehicle, take an adventure or safari or visit a specific city, country or part of the world?

> ***Hint:*** *Choose your destination, season and intensity of the trip with your goals in mind.*

The Four Questions

Before any real planning can begin consider the following questions:

1. ***Where you are going*** - *are you going to stay in one place or many places?*

2. ***How long you are planning to go*** - *will you be away for days, weeks, months?*

3. ***Who is going*** - *do you plan to go alone, with family, a group or friends?*

4. ***When you are going*** - *what dates are you planning to leave and return?*

Transportation

If you are planning your own trip, you need to make decisions about the type of transportation you wish to use. When it comes to transportation think of your travel in two parts. The first part is what type of transportation you will use to get to your destination? Will it be plane, train, bus, boat or car? Will you be using frequent flyer miles? Will you be using your own car? The second part to think about is the type of transportation or vehicle you will require to get between places. Will you be staying in a city that offers many forms of public and private transportation? Do you need to make additional plane, train or bus reservations to get from one city or town to another? Do you plan to rent a car? Will you need to consider car rental insurance? How expensive is gasoline and how frequent are car services where you are going? Do you need schedules for a train, bus or ferry? What about an Amtrak or Eurail train pass? When you do your research and comparison shopping - compare the rates, discounts and various incentives.

> **Hint:** *Try a variety of permutations of dates and times as a slight difference in time or routing can alter the cost.*

Accommodations

When it comes to a place to stay you have many choices. Only your price range will limit your selection. Do you wish an all-inclusive vacation or a package tour where you do not have to handle a cent? How about taking a cruise? Would you like to vacation at a health spa or on a ranch where everything is taken care of for you? Do you wish to stay at a hotel, motel, inn, bed and breakfast (B&B), hostel or condo? Do you wish to go tent camping or tour around in a trailer? Do you wish to be located in the center of town or close to your destination? Would you care to exchange your home for someone else's and save money? Think about your comfort zone. What level of luxury do you need or amount of roughness will you put up with? The physical locale, environment, weather conditions and temperature will dictate many of these decisions and limit your choices. When making a reservation - compare prices, discounts and incentives.

Getting Good Value

When planning a trip on your own you want to make sure you are getting the best deal possible. If you can travel during the off-peak or shoulder seasons you will pay less and encounter fewer crowds. Early morning and midweek flights, when planes are least crowded, are more economical. Rental car and hotel room rates generally drop on weekends, when business travelers go home. While looking for vacations, airfares or hotel reservations check the Internet for last minute offers. There are numerous websites that offer reduced prices on many last minute deals. If you can afford to wait till a week or two before you make your plans you can take an expensive trip at an inexpensive price. For special rates, discounts and promotional rates call airlines and hotels directly. I have discovered that depending upon when you call - the price changes. I usually call an airline or hotel at least twice to confirm the best price or to find out about a special discount (AAA, AARP or Entertainment coupon) or value (senior, student, military or corporate rate) arrangement.

Hint: When calling during nighttime hours I usually get someone who likes to chat and I have been informed about deals that I had not known about previously.

Pre-Trip Planning

Pre-trip planning is more than just gathering equipment, selecting your luggage and making a checklist. It requires examination of the possible interaction and consequences of the activity, location, season and people. Many accidents or close calls happen because people do not properly plan their trip and identify the risks. After you have decided on a destination the next step is doing the proper research. After I choose my hotels and transportation I further research my destination. I read a book about the location and educate myself on all it has to offer. Not only do I learn about the major sights but also festivals, concerts, events and cultural happenings at the time of my visit. I find out the opening and closing times of museums, monuments or places of interest I wish to visit. I select the sites that interest me and decide what I can group together. What activities can I do at the same or nearby vicinity? The better research you do beforehand will lead to a safer and more enjoyable adventure.

Museum Tips

Read up on the museums in the location you are going to ahead of time. Make a list of museums you wish to visit and plan to see the museum's top sights. Make a note of the days and hours the museum is open. Most museums are closed one day during the week, usually Monday or Tuesday and tend to offer one free day or evening admission. If your goal is to save money, schedule a visit on the free admission days. If you would rather visit during the least crowded times, stay away on the free admission days and plan your visit closest to the museum closing hours, when attendance has dwindled down. Although most museums have a pre-set admission fee some have a pay-what-you-wish policy. When you get to the museum focus on what you had planned to see first and then spend the rest of the time wandering around as your eyes desire.

> ***Hint:*** *To get the most of your visit join a tour of the museum, rent an audio recording of a particular exhibit or just eavesdrop on a passing tour guide.*

Itineraries

On the following pages you will find two sample itineraries I compiled and used on recent short trips. These give you a good idea of the type of information to assist you in creating your own itinerary.

You should include:

1. Location of the Trip
2. Dates of the Trip
3. Flight, Train or Bus Numbers
4. Departure and Arrival Times
5. Hotel Reservation Numbers
6. Hotel Addresses and Telephone Numbers
7. List of Places to Visit
8. Chronological Order of Visits
9. Times and Days Place is Open
10. Admission Prices

Each piece of data is important. Each day was planned to centralize activities within a given area of the city. Having done all the research beforehand, of what to see and do gives you more time to enjoy your new surroundings. You are not preoccupied with planning your day on the spot, can have more fun and avoid arguments with others. For both cities I equipped myself with a local map and a metropolitan transportation map. I did not need to depend on others to get around and always knew how to get to the next location on my schedule.

Hint: For locations inside the USA use websites such as www.mapsonus.com to plan your easiest route or find an exact location.

Prague Trip - March 4th thru March 12th, 2005

Lufthansa (800) 645-3880 in Terminal #1

#LH401- Depart JFK: Friday 3/4   Arrive Frankfort: 5:30AM
       4:05 PM 25A,C,D
#LH3260 - Depart Frankfort: 3/4   Arrive Prague: 9:25 AM
       8:25 AM

#LH3261 - Depart Prague: Sat. 3/12   Arrive Frankfort: 11:30 AM
       10:15 AM
#LH404   - Depart Frankfort: 3/12   Arrive NYC JFK: 7:35 PM
       5:10 PM 28A,B,C

Vysehrad Hotel   "C" Line Prazskeho Povstani
Marie Cibulkove 29, Prague 4   Metro 7-Day Ticket   250kc
Telephone 011422436003

                         AAA Limo Service on VISA
                         (800) 932-7789 USA
                         (908) 735-6499 Abroad

Suggested Itinerary:

      Saturday   Day 1 -   Arrive at Ruzyne Airport
                               Hotel Check-In

      Sunday   Day 2 -   Walk Around - Municipal Hall, Powder Gate
                               Old Town Square, Charles Bridge,
                               Mala Stana/Lessor Town in Hradcany.

      Monday   Day 3 -   Hradcany/Prague Castle(9-4) 200 czk-100 czk
                               Golden Lane, Old Royal Palace, St. Vitus
                               Cathedral, Nerudovan Street, Katva
                               Department Store, Classical Concert in
                               Smetana Hall in Municipal House 7000 czk.

      Tuesday   Day 4 -   Nove Mesto / New Town & SONA
                               Mucha Museum-Panska 7 (10-6) 120 czk-
                               60 czk, Wencesles Square, Tesco Department
                               Store, Globe Bookstore.

      Wednesday Day 5 -   Josefov/Jewish Quarter (10- 4:30) 300 czk -
                               200 czk, Jewish Museum, Ancient Cemetery,
                               Maisel Synagogue, Old-New Synagogue,
                               Pinkas Synagogue 200 czk - 160 czk.

      Thursday   Day 6 -   Stare Mesto / Old Town Astronomical Clock &
                               Tower, Old Town Square, Kinsky Palace,
                               Museum of Communism-Na Prikope 10 (9 -8)
                               180 czk - 140 czk.

      Friday   Day 7 -   Loreto, Strahov Monastery, Changing of the
                                 Palace Guards at noon
                               Cubist Museum at House of Black Madonna

      Saturday   Day 8 -   Car Service to Ruzyne Airport
                               Prague Airport Shuttle +42 0602 395 421 $26.

*NOTE - **Prague Post**:* Prague's English newspaper for concerts, theatre, etc.

Chicago Trip Saturday October 15th - Saturday October 22nd, 2005

Amtrak

Leave NYC: 10/15
    9:10 PM
	Arrive Chicago: 10/16
	    2:50 PM
		$246.60

Leave Chicago: 10/21
    7:00 PM
	Arrive NYC: 10/22
	    1:50 PM
		+ Sleepers
		$75. each way

Best Western Inn of Chicago
162 East Ohio Street
Telephone: (312) 787-3100 - Front Desk or (800) 557-2378
Reservation Number: 813934671   Reserved on VISA 9/5/2005
Arrive October 19th for 5 nights   2 Double Beds Night   1= $79.20
                                     Nights 2-5 = $95.20   AAA Rates + Tax 14.9%

Sunday	**Day 1**

Robie House (Tours $9. at Mon-Fri 11am, 1pm, 3pm & Sundays 11am - 3:30pm)
Check-In to Hotel
Navy Pier & Navy Pier Walk - 36 Sculptures (Sunday - Thursday 10am - 8pm)
Smith Museum of Stained Glass Windows at Navy Pier

Monday	**Day 2**

Adler Planetarium & Astronomy Museum (Daily 9:30am - 4:30pm) Free Mon & Tues
Shedd Aquarium (Daily 9am-5pm) Part of Museum Free Mon & Tues or Discounted to
$13 Non-Residents
Buckingham Fountain in Grant Park (6PM) Lights and Music

Tuesday	**Day 3**

Get Hot Tix - Opens 8:30am at Randolph Street - Top Dog/Under Dog at Steppenwolf
Theatre
Architecture River Cruise $23. (Daily 11am, noon, etc.) Tour is 90 minutes
The Field Museum (Daily 9am - 5 pm) Free Mon & Tues

Wednesday	**Day 4**

Get Hot Tix - Opens 8:30am at Randolph Street - Blue Man Group at Blair Theatre
Frank Lloyd Wright House and Studio (Weekday Tours $9. at 11am, 1pm, 3pm)
Unity Temple ($7. Entrance Fee)
Walking Tour of Frank Lloyd Wright Homes in Oak Park

Thursday	**Day 5**

Get Hot Tix - Opens 1am at the Water Tower = The Secrets in the
Wings at Lookinglass Theatre
Museum of Science and Industry (Daily 9:30am-4pm & Sunday 11am-4pm)
Free Mon & Tues or $9.

Friday	**Day 6**

Early Morning Walk around the Gold Coast Area
The Art Institute of Chicago (Daily 10:30am-4:40pm & Sunday 10am-5pm) $10 or pay
what you wish
Chicago Architecture Foundation

Train Station Departure

RESEARCH

What to Know About Before Planning Your Trip

1. *Passport or Visa*
   - Is your passport up to date?
   - Do you need a VISA where you are planning to go?

2. *Converting Currency*
   - What denomination is the foreign money?
   - Compare the currency and know how many equal the dollar.

3. *Health Resources*
   - What resources will be available in case of a medical emergency?
   - Do you require any special accommodations for a health or physical disability?

4. *Money*
   - Do you plan to get travelers checks before you leave?
   - Where you will be able to find an ATM at your destination?
   - Will you be charged an extra fee on each of your credit card transactions?

5. *Restaurants*
   - Do you need to make reservations?
   - Find dining locations that have been recommended.

6. *Weather*
   - What months are considered high season vs. off-season?
   - Research the climate at your destination at different times of the year.

7. *Maps and Routes*
   - Calculate daily travel mileage.
   - Plan routes and daily destinations.
   - Obtain good maps and routes to travel on to avoid getting lost.

8. *Transportation*
   - Investigate your transportation options?
   - If you experience car trouble, know what alternatives you have.

9. *Health Vaccines*
   - Does your destination require you to have any vaccinations?
   - Has there been a recent health warning in the area you wish to visit?

10. *Politics*
    - Check the political situation in a foreign country.
    - Do you need to be concerned for your personal safety?

PREPARATION

What to Think About When Preparing for Your Trip

1. *Luggage*
   - Will you check your luggage or carry-on luggage?
   - Will you need to take an extra bag to bring back purchases?
   - Decide on what size bags and how many bags you will need.
   - Will you take a backpack, soft-sided suitcase or a wheeled bag?

2. *Carry-on Allowance*
   - Airlines differ in the weight and size of carry-on luggage.
   - Check into the allowable dimensions and weight allowance.

3. *Do Not Bring*
   - Knives, scissors, nail files or cigarette lighters can be placed in your checked luggage.
   - All the above items will be confiscated from your carry-on bags.

4. *Checklist*
   - For each item on your checklist note the number you will need.
   - Prepare a list of things to pack and then check them off your list as you pack.

5. *Pre-pack*
   - Lay out everything you would like to take and pack half of it.
   - Try various packing arrangements within your luggage for maximum room.

6. *Travel Light*
   • Take comfortable, easy to clean clothes.
   • Dark clothing hides stains better but in warm weather black absorbs heat.

7. *Plastic Bags*
   • Wrap toiletries, squeeze bottles or anything that can leak or needs extra protection in a plastic or zip lock bag.

8. *Watches and Umbrellas*
   • Take a wristwatch with a built in alarm or else a travel alarm clock.
   • For inclement weather pack a small collapsible umbrella or poncho.

9. *Itinerary*
   • Leave a copy with a relative, neighbor, co-worker or boss in case of an emergency.
   • Pack a copy of your itinerary inside each bag so if your luggage is lost and then found, you can be easily located.

10. *Home Preparations*
   • Notify any newspaper delivery service of your return date.
   • Notify the post office to resume mail delivery on your return date.
   • Leave money and arrange to have someone (who looks after your house and pets) buy milk and other needed perishables for your return date.

PACKING

What to Take on Your Trip

1. *Mix and Match*
   • Match solid colors and prints to coordinate a complete outfit.
   • Select a mixture of pants and skirts that complement your shirts and tops.

2. *Shirts*
   • Take long and short-sleeved shirts.
   • Select a mixture according to the season.
   • Cotton/polyester blends resist wrinkles and dry quickly.

3. *Sweaters*
   - Sweaters never look wrinkled.
   - For both winter and summer take one to dress up or layer.

4. *Pants*
   - Linen or cotton pants are the lightest.
   - If you bring jeans, bring at least one pair of other pants for modest dress codes.

5. *Underwear and Socks*
   - The lighter they are the quicker they dry.
   - Bring enough if you do not plan to do a wash.

6. *Shoes*
   - Wear the right shoes and test out new pairs before your trip.
   - Select comfortable, lightweight shoes with a good sole for traction.

7. *Ties or Scarf*
   - Bring one or two along to dress up an outfit.

8. *Necessities*
   - Retractable clothesline for drying.
   - Carry medication in their original packing to avoid delays at Customs.
   - Bring packets of Woolite or laundry lotion for small overnight washes.
   - Bring soap, shampoo, deodorant, toothpaste, toothbrush, insect repellent, sunscreen, contact lens cleaning gear, lip balm and medical prescriptions.

9. *Camera*
   - Bring enough film or memory disks to last your whole trip.
   - Clean, check and put new batteries in your camera before you go.

10. *Tag Your Bags*
    - A brightly colored tag can be more easily identified in a crowd of luggage.
    - If you write your home address on your tags cover it so potential thieves cannot readily see it.

BEFORE

What to Do Before You Leave on Your Trip
Besides making sure you turn off the stove before you leave your house.

1. Set up any pet sitting arrangements.
2. Get your seat assignments in advance.
3. Confirm pre-arranged hotel and/or tour reservations.
4. Xerox your passports, credit cards and any other cards in your wallet.
5. Arrange for others to take care of things for you during your absence.
6. Arrange for a car service or find out about parking at the airport or train station.
7. Give a copy of your itinerary to someone, so if you are needed, you can reached.
8. If going overseas take extra passport photos in case your passport is lost or stolen.
9. Check the flight time, terminal number and find out about any delays with the airline.
10. Arrange someone to pick up your mail and newspapers or have the post office hold it.

DURING

What Tips to Follow While On Your Trip

1. Always keep all your tickets in the same place.
2. Keep track of your expenses and receipts in a small notepad.
3. Leave early to stay on schedule in case of delays or the unexpected.
4. Come home a day early to prepare for work or school or relax from jet lag.
5. Note down your car location in case you don't remember where you parked it.
6. Use the phone to solve problems quickly, such as: flights cancelled or delayed.
7. Take a project or a good book and make good use of your uninterrupted travel time.

8. Fill out a journal or note down your trip experiences and places you photographed to save as a personal memoir or souvenir.
9. Carry important phone numbers with you at all times of people who can give you the information you need at the last minute.
10. If your luggage arrives damaged or fails to arrive, file a written report before leaving the airport or station and let the personnel know where you can be contacted.

AFTER

What to Do Once You Are Home

1. Pick up your mail.
2. Sort through the mail.
3. Unpack all your bags.
4. Store away all luggage.
5. Get back keys to your home.
6. Slowly readjust to your old routine.
7. Sort and label all your travel photographs.
8. File away photographs in an album or on your computer.
9. Sort out travel memoirs (tickets, brochures, etc.) to keep.
10. Track all of your expenses to see if you were within budget.

Chapter 10

AN APPLE A DAY KEEPS THE DOCTOR AWAY

"The first wealth is health."
Ralph Waldo Emerson (1803 -1882)

Businesses must think towards the future and develop preventative strategies to head off impending disasters. They develop methods to check their financial health and plan for future growth. Businesses schedule periodic reviews and financial audits to check for accuracy and a certain standard of quality. Businesses execute cutbacks and perform employee downsizing when they determine they are *"too fat"*. Likewise they increase hiring when they have the need to add to their staff. Businesses maintain productivity schedules and long-term targets. As individuals we think similarly towards the future in terms of taking care of our bodies. We schedule periodic preventative medical checkups and are constantly in touch with how we are feeling. When we feel our bodies are too large or heavy, we diet. When we need to increase our metabolism and productivity, we exercise. When we believe smoking or too much alcohol is detrimental to our health, we attempt to stop. Our bodies are our mainframes and we need to maintain its durability to carry us into our future. This chapter describes how health planning involves caring effectively for our physical body, eating the right kinds of foods, getting sufficient rest, relaxation and exercising on a regular basis.

Health Planning

The most important thing about having a medical check-up is remembering you are due for one. With all the things you need to do and remember it is almost impossible to remember your last visit to a particular doctor. If you are a parent you must also arrange medical appointments for your children. Unless you have a chart of who went to which doctor for what reason, you will never have it straight. Besides your family physician you may require visits to a gynecologist, cardiologist, dentist, podiatrist, orthodontist, chiropractor, etc. By keeping track of your prior visits and marking them in advance in your date book you can maintain a regular schedule of medical appointments.

Medical Files

One of the best ways to keep track of doctor visits is to create a master medical list. A listing of each member of the family, what doctor they routinely visit and dates of their last three or four appointments. If you look ahead you can pencil in when the next appointment should be scheduled. In one glance you will be able to see what's next. In addition to a master medical appointment list you should set up a medical and dental file for each person in your household. Keep a record of surgeries, vaccinations, illnesses and injuries for each member of your family. Medical and dental insurance is extremely complicated and paper intensive. Past statements from your doctor and insurance company can clear up many discrepancies that tend to arise. Keeping a folder for each member of your family will help you find a specific paper when you need it, without having to look through a ton of unassociated papers.

Finding a New Doctor

Choosing the right physician is fundamental to your health care. The doctor you select will be affiliated with specific hospitals that will also dictate your level of care. It is important to choose a doctor you feel at ease and comfortable with. You want to be able to trust the doctor for their medical experience and knowledge. Ask friends, relatives and co-workers for personal recommendations. Ask what doctors they see and whether they are satisfied with the quality of care they receive. To help you make your choice here are a few things you will want to check out ahead of your first appointment:

- How are office visits booked?
- Does the doctor accept new patients?
- What is the availability of appointments?
- How heavily booked is the doctor's schedule.
- How many people are given the same time slot?
- Find out about the doctor's education and licenses.
- What is the average waiting time for an appointment?
- What are the doctor's office hours and office location?
- Does the doctor accept your insurance plan or Medicare?
- Does the doctor belong to your HMO or other managed care plan?
- Do the hospitals the doctor is affiliated with have good reputations?
- Does the doctor have a list of specialists to whom he refers patients?
- How does the medical office handle requests for prescriptions and refills?

- Find out how you can get in touch with the doctor in case of an emergency.
- If you have a medical condition, does the doctor have expertise in this area?

Doctor Appointments

Schedule all your doctor appointments in advance to select the dates you want that are best for you. Lots of time I set up an appointment for my next visit before I leave the doctor's office. I jot it down in my date book and do not have to worry about forgetting it or need to spend extra time making the next appointment. Make your health one of your main priorities. By scheduling an appointment ahead of time you can plan your remaining schedule around your doctor appointment instead of squeezing it into your schedule at the last minute. Nothing is worse than being on a doctor's call list when you desperately need an appointment. It is a good idea to call the medical office a few days prior to your appointment to confirm the date and time.

Hint: Take all your medical information and medical insurance cards with you to your appointment.

Preparing for a Doctor Visit

When preparing for a visit to a doctor write down an agenda of questions you wish to ask. If you try to remember them all when you are facing the doctor you may forget one or two. Many times you are not totally able to concentrate and take in all the doctor is saying. If you are going for a consultation or for a second opinion bring someone along with you. Someone whom you feel comfortable with, who can also listen to what the doctor says and jot down notes or items for you to follow-up on. Having someone else there not only brings a sense of comfort but also allows you to have someone who knows about the situation that you can have discussions with later.

Medical Insurance Forms

As time goes go on, thanks to the computer and Internet age, medical insurance becomes easier. Soon you will be able to use a swipe card at your doctor's office to check your eligibility and benefits. In the future an eye scan may be developed to uniquely identify you and your existing medical coverage. Until then you must keep track of things the hard way. I am lucky enough to have two medical insurances and the insurance companies must coordinate the benefits (COB). Once I find out what the first insurance carrier paid, my doctor's office submits the claim to the secondary insurer. I am responsible for the amount that is not paid between both insurance companies. I need to keep close track of when the claims have been sent to each insurance company, how much each paid, what charges they each paid and how much of the bill I am responsible for. To organize all this I devised a simple chart. It's good to keep a record of all your medical and dental insurance claims and statements even if you have one insurance carrier.

Hint: *Most medical insurance companies provide a website for you to track claims that are in progress and ones that have been processed.*

Reimbursement Worksheets

Looking at the example on the next page you can easily keep track of:

- Claims still outstanding.
- All your co-pay amounts.
- Doctor visits for the year.
- How much you owe a physician.
- How much you paid for dental expenses.
- How much you paid for medical expenses.
- Amount your insurance company has paid.
- The last date you visited a particular doctor.
- Your total medical and dental expenses for tax purposes.
- Charges that have not yet been processed through insurance.

MEDICAL / DENTAL PAYMENTS AND INSURANCE REIMBURSEMENTS FOR YEAR 2005

MEDICAL	Date of Service	Total Charge	Copay	Date Sent to Insurance	Insurance Paid	Amount Left to Pay	REMARKS

DENTAL	Date of Service	Total Charge	Copay	Date Sent to Insurance	Insurance Paid	Amount Left to Pay	REMARKS

Food Planning

When you stop to think about it, lots of activities in your life involve food - the three meals that you eat everyday, meal planning, grocery shopping, meal preparation, dish washing, kitchen clean-up, dining out and even socializing at a party. Being organized in each of these areas can help you to stay on track and eat healthier. If you plan meals ahead of time and buy the necessary ingredients to prepare your meals, you will always have what you need on hand. If you plan a meal that you do not have the ingredients for, you will ultimately eat something different. This will take you off track and off your meal plan. So get into the habit of making a weekly menu, listing the foods you need on your grocery list and buying them on your next grocery-shopping trip. Dining out and partying can easily get you off track if you do not have a plan. Find out what the restaurant or your host is serving and decide beforehand what you plan to nibble on and eat. This way you can look forward to a particular food and feel satisfied when you receive it, other foods may not be such a big temptation.

Grocery Shopping

Meal planning and grocery shopping is a science in itself. I now live seven miles from a supermarket and shop only once a week. However, I also shopped once a week when I lived in Manhattan and the supermarket was one block away. Shopping is fun for some but I see it as a chore and try to minimize the pain whenever I can. I created a grocery shopping list detailing what products are contained in each aisle of my favorite store. I sit down once a week and go through the sale circular from the supermarket looking for the specials. I write down each item I need and want under the correct column. I then decide what foods I will be serving as dinner or meals for the upcoming week. If I need extra ingredients to prepare the meal, I add them to my list. Whenever I go to the grocery store without a list I tend to buy items I really don't need or I never buy what I really do need. It is also a good idea to have a grocery list handy in your kitchen so anyone in the household can quickly write down anything you run out of.

WEEKLY SHOPPING LIST

PRODUCE
apples, onions, nuts, grapes,
oranges, potatoes, bananas

BAKERY & APPETIZERS
donuts, bagels, bread, cakes,
deli, gourmet cheeses, salads

SEAFOOD
salmon, sushi, crab,
flounder, shrimp, lobster

MEAT
fresh cut meats, frozen meats,
gourmet meats, marinades

AISLE 1
water, water filters,
fruit juices, Gatorade

AISLE 2
hot & cold cereals, candy,
natural cereal, drink mixes

AISLE 3
cookies, coffee, tea, crackers,
powdered milk, hot cocoa

AISLE 4
baking needs, spices, sugar,
canned fruit, gadget, popcorn

AISLE 5
condiments, dressing, oil,
olives, pickles, tuna, soups

WEEKLY SHOPPING LIST *(cont.)*

AISLE 6 - 7 - 8 - 9
vitamins, cards, cosmetics,
stationary, first aid, batteries

AISLE 10
baked bean, pasta, kosher, rice,
spaghetti sauce, canned vegs

AISLE 11
beverages, cocktail mixes,
canned nuts, snacks, soda

AISLE 12
auto, insect spray, matches,
light bulbs, pet food, shoe care

AISLE 13
soap, detergents, vacuum bags,
household, laundry detergent

AISLE 14
paper products, tissues,
toothpicks, trash bags

FROZEN
veggies, entrees, dinners, ice,
pizza, juices, ice cream

DAIRY
butter, cheese, milk, yogurt,
hot dogs, grated cheese, eggs

AISLE 15
desserts, peanut butter,
jelly, rice cakes, bread

Food Categories

Walking through the grocery aisles you most probably place selected items anywhere you find an empty spot for them in your shopping cart. When you are done shopping, while waiting for your turn at the checkout line, begin to separate your items by category: dairy, canned goods, meats, etc. When laying your items on the checkout counter, try to order them as you have them arranged at home. Place all your refrigerator goods together and your sodas or fruit juices together. With any luck the grocery bag packers will pack your groceries as you have them arranged. Once you are at home, unpacking and placing items where they belong should become a quicker process.

Eating Healthy

I believe that we all know how to eat right. Sometimes we do and sometimes we don't. Depending on your body weight and age, eating healthy can keep you feeling fit. However many people are overweight or diabetic, have high cholesterol or just gravitate to the wrong types of food and must closely watch what they eat. Eating healthy is making the right choices. You need to select foods that are low in fat, sugar, salt and sodium. Including lots of vegetables, fruits and grains as part of your daily diet is much better than filling up on simple sugars and starches. Being organized can help you to eat healthier. Learning how to shop wisely, ordering menu selections carefully, planning your menus ahead, knowing what times of day trigger eating, making shopping lists and preparing meals ahead of time can all help you to eat properly.

Tips for Eating Healthier

1. *Allow yourself to enjoy what you eat.*
2. *Don't eat when you are in a rush or on the go.*
3. *Take small portions, you can always get more.*
4. *Don't shop for groceries when you are hungry.*
5. *Read and compare label ingredients and fat counts.*
6. *Prepare drinks and snacks for long trips or car rides.*
7. *Take your time eating and put your fork down after every bite.*
8. *Use a small fork or spoon to slow you down and chew more times.*
9. *Bring fruit and vegetables to work and avoid using vending machines.*
10. *Prepare your meals ahead of time so they will be ready when you are hungry.*
11. *Savor each bite and be aware of the aroma, texture and appearance of the food.*
12. *Plan your meals ahead of time so you will have the ingredients to prepare them.*

Tracking What You Eat

There are times in your life when you decide to become more conscious of what you eat, how much you eat, and when you eat it. Keeping track makes you more aware of what your limits are, for the day and for the week. It can help you to understand your eating patterns. Maintaining a simple food log or daily list of what you eat for your meals and snacks is fine. There is no need to get elaborate and buy a computerized calculator. Just jot down what food items you eat for each of your meals and the portion or quantity as best as you can judge. For easy portion control store a handy portion basket on your kitchen counter. All you need is a golf ball to measure nuts and shredded cheese, a deck of cards for 3 ounces of poultry, pork or beef, a die for oils and fats, a tennis ball for fruits and vegetables and a computer mouse for potatoes and cooked grains. Don't forget to write down all your little snacks, even the one before bedtime, they all count.

Hint: By keeping track of what you eat you are reporting to yourself and making sure that you do not exceed your limits.

Food Cravings

We all have a food craving now and then. When you have a food craving whatever you eat will not satisfy you until you eat that one food that you crave. Your body is trying to tell you something. Do not be tricked into believing that the food you crave will always be a sweet one. Lots of time your body craves what it lacks nutritionally. Eating a banana, a piece of bread or just a few pretzels may satisfy a craving. It is important to think about what your body craves. If you eat the wrong item you will just keep on eating until you find the right item. So ask yourself what taste or flavor you need, what texture you want to feel, what aroma you wish to smell, what will satisfy you, do you want something dry or juicy, soft, smooth or hard? After you have quizzed yourself and found the food you have been craving, eat it, enjoy it, savor it and feel satisfied.

Hint: Organize your kitchen to have foods you usually crave handy and keep the tempting ones out of sight.

Body Energy

You need to take care of your body and have enough energy to do all the activities you wish to do. There are certain behaviors that drain and others that fuel energy levels.

ENERGY BOOSTERS
Eating Healthy
Drinking Lots of Water
Exercising Often
Taking Vitamins
Getting Enough Sleep

ENERGY DRAINERS
Skipping Meals
Drinking Soda
Watching TV and Movies
Eating Junk Food
Not Getting Enough Sleep

Activity Planning

Everyone wants to look good, feel good and live longer. Exercising can help you achieve these ideals and improve your body image. No matter how old you are, how unfit you are or your body weight, you can exercise. Participating in a sport or exercising a few days each week will give you more energy, lessen your stress, improve your sleep and increase your mental abilities. Exercise can also tone your muscles, improve your posture and increase weight loss. A healthy exercise program includes three kinds of exercise: aerobic activity, muscular strengthening and flexibility exercises.

• *Aerobic activity* is defined as prolonged, continuous movement of large muscle groups. This means doing something that keeps you moving - walking, biking, running, cross-country skiing, hiking, dancing, swimming, etc. It is good for increasing your cardio-vascular health and fitness. It is the best exercise for burning calories and helps lower the risk of heart and other diseases.

• *Muscle strengthening* is not just about body sculpting. It maintains muscle mass, bone mass and helps with weight loss. Resistance training builds bone density which guards against osteoporosis. Muscle strengthening can be achieved by simple calisthenics such as push-ups, pull-ups and sit-ups. You can also lift weights or use weight machines.

• *Flexibility* is a joint's ability to move through a full range of motion. You gain flexibility through stretching and lifting. It can help reduce muscle soreness, improve your posture, reduce lower back pain and improve your coordination. You can do a set of exercises, practice yoga or get the same benefit by doing simple housework, gardening or raking.

Whatever you choose to do, get yourself into a pattern and stick to it. Find out what physical activities you like to do, get whatever gear you need to do it, arrange a time to do it and then do it. It sounds so easy and it is.

> *Hint: No matter what your age your body requires a minimum number of hours of sleep to keep your senses sharp and keep you active during your waking hours.*

Find Out What You Like

Choose an activity you enjoy doing or used to like doing. If nothing comes to mind then try biking, playing tennis, playing golf, running, walking, skiing, skating, yoga, baseball, volleyball, etc. the list can go on and on. Choose an exercise or sport that fits your lifestyle.

If you try something and it is a strain on your body, make a change or adjust to it. Don't get discouraged if you do not immediately love it. Try to find a friend, co-worker or exercise partner to do it with, to motivate you and socialize. It's always a good idea to check with a physician before starting any physical exercise plan. Listen to your body and if you have any difficulty breathing during or after exercise consult your physician. Mornings may be a good time to exercise, as you may be too tired after work. If you lack time, use your lunch break to get out of the office. If you have lots of stress at work try to schedule in an exercise session right after work. Select more than one type of exercise. This will give your body a thorough workout and help prevent boredom.

Burning Calories

If your goal is to lose weight you will need to burn off 3,500 calories to lose one pound. Besides limiting your intake of food and selecting low calorie foods you can increase the amount of exercise you do or change your activity to one that burns more calories. Running or stair climbing are more aggressive ways to burn calories than walking. Jumping rope and swimming will burn off more calories than a leisurely bicycle ride. Remember to select your activities to fit the season. You may switch to an indoor activity for the winter and an outdoor one for the warmer months. In the summer exercise in the morning or evening when it is cooler and wear lightweight loose fitting clothing. In winter, for outdoor activities, dress in layers and drink fluids as you can get dehydrated in the winter too.

Hint: For year round safety warm up and cool down to decrease the risk of injury.

Small Ways to Exercise

1. *Take a walk during lunch.*
2. *Plant your garden in spring.*
3. *Mow your lawn in summer.*
4. *Rake your leaves in autumn.*
5. *Shovel your snow in winter.*
6. *Pack your groceries at the store.*

7. *Play music and dance around the house.*
8. *Use the stairs instead of an elevator or escalator.*
9. *Park a block or two away from your destination.*
10. *During the wintertime take a long walk in an indoor mall.*
11. *Do stretching exercises at work while sitting at your desk.*
12. *Walk over to a friend's house to chat instead of telephoning.*
13. *Walk to your phone instead of keeping your cordless with you.*
14. *Use a small coffee cup and walk back to the coffee pot for more.*
15. *Disembark the bus or train a stop before & walk the rest of the way.*

Exercise Logs

Exercise logs are great for keeping track. You can record what days you do what activity, how long you do it and what you do. Looking at your log can tell you a lot. You can quickly identify why you may be getting bored or see how much time you spend exercising in the total of a week. You can use your log to plan your schedule, allowing time for you to exercise or do an activity. Once you have settled on your routine you can easily include an acquaintance, friend or co-worker to join you. You can set a regular place and schedule a time to meet, to make sure you stay with your exercise plan. You can plan to increase the amount of activity you do or just the repetitions you do for a particular set of exercises. Looking at the log you can identify what you need more of or less of and can adjust and plan your exercise schedule accordingly. If you cannot devote enough minutes in a day, or days in the week to exercise, increase your intensity when you do exercise.

> **Hint:** *Use your exercise log to track your progress for endurance and muscular strength. Update your exercise log immediately after the completion of your workout. Try to add new exercises to your daily routine to prevent boredom.*

EXERCISE LOG - RECORD NUMBER OF MINUTES

WEEK OF _____

TYPE OF ACTIVITY	Day 1	Day 2	Day 3	Day 4	Day 5	Day 6	Day 7
STRETCH							
AEROBIC CARDIO							
STRENGTH TRAINING UPPER BODY							
LOWER BODY							
ABDOMINALS							
FLEXIBILITY TRAINING							
YOGA							
RELAXATION							
OTHER							
TOTAL TIME							

Chapter 11

HOW TO LIVE WITH DISORGANIZED PEOPLE

"The shoe that fits one person pinches another,
there is no recipe for living that suits all cases."
Carl Jung (1875 - 1961)

On the job you will find a mix of organized people and unorganized people. Business management attempts to teach a standard way and method of good organization on the job. Some people decide to go along with it and some don't. Management knows that workers who have good organization skills are more productive and effective than workers who have not developed these skills. Businesses hold seminars to teach and institute new procedures, skills and techniques. Within a company there may exist a very disorganized person, who is valuable to the group yet very difficult to work with. They may have their own way of doing things and unless you meet them on their turf you cannot get any information out of them. Because of their lack of organization it may be difficult for them to locate needed information. Or due to their poor time management skills they are always late. The fact that many times we are forced to deal with difficult people is what makes learning how to cope with them useful and necessary. Since the main purpose is getting on with your business, coping, rather than changing or finding fault with them should be the optimum goal.

Difficult People

You may encounter situations in which others cause you difficulty. If you must deal with others who are disorganized, either in your workplace or in your personal life they will most probably hinder you from accomplishing even the simplest jobs. Fortunately, they are small in number but their impact can be large. They irritate you and are difficult to understand and work with. They may be people who stall making any decisions until the decision is made for them. Some people stall until the last possible minute. There are those who gripe incessantly but never try to do anything about what they complain about. The worst are those who refuse to take on any responsibilities.

Have You Encountered People Who:

- Do not show up.
- Are continually late.
- Do not communicate.
- Are reluctant to begin.
- Do not carry their load.
- Stall making a decision.

- Decide at the last minute.
- Find fault with everything.
- Will not commit themselves.
- Continually change their minds.

The Problem of Dependency

Living in a society, people are dependent on others. When you depend on others to do things for you - sending important letters, signing checks or forms, doing research, writing a report, being there to pick you up, placing a call, depositing money, etc. nothing is more maddening than to find out that those people forgot. It may not be that they forgot, sometimes people procrastinate so long that the need for any action or decision disappears. The events of life have a wonderful way of rapidly moving on causing unmade decisions to become quickly irrelevant. It is precisely your dependency on others that frustrates and maddens you. It is unproductive for you because that action which you depended on was not done. Even worse are people who are never on time but refuse to acknowledge it or apologize for it. This is more than bad manners; they are saying their time is more valuable than yours.

Interpersonal Communications

In the business world relationships and communication are integral parts of any success or failure. Business relationships play a major role in the productivity and success of every individual involved. Either at your workplace or in your personal life, miscommunication with others is guaranteed to complicate a situation. Things poorly said or left unsaid altogether can create problems in every area of your life. It is important to approach interpersonal communication with a sharp mind. Think before you speak. Be clear on what you intend to communicate. Organize your thoughts beforehand to convey the gist of your message. Saying the first thing that pops into your head can be dangerous since this is how people come to say and do unintentionally rude and regretful things. Try to maintain a friendly tone and bring diplomacy into your conversations. Be attentive to your body language. Listen attentively, understand and acknowledge the other person's messages. Don't be afraid to speak your mind but think before you speak.

Relationships

Two individuals interacting with each other, without ego involvements, characterize a mature relationship. In a healthy mutual relationship the one-upmanship aspect that characterizes so many other relationships is absent. Each person is autonomous and each supports the autonomy of the other. In an optimal relationship each person is able to give to the other, expecting nothing in return and creating no obligations of the other. There is a balance of getting what one needs for oneself and giving to the other person. In a controversy, through compromise and negotiation the needs of both sides are satisfied. Each person expresses his or her feelings freely and each can hear the others feelings without being defensive. Being aware of feelings is important for the development of communication. When people understand that their feelings are caused by the relation of events to their own wants, needs and expectations they will be able to express their feelings constructively, without feelings of aggression. This allows people to think how to get what they want or need without necessarily requiring that the other person change.

Hint: Acceptance is one of the keys to a happy relationship.

Roommates

In summer camp, on a college campus, on a business trip with a colleague, on vacation with a friend or at home with a sibling, husband, wife or living partner having a disorganized roommate can be frustrating. It is difficult to establish order in a room shared with someone who is only too happy to live in a pigsty. It is equally frustrating to have your personal belongings organized and have your roommate borrow something without returning it because they can never find their own. The answer is to try to organize and focus on your own area. Let your roommate know that you are not trying to convert them. Explain that you just want your space to be organized.

Here are some additional suggestions:

• Label your belongings and keep them separated.
• Use screens, beds, bookcases or curtains as a room divider.

- Subdivide the space in a way that gives each of you an individual area.
- If you hate to walk through the mess, take the part of the room closest to the door so you don't have to walk through your roommate's clutter.
- If you want privacy, take the part of the room away from the door so your roommate does not have to walk through your space to get to theirs.

What Not To Do

There are many things that you can do or not do. Here is what you should not do:

1. **Don't expect the person to know how you feel -**
   Tell them how you feel.

2. **Don't expect the person to know what you like and dislike -**
   Tell them what you like and dislike before a situation occurs.

3. **Don't expect help without asking for it -**
   Ask for help or assistance politely.

4. **Don't criticize their taste, preferences or behavior -**
   Act the way you would treat children to instill good behavior.

5. **Don't keep track of their mistakes -**
   Remember your last goof or blooper.

6. **Don't criticize everything -**
   Say something nice before you make suggestions.

7. **Make suggestions how they can improve -**
   Notice positive and appealing things they have improved lately.

8. **Don't always note the negative -**
   State the positive in every negative (the dress is beautiful but a bit too short).

9. **Don't refuse to compromise** -
Ask yourself why it may be important for you to win every argument.

10. **Don't blame anyone** -
Try to understand their behavior and why it may have occurred.

Scarce Resources

In the community, at work, at school and even at home, decision-making always concerns distributing valuable and scarce resources. These resources are: time, money, attention and caring. They are tied to people's wants and needs. These decisions may mean more to others than you may think. Sometimes people cannot reach a decision because they do not want to take the responsibility or they just procrastinate. However some people simply do not wish to hurt anyone. By making a decision they are doling out a scarce resource to one person instead of another. Think about your relationships with others and your everyday interactions with them. How many of these relationships relate to your time or your money? How many relate to getting your attention and invoke feelings of caring?

The Cost of Indecision

Indecisive people may cause discomfort for you. They attempt to lower their own internal pressure by procrastination. Although they are not motivated to manipulate, they put others at a disadvantage by keeping them off balance and incapable of effective action. As life goes on, if a decision is left unmade it rapidly becomes irrelevant. Indecisive people hint and beat around the bush as a compromise between trying to be honest and trying not to hurt anyone.

Not making decisions on a timely basis does have some negative implications:

- Leaves others feeling confused
- Shuts down discussion of a topic
- Reduces enthusiasm and commitment
- Causes anxiety and friction among people
- Prevents people from finding alternate ways of doing a job

When People Procrastinate

As previously mentioned in Chapter 4 - Time Management Skills, there are many reasons why people procrastinate. You can usually anticipate how others will react. If a disorganized person procrastinates, prepare yourself to have a talk with them. In order to help you accomplish your goals you need to make them understand what your goals mean to you and why they are important. The other person may not even know how much their behavior affects and frustrates you. Even in the most innocent situations where it seems there can be only one way to interpret the situation, there's always someone who sees it differently. You should try to gain some perspective on their actions. Seeing their patterns of behavior and understanding the source of these patterns can help you devise an effective strategy. It then pays to take the time to discuss and help them see the reason why they procrastinate. Once they understand the reason, they can face the problem and if they wish, they can take the first steps to stop procrastinating.

Hint: The first step to changing a behavior is realizing that you do it and how it affects others.

Work Effectively

If you work with other people your main objective will be to increase your own ability to work more effectively with them - as you cannot change someone else, you can only change yourself. Working with difficult or unorganized people will never be enjoyable but it can get easier. You may need to take the other person's perspective, not make unreasonable demands and not create any inappropriate stresses. Thinking through what needs to be done and how you are going to do it, is worthwhile. The best way to work together is to involve others in the process. You need to balance your mutual interest by producing a situation in which you can both function and be as productive as possible. At the least, you wish to minimize the discord caused by the difficult person. At the most, you wish to highlight shared values. While helping yourself, you have to find ways to make it easier for the other person.

- *Give them support* - be around to listen
- *Propose a resolution* - devise a plan to work on and follow
- *Be direct with them* - explain the consequence if a task is not done
- *Follow up with them* - do not allow them to feel they are in it alone
- *Consider it may be you* - you may be too perfect or asking too much
- *Educate them* - they may not have the knowledge, skill or experience
- *Cut it down* - you overestimate the difficulty of what you ask them to do
- *State all the facts* - make sure they understand what you want them to do
- *Link your plan to values* - make them feel they are doing beneficial work
- *Rank your alternatives* - limit the number of solutions and alternatives to consider

Are You a Perfectionist?

Consider the fact that you may be a perfectionist and may ask too much of someone else. A perfectionist is a person who expects perfect results or perfect performance for everything. Perfectionists make everyone around them feel inferior. The ongoing struggle to achieve perfection is a learned behavior. People tend to learn perfectionism from a parent who is never satisfied with what the child does or tries to do, or a teacher who spends all of their time with only the best students, rewarding them and ignoring the others. Besides doing things over and over until they feel it is perfect perfectionists often expects their spouses or close friends to do everything perfectly too. They place unnecessarily high expectations on the other person and tend to view others as disorganized. If you feel you are a perfectionist retrain yourself to expect the best of yourself rather than perfect results. You may also want to rethink your expectations of others.

Hint: Excellent is great, but sometimes good is good enough.

Right the Balance

Individuals may behave in an unorganized manner because they have learned that doing so keeps others off balance and incapable of effective action. Unaware of the long-term cost they put you through they manage to gain control over others. There are techniques you can use and actions that you can take to right the power balance and minimize the impact of their behavior in the situations you find yourself in. Coping involves reflective listening, identifying nonverbal cues, responding with understanding, effective problem solving but most importantly, reaching an equal ground. Working on equal terms allows you and the other person to respond in different ways from those that are expected. By making a practical decision to cope, you remain the one in control of your own behavior. You can go about your business and the other person is provided with an incentive and an opportunity to develop other more constructive behaviors.

Effective Coping Techniques

Most of us hold off on coping until we can no longer stand the situation (which is not coping but reacting). A better approach is to start coping as soon as possible. A lot of coping is learning how to take the pressure off. By applying some coping techniques you can benefit in situations that formerly left you angry or frustrated. Assess the situation and determine whether or not you are dealing with someone who is always disorganized or unable to accomplish anything. You may be in a temporary situation that brings out the worst in an ordinarily organized person. If the person does not act as you would expect or would like them to act, stop wishing they were a different type of person. Hoping will not result in any changes. If you feel angry then get some distance between you and the other person. Try to see the other person's patterns of behavior and understand the source of those patterns. Introduce any plan you may have when the timing is right and the other person is not over-burdened by other problems and you also have time to devote to them. By giving your time to the other person you are showing them how important the matter is to you.

> **Hint:** *You always have the ability to change the nature of the interaction you are both caught in by changing your behavior.*

Allowing Choice

Providing choice enhances people's motivation. If you think about it ahead of time you can present data with an alternative set of choices rather than only one solution or option. Offering alternatives gives people the opportunity to choose a preferred process or resolution after careful thought and judgment. Working together to make choices has advantages. When the person who will be carrying out a decision actively participates in making that decision, the decision will be of a higher quality. When people participate in decisions about what to do and how to do it they will be more motivated and committed to the task. They will try harder to make sure that the task gets done well. They will be more satisfied working on the task and will be more positive with their response and enthusiasm.

> **Hint:** *Take on the challenge of figuring out how to offer choice and alternatives.*

Clarifying Expectations

The cause of almost all relationship difficulties is rooted in conflicting or ambiguous expectations around roles and goals. Many expectations are implicit; they have not been expressed, discussed or understood. Unclear expectations bring about misunderstandings, disappointments and withdrawal. That's why it is important whenever you come into a new situation to get all your expectations out on the table. When you begin any discussion have everyone state what he or she wishes the outcome to be. You will find that you begin to judge others through those expectations and when you feel like the basic expectations have been violated, trust is diminished. Keeping promises and having clear expectations builds bridges of trust between people and avoids personality clashes. Clarifying roles, routines and rules is important to setting mutually agreeable expectations.

Roles

In any group or partnership, roles cannot be assumed. People all have individual skills, experience and knowledge. Some are better at one thing than others. In order to effectively live or work together you avoid friction and future difficulties by clearly defining roles. When living with a disorganized person one very effective technique is to go through and agree on who is responsible for performing a particular task. Make sure they understand what the task entails and how to get it done. Once you have reviewed them together, write down and post them, so there will be no disagreements later.

Here is a basic list of household and family tasks that should be decided upon. Add any special circumstance that your family may have to account and plan for.

Decide who:

1. Pays bills
2. Does laundry
3. Walks the dog
4. Takes out trash
5. Researches trips
6. Does the yard work
7. Does the gift shopping
8. Does the house cleaning
9. Drives the kids to school
10. Keeps the social calendar
11. Does the grocery shopping
12. Watches the kids and when
13. Is responsible for car repairs
14. Sends cards to friends and relatives
15. Makes weekly dinners and other meals

Routines

Following a regular routine keeps you on track and assures that things get done on time. When living with a disorganized person, getting into the same routine on a regular basis will definitely help the situation. It should clear up any misunderstandings by providing detailed procedures to follow and setting a specific time for all tasks to be performed.

Here is a basic list of household and family routines that should be decided upon. Add any special circumstance that your family may have to account for.

Decide:

1. When to visit relatives
2. When to change the linens
3. What time dinner is served
4. What time to get up for work
5. What day the housekeeper comes
6. When to clean out the refrigerator
7. What time you go to religious services
8. What day of week laundry should be done
9. When the kids must go to bed on weekdays
10. What night of the week to go out for dinner
11. What day of the week to go grocery shopping
12. When to pay the bills (1st or 15th of the month)
13. What time the television goes off for the evening
14. When to change the fire alarm battery July 4th and Christmas
15. What time sequence everyone uses the bathroom in the morning

Rules

Rules standardize how to act in a given situation. Although it is not mandatory to have rules in a household, it sure helps. Rules keep things in line. They act as barriers for procrastination and excuses. If everyone follows the same rules you show equality and respect for the others.

Here is a basic list of household and family rules that should be decided upon. Rules, even more than roles and routines, need to be posted for everyone to see.

1. Keep your room clean and tidy
2. Come to breakfast fully dressed
3. If you plan to come home late, call

227

4. Brush your teeth before going to bed
5. Do not bring food into your bedroom
6. Being unkind means you must apologize
7. Do not bring outdoor pets into the house
8. Place all read newspapers on the back porch
9. Agree upon discipline to support good habits
10. Leave a phone number where you can be reached
11. If someone goes over budget, they get to pay the bills
12. Do not bring a guest for dinner before getting consent
13. Agree on what constitutes a good grade or a bad grade
14. Make your bed before leaving the house in the morning
15. Clean up before going out so the house will be neat when you get back

Different Strokes for Different Folks

When looking at various businesses you will not only find contrasting corporate cultures but also different approaches to the work environment. Some businesses encourage an informal setting while others prefer a smart suit as the daily attire. Some tend to promote shorter days in the workplace with work at home in the evenings while others try to stretch the workday in the office by extending into lunch hour and before or after core working hours. As each business operates to proceed and work towards a common goal, each business facilitates the process of getting to the goal differently. It's the same with people. Each person has their unique personality, own way of doing things and works at their own pace. Working or living together the challenge is to make use of everyone's positive characteristics and distinctive abilities while minimizing any of their negative qualities. Acting in this manner each person brings a benefit and contributes to the process while working towards a common goal.

Money Matters

Couples, either married, living together or just dating seem to disagree and argue about money and financial matters more than any other issue. In most cases one is a planner and a budgeter while the other is not. One has a different saving or spending philosophy than the other. People tend to evolve into their own investing and consumption style, each following different strategies. It's a challenge to blend and organize financial habits and values. Make it a point not to disagree over money. Rather, sit down and talk about each monetary issue that arises. For parents who have different approaches to money, create a single response to issues like allowances and shopping as children can manipulate and play one parent against the other to get what they want. Air your views on the type of lifestyle and standard of living you each want. In every partnership one partner tends to be more financially savvy than the other. Set time aside to discuss your feelings and ideas about money to boost the other partner's money IQ and get you on the same financial page. Then, mutually agree on how to organize your finances and prioritize your financial objectives.

Being Neat and Clean vs. Being Organized

There is a very big difference between being neat and clean versus being organized. Many people think they are the same thing but that's not true. There are some people who are both, but most are not. Being neat and clean is having an outward appearance of organization however there may or may not be any personal organization involved. You can have neatly stacked piles of magazines and newspapers but have been saving them for no reason. An organized person would have cut out the articles or sections of magazines and newspapers they decide are important to keep. They may not keep their clippings in a tidy stack but they have pared down the paper. These organized people have already learned that garbage can be your friend. You can live an organized life by simply refusing to live with piles. Neat and clean people think that they are organized but in actuality they may not practice good organization techniques in their personal lives or on their jobs. They can fool everyone but themselves.

Reacting to Change

The world is constantly revolving and circumstances are changing around us on a daily basis. The speed of change can be blinding and there is nothing we can do about it except go along. When change occurs in the world it affects each of us. When change occurs in our own lives, most of the time, we have control and can respond well. New situations may call for different ways of thinking and acting. We can fight the change, learn to conform to the change or alter our habits to encompass the change. Most people think that change is bad because it takes them away from the routine that they are used to and accustomed to everyday of their lives. Sometimes a small change for one person is a big change for someone else. The best made plans and schedules can fly out the window if a small change occurs, so it is best to plan on being flexible. In terms of news, no one likes to hear bad news. However, learning bad things early on makes it easy to correct the course of action and avoid a major crisis later.

> **Hint:** *No one is ever prepared to handle everything in a crisis.*

Being Flexible

It's a good idea to learn how to be flexible and adapt to the changing conditions around you. The world is going too fast and you need to constantly readjust your pace. Sometimes the old ways just don't work anymore and you need to learn new ways to cope and new techniques to negotiate ways to live with a change. You constantly adjust to new weather patterns, new people on the job, a new boss and new government taxes. Most of the time change offers new choices and you must reassess your goals and decide whether or not to take advantage of new opportunities. Sometimes you must adjust to the loss of something; no bonuses at work this year, mandatory overtime or higher auto insurance rates. You must rationalize that this is something you must do to get a higher reward. Hopefully it is only temporary. A change for the worse will eventually make you angry, depressed and miserable. Once that occurs, it is time for you to initiate change and get out of a situation you are currently in. This may involve hardship in terms of time or money but may be worth it in the long run. It is also important to remain open to new things and not let your pride determine your decisions.

Accepting Oneself

The starting place for change is accepting yourself and taking an interest in understanding why you do things. Learning your own characteristic style of thinking and those of others can enrich your understanding. People adopt a certain pattern of behavior because those behaviors were the best ways they could find to deal with a situation. Discovering the reason behind why they do something or react a particular way can be a helpful start to changing it. Just as the process of change is facilitated by awareness of why people are doing a specific behavior it is hindered when they blame themselves, or others, for the behavior. When people are truly interested in why they do something and are personally committed to making a change, blame is irrelevant.

> ***Hint:*** *Not fighting change, learning to be flexible and adapting to change will make you a more effective and happier person.*

Chapter 12

LIFE CHOICES AND DECISIONS

"The wise man bridges that gap by laying out
the path by means of which he can get from
where he is to where he wants to go."
John Pierpoint Morgan (1837 - 1913)

E veryday in business there are decisions and problem solving situations that must be handled. Sometimes they are major, involving people's lives or money matters. Your personal life is also full of problem solving situations and decisions. Situations that require major decisions seem to pop up pretty often. They are usually very difficult to sift through and in the end you still do not know whether you have made the correct decision. These passages of life can evoke fear and anxiety in us. They all carry with them an element of risk. However you cannot let your fears hold you back from experiencing the joys that they can lead you to.

Being organized can help ensure that you make the decision that is best suited for you. Getting and staying focused will allow you to operate efficiently. A logical starting point will help you to determine your purpose. If you have a vague idea or a fuzzy notion, give it some thought and write it down to solidify your purpose and make it less ambiguous. Being organized can help you decide what data you need to obtain or research you need to collect to intelligently make choices and have a solid basis for your decisions. It's all about being prepared so you mentally, physically and emotionally know what to expect and know where you are going. Being organized means spending the time analyzing your choices and options.

- **Be very clear on what you have to decide.** Understand why it is important to you.

- **Decide on the optimum outcome you wish to attain.** Brainstorm and list all the ways that can get you to that outcome.

- **Do not make a situation bigger than it is.** Break down your situation into the most major factors that you will have to decide on.

- **Educate yourself and learn more about the topic.** Research and gather information that you can read, understand and refer to while making your decision.

- **Go over the list with someone who cares and discuss your reservations.** Examine all the advantages and disadvantages and weigh each point in terms of their priority to you.

- **List all your available options and then evaluate each one.**
  Create a pro and con list that states all your likes and dislikes.
  Learn about all your choices and alternatives.

- **Stick to the facts.** Try to be logical, not emotional.

Good organization eliminates the frustration, anxiety and unpleasant surprises that go along with making life choices and decisions. It is often hard to think of the right question to ask at every step of the way. I discovered that if you do not ask the right question you will probably not get the correct answer. I have tried to expand the thought process that goes into specific life changes and events that occur in our lives. These may not pertain to each situation you individually face but it will give you a general starting point. Once you review the topic you can start looking for more information to increase your knowledge on the subject. Aim to educate yourself enough to make an informed decision and to prepare yourself for an exciting future.

I have listed specific life events concerning several transitions, financial decisions, major purchases and actions that can take place during a lifetime. Each life event contains a list of items that you will need to consider and learn about or prepare for as you make your decisions and choices. Each category is designed to help you better understand the issue you are facing. By breaking down the process into smaller pieces you can clearly understand what your options and opportunities are. This can help you determine the right resources you will need to analyze an opportunity or a problem and allow you to move through these life events as smoothly as possible.

Once you are aware of and fully understand the implications of each of your options analyze your choices and decide on a specific action. Then you will need to create a plan. Logically break down the steps or actions that you will need to perform to carry out your life transition, financial action, big purchase or major decision. Compile a list of all the tasks or activities you will need to complete to attain your goal. Look back at all the tips in Chapter 3 - Setting Goals and Making Plans to help you overcome any obstacles and achieve successful results. Be assured that being organized and staying on track can turn your dreams into your reality.

NOTE: If you are confronted with a topic that is not listed, use one of the listed topics as an outline to help you breakdown the components of your particular situation. Hopefully these will serve as a guide to help you deal more effectively with the opportunities and challenges that life presents.

Life Choices:

Major Transitions -

    1 - Going Away to College
    2 - Getting Your First Job
    3 - Getting Married
    4 - Becoming a Parent
    5 - Moving
    6 - Getting a Divorce
    7 - Losing Someone Close

Financial Actions -

    8 - Doing Your Taxes
    9 - Selected For an IRS Audit
    10 - Selecting Medical Insurance
    11 - Buying Life Insurance
    12 - Buying Disability Insurance
    13 - Making a Will
    14 - Starting Your Own Business

Major Purchases -

    15 - Buying a Car
    16 - Renting an Apartment
    17 - Buying a Home
    18 - Making Home Improvements
    19 - Selling a Home

Major Decisions -

    20 - Choosing Child Care
    21 - Deciding Where to Live
    22 - Selecting a College
    23 - Changing Your Job
    24 - Caring For Your Elderly Parents
    25 - How and When to Retire

1 - Going Away to College

You are about to embark on an exciting, life changing experience. However, you feel unsure about the transition and are consumed with thoughts and apprehensions about college life. You probably have lots of questions about what to expect and what to plan and pack. Here are some things you need to prepare for -

Pack Clothing - you will wish to wear for most activities, mostly casual wear. Then pack a few dressy outfits for special occasions. Take enough clothes to last at least two weeks or until you usually do your laundry. Include umbrellas, boots and gloves. If you are close to home, bring clothes you will need for the fall season, storing winter things at home until you need them.

Take Appliances - you and your roommate may want to share. Try to talk to your roommate beforehand to decide who takes what. You only need one iron, coffeepot, CD player, refrigerator and television. Some colleges have strict rules about what you are allowed in residence halls and dormitories. Check with them first about your microwave, refrigerator and the use of extension cords.

Study Aids - will make homework a lot easier. Take along a good dictionary and thesaurus. Take folders, notebooks and notepads to take notes and organize your assignments. Stock up on personal and business size envelopes and stamps for correspondence. It will be cheaper to buy most of your supplies at a discount store before leaving for college than the college bookstore.

Personal Items - such as toiletries, linens, brushes, combs, manicure kit, hair dryer, sewing kit, first aid kit and laundry detergent are things that you use each day at home. Make a list of everything you use and recheck to make sure you have not left off anything. If you require medications have a prescription or a doctor's note sent in advance to the college health center.

Buy an Alarm Clock - to ensure that you will wake up in time for classes. Your mother won't be around to hound you out of bed, make your breakfast or make sure you get out of the house in time. A big part of college life is learning to be responsible for yourself and accountable for your actions. You will have no one to blame but yourself if you sleep in. By making lateness or absence a habit you will miss vital information in your classes and not be taking full advantage of all you can learn.

Meeting New People - will become an everyday occurrence to you. In addition to your roommate, you can meet people at freshman orientation, in the dining hall, in the laundry room, recreation center and in your classes. Participate and join activities or clubs, attend sports and cultural events and exchange names with people in your classes. If you wait too long you may find it more difficult to make friends as other relationships have been formed. Be open to meeting new people and take their phone number or email address so you can contact them.

What Courses to Take - will be decided between you and your college advisor. It is up to you to find out what the basic requirements are and to select courses that fit into your program and (if you know it already) towards your major. Become familiar with the college course catalog. It contains information on graduation requirements, requirements for all the subject majors and specific details about all the courses offered. It also contains a listing of professors and their backgrounds and degrees.

Drinking, Drugs and Sex - are all personal decisions. By the time you attend college you will have formulated your own set of values. College life brings you face-to-face with even more choices. Remember that this time in your life is for personal growth. You will be happier and healthier if you always think about the consequences, do not cave into peer pressure and act responsibly by setting your own limits. At college there is lots of support available from peer group counseling. Take advantage of individual psychological services in the health center or talk to your resident assistant.

2 - Getting Your First Job

It is time to find your first job and start making your own money and begin thinking about building a career. This can be one of the most exciting times of your life. Whether you are looking for a temporary job or an entry-level career position these are some things you need to consider -

Introducing Yourself - is the first impression an employer will get from you. Be prepared by asking yourself what you like to do and what jobs would fit your skills, hobbies and interests. Look up the company's website to get additional information on the company, their goals and principles. Determine how you would like to contribute to the company and how they can make use of your skills.

Create a Resume - and a cover letter. A resume is a brief description of your education, work experience, skills and accomplishments. A cover letter is a one-page introduction that accompanies your resume. It should state why you wish to work at this company and what you can contribute. Your resume is a self-promotional document that should show off your abilities in their best light. The main purpose of both of these is to get to the next step, an interview.

Prepare for the Interview - by emphasizing your good traits and those skills that relate to the job for which you are interviewing. Be ready to explain why you want to work there and how you can apply your skills, interests and goals to the job. Take the opportunity to highlight your unique qualities. Prepare an agenda of questions you wish to ask the interviewer about job benefits, promotional opportunities, starting salary, etc.

When You Go to the Interview - arrive on time to make a good first impression. Dress appropriately in professional attire that makes you look responsible, well groomed and neat. Listen to questions carefully and answer them directly. To prove your interest in the company and discover if the job is right for you, ask questions. Remember to maintain eye contact during your conversation to show that you are confident and honest. If you can articulate your passion, you'll impress potential employers.

When You Get the Job - you will be notified of the starting date and where and to whom to report to. Most probably you will be asked to attend an orientation session. Here you will be introduced to the company, the facility and learn about employee policies, practices and company standards. Take home all the literature you are handed and look over their contents before your first day on the job.

Fill Out the Paperwork - when you become an employee for health insurance, life insurance, savings plans and other employee benefits. Ask the Human Resource department or the person who hired you about your benefits and various options. Here is your chance to learn about all the perks that may be available to you. You will also have to fill out Federal and state forms for withholding purposes.

You May Be Asked to Take a Drug Test - or a physical exam. Many companies now ask new employees to take a drug test prior to being hired. A physical exam is sometimes required for health insurance reasons and to assess pre-existing medical conditions. The company may also do a security review on you to check if you have been involved in any criminal or fraudulent activities.

Your First Week On the Job - you should introduce yourself to as many people as you can. Pitch in to help out fellow workers wherever possible to show that you are a team player. Show that you are willing to take on challenging assignments and follow through on your assignments. Hook up with others during lunch to get to know some of your co-workers. And do not hesitate to ask a question whenever you are uncertain of a procedure.

3 - Getting Married

Your dream has come true, you have met the love of your life and you are planning a day that you will remember for the rest of your life. While preparing for all the details of your big day, remember to keep things in perspective. If you stick to your budget and avoid handling all the preparations alone you can enjoy the planning process as much as your wedding day. Here are some things you need to prepare for -

The Number of Guests - is the first decision you must make. You will not be able to decide on a budget until you estimate the number of guests you want to invite. Write out a guest list that includes people you truly want at your wedding and do not overlook people you really want to share this special day with. Include family, friends, relatives and business associates. Then try to par down the guest list to a reasonable size.

A Wedding Gown - can be very expensive. Many brides have their wedding dresses custom-made but you can also purchase a dress off the rack, buy a sample dress, find a dress at a secondhand store, rent a dress or borrow one from a friend or relative. Take a camera with you so you can compare dresses when you are back at home. Look through magazines or on the Internet to first decide the style and dress design you look best in.

Honeymoon Plans - usually go into affect soon after the weeding. The honeymoon gives you an opportunity to relax after the stress and excitement of the wedding. Make plans early so you will get your first choice and not have to make calls at the last minute. This gives you time to look for discounts on airfare, car rentals, accommodations and cruises. Engage a travel agent to look for a package deal to give yourself more time to arrange other wedding details.

Wedding Costs - can get out of hand if you plan to get everything you want. Think hard about your choice of ceremony, stationery, bridal gown, wedding party gowns, reception, food, cake and entertainment. Plan a budget and compare potential expenses with what you can afford. If you are accepting money from your family be prepared to accept the advice that goes along with it.

Premarital Agreements - also know as prenuptial agreements are becoming more popular. They are a way for you and your spouse to define equality in your partnership. They cover your pre-marriage nest egg and protect any gifts or inheritances you receive during your marriage. In the event of death or divorce it will avoid difficult disputes about property and ensure that children from a prior marriage receive their inheritance.

For the Wedding Day - create a plan and put it on paper. Be as complete as possible. One list should be a pre-wedding checklist and the other devoted solely to the details of the wedding day. When the day arrives it's natural to feel nervous. However, you will enjoy your special day and celebration much more if you carefully plan ahead and avoid having to make any last minute decisions.

Thank You Notes - should be sent out as soon as you get time to acknowledge all the gifts. The note should thank the giver by mentioning the specific gift and describe how you intend to use it. To be really organized, select your note cards and address and stamp envelopes prior to your wedding so you will have less work to do after.

Couple Finances - will be your first attempt to develop compatible saving and spending habits. Decide which partner will have the financial responsibility but make sure that you make big decisions jointly. Think about joint or separate banks accounts, using the same medical benefits plan, the terms of your will and beneficiaries on all your retirement and life insurance plans.

Your Last Name - will change if the bride decides to take her husbands name. She should legally change her name on her social security, drivers' license, income tax forms, voter registration, passport, bank account, credit cards and all insurance policies. If you decide to keep your maiden name there is nothing you need to do.

4 - Becoming a Parent

Becoming a parent is a big responsibility. From now on you must constantly think about another person. You are in for moments of sheer happiness and many sleepless nights. You may have to make adjustments to your life to accommodate your larger family. You may have to revamp a guest room or even buy a bigger house. You may need to make modifications to your lifestyle to acquire more time. Here are some things you can look forward to -

Who Stays Home - with your newborn for the first few months is a big decision for a couple when each of you has a full-time job. After the customary maternity leave for the mother, one of you can decide to take an extra leave, work part-time or work from home. Other choices such as live-in child care or a day care center may be an option for you, if you can financially afford the extra costs.

Leaving Your Job - is always an option but unless you have enough money saved up, not such a common option. It takes more and more money to raise a family, save for college and even buy diapers. Try investigating taking a leave from your job, working part-time, working from home or job sharing. If you decide to stay home, enjoy your time with your baby. You can always develop a strong interest or hobby into your own home based business.

Making Room - for your newborn may require you to start thinking about a bigger apartment or house. When a child is young it makes sense to place a crib in the corner of your bedroom but as they get older they will need their own private space. Start to think and plan for all your living options and consider any financial goals you may have to buy a condo or house.

Money and Finances - can become a problem if you do not plan ahead. The major expense after having a child can be medical expenses and college tuition. A medical problem or emergency can be very costly so make sure you list your newborn on your medical insurance policy and have them covered right away. Investigate various college investments and 529 state college savings plans. As soon as you possibly can, start saving for their college education.

Baby Care - can come naturally to you, if you have been around other babies, or may come out of a Dr. Spock book. Many hospitals give classes on baby care before you leave the hospital. Your first responsibilities are to make sure you keep the baby's doctor appointments, get their vaccinations on schedule and maintain your baby's healthy growth and good nutrition.

Rules and Discipline - can make or break your family. Start early in discussing with your spouse what type of behavior is allowable and what punishments you believe will work. It is never too early to develop rules as bad habits can start forming early. You may find that you both share the same values or that you have contrasting views on the subject. Have serious talks with your spouse to decide on common strategies.

Safety - must be considered with your newborn. Having a car seat is mandatory and most probably will be given to you as a baby gift. Many auto insurance companies provide them for free. Also think about child proofing your home: cover up electrical outlets, hide wires, soften sharp edges, block entrances to staircases and be generally conscious of breakable objects.

Development - of your baby begins as soon as you see them. You must begin to concern yourself about their health and emotional well being. Expose your newborn to music, art, color, shapes, toys and all different types of stimulus. Give thought to their social interactions and join a playgroup. Start reading to your child as soon as you feel comfortable. Cuddle and hold them often to build a physical bond. Whatever you do, you are in for a lifetime of love.

5 - Moving

The simple, or not so simple, act of moving can change many aspects of your life. Whether you are moving to a different state or just a few blocks away it will affect your daily commute, where your kids go to school, where you grocery shop, your friends, your medical doctors and lots more. Change is always good but it takes some time getting used to. Here are some things you will need to plan for -

What You Are Moving - will affect your moving costs? Besides your personal belongings, what furniture are you planning to move? Will you be moving a piano, a motorcycle, an automobile or a lawnmower? These large and heavy items can considerably increase your costs. To lower moving costs try to move some items by yourself.

Movers - can do everything for you if you wish. They can provide boxes and wardrobes, pack, move and unpack if you are willing to pay the price. You can move yourself by renting a van, or pack yourself to save. Last minute moves will be more expensive because you will not have the luxury of time to shop around for the lowest costs. Like other businesses, movers are quite competitive and come with a service reputation. Compare prices and get recommendations from others.

Storing - your furniture and belongings may be part of the total moving costs if you must vacate your current dwelling and cannot move into your new home. You may also need to arrange for temporary housing until your new home is ready to be moved into. Some people rent storage space for items they wish to take with them but decide to get rid of later on. Try to rid yourself of unwanted stuff before paying to store them.

Utilities - must be turned off at your old residence and either transferred or turned on at your new residence. Allow plenty of time to arrange your electric, telephone, garbage, water, cable TV, fuel delivery, garbage, etc. services. While you are at it, notify your post office of your change of address. Also notify all your magazine and newspaper subscriptions of your new address.

Packing - the bulk of your stuff by yourself will save you a lot of money. Get the proper size boxes for your items. Take the time to pack everything carefully. Buffer and separate the fragile items. A good rule of thumb is if you cannot easily lift the box you have packed too much. Pack heavy items in smaller boxes to avoid overloading the box.

Valuables - should be packed and carried with you. Pack your jewelry, computers, electronics, family heirlooms or other priceless items yourself and bring them with you to your new home. Make sure the value of your moving insurance is set correctly to cover the cost of replacement or repair in case of damage or breakage. You decide on the amount of insurance and coverage when you sign the moving contract. Also discuss how damages are handled.

Establish New - relationships with medical doctors, a new school for your kids, a new bank, a new babysitter and a new favorite restaurant. If you move far away going to your old neighborhood may not be an option. You will need to find new places to go for all the services your family requires. Ask your new neighbors and investigate all the options available to you before you move in. To lessen the anxiety try to make decisions prior to your move for selection of doctors, schools and other activities you regularly perform.

Allow Extra Time - to adjust and get used to things. Moves and relocations need time for you to settle in and get acquainted with your new surroundings. Get to know your neighbors and use them as a resource for information in your area. Always allow extra time to travel to new places and try new routes. By allowing additional time in your schedule or daily plan you will avoid stressing out or being late for appointments.

6 - Getting a Divorce

Divorce can be heart wrenching. Not only is it a very emotional experience but you are also faced with dealing with many legal and financial issues. Divorce goes to the root of your self-esteem and you may feel anger, guilt, sadness, depression or fear due to the loss of the relationship. Taking positive actions and planning ahead will help you to feel better. But before you get ready to build your new future here are some things you need to think about -

Legal Arrangements - can be made by you (if you and your spouse agree to the terms of the divorce) or you can hire a lawyer to negotiate a settlement and represent you in court. Unfortunately many divorcing couples are not on friendly terms. Legal fees vary by the complexity of the divorce, the size of the marital estate or custody issues involving your children.

Before Your Divorce Is Final - several issues must be settled. The most important ones are deciding on the division of all assets and property, the custody of the children, parenting arrangements for after the divorce, establishing child support and/or alimony payments, determining liability for outstanding bills, grandparent rights, etc.

Money Matters - are always a consideration when a couple separates. First comes the division of bank accounts, your home, your cars and your investments. Then there are monetary issues: (1) whether or not the court orders an allowance to be made to the husband or wife to maintain their cost of living (2) if underage children are involved, child support payments must be agreed upon, as well as educational support beyond high school, who will be covering the child's medical insurance and who may claim tax benefits such as an exemption of children (3) court costs (4) lawyers fees. Financial planning should be performed after the divorce is finalized to analyze your present cash flow and estimate for your future needs. New investments may need to be funded as well as creating a new budget and money management system.

Building a Single Life - means reorganizing many of your affairs. You will need to find a place to live. You may not be able to afford the same standard of living that you were used to. You will need to open a new bank account, establish lines of credit and pay off existing bills in your name. You may decide to go back to school, re-enter the job force, move away from the area, find a new job or just keep on doing what you are doing. The possibilities are endless.

Your Children - if you have any, will also be experiencing emotions connected to the divorce. Not only may your children be losing daily contact with both their parents, they may be losing their home, their school, and their friends. It is important to talk truthfully with your child and clearly explain the situation to them in words that they can understand for their age. Be honest with them and do not give them any false hopes. Children need to understand that the divorce is not their fault. Many children go through periods of stress trying to deal with all the issues that they are facing. Teachers and counselors need to be informed of the divorce and be on the look out for changes in their behavior. Try to get other family members to spend more time with them. Children need continuum in their lives, assurance and lots of love, so try to make the least amount of changes to their lives. Given time, they too will adjust.

New Opportunities - will open their doors to you, when you are ready. Given time you will adjust to your new life and become more comfortable in your new situation. Be open to trying new things, meeting new people and going to new places. There is no telling how far a relationship can go with a newfound acquaintance.

Life Coaching - can help you identify and work through setting new priorities in your life. Your life coach can help you focus on areas in your life that need attention or even challenge your perspectives and values. They can help you identify your goals, strengths and weaknesses. They can work with you to overcome obstacles and assist you in changing what you want - to get more out of life. Consider therapy to help resolve deeper feelings of depression or loneliness.

7 - Losing Someone Close

Being prepared and having as many details as possible pre-arranged can ease the stress in a difficult time. It will allow you to devote your energy to the emotional needs of your family and yourself. Some day you may be called upon to make the final arrangements when someone close to you dies. Here are some things you need to thing about -

Funeral Arrangements - can be made and/or pre-paid beforehand (before your death). They can also be made with the help of a lawyer or family member or friend. If no arrangements have been made try to locate any written instructions the deceased may have left or try to recall the wishes of the deceased.

Memorial Services - may be a less expensive option than a funeral. Both bring friends and family together to bring comfort to one another through the grief of the occasion. Holding a funeral or memorial service shows respect to the deceased and observes any religious customs. Most funeral homes can provide a service within your budget. Before you sign any agreement figure out how much you can spend and what the total price includes.

Immediate Care of the Body - must be taken if the deceased has made provisions to donate his or her organs before any procedure can be carried out on the body. There must be a decision whether or not the body will be embalmed. Some states require it and some religions prohibit it. Try to determine the prior wishes of the deceased.

Final Care of the Body - depends upon the wishes, religious beliefs and customs of the deceased either a burial, cremation or entombment. Additional decisions would be an open or closed casket, what clothing the deceased should be buried in, who will conduct the service, who will speak at the graveside, preference of flower donations or contributions to a charity.

Death Certificates - report the cause of death and helps settle the legal and financial affairs of the deceased. It is a good idea to request additional copies of the certified death certificate as individual ones need to be submitted to claim death benefits, close bank and investment accounts, file tax returns, get mail from the post office, stop Social Security payments and sent to any creditors. The doctor must sign the death certificate, stating the date and cause of death. The funeral director will add additional information. Eventually the certificate will be filed with the county health department.

Financial Affairs - of the deceased must be finalized after the funeral or memorial service. The complexity and expense depends upon the size and type of the estate. The named executor will handle many of the financial affairs. The estate may involve a trust agreement or the probate process that determines the authenticity of a will. If there is no will the property will be passed onto the heirs according to state law.

Other Issues - that will have to be addressed will be contacting the Social Security Administration, notifying all insurance companies, notifying the employee of the deceased, submitting outstanding medical claims, notifying banks, notifying creditors and submitting the last tax return. If a young child is involved a legal guardian may need to be assigned according to the wishes of the will or the court system. The personal effects of the deceased must be taken care of and the sale of a residence may even be involved. You may do all of this yourself or feel more comfortable hiring or consulting a lawyer.

Grieving Process - consists of a complex series of emotions. People tend to move from one stage to another or go back and forth between stages. You will most probably go through denial or shock, anger, depression and finally to acceptance. Try to concentrate on the good times and think positively. If you need extra help dealing with the situation or getting through it, seek out a support group, speak to a counselor or friend, ask your employee assistance program where you work and keep close ties to other family members.

8 - Doing Your Taxes

April 15th is the day that every taxpayer dreads. It is the date when the IRS requires you to submit your tax return for the previous year. Not doing so or filling it out incorrectly can bring interest, late payment fees and penalties. That is why it is important for you to understand what and how you need to calculate and report. If you need help you can use a computer program, hire a professional tax preparer, contact the IRS, purchase a current book on taxes or order Publication 17 from the IRS which explains all there is to know on the subject. Here are some things you will need to prepare before you finalize your return -

How You Identify Yourself - will affect your taxes. There are five ways you can identify yourself to the IRS: (1) single (unmarried or legally separated or widowed), (2) married filing jointly (you and your spouse on one return), (3) married filing separately (you and your spouse on separate returns), (4) head of household (a special status that is taxed at a lower rate), (5) qualifying widow(er) with dependent child (your spouse died within the last two tax years, you have a dependent child and meet other requirements).

Which Forms - do you use. Everyone must file the basic 1040 tax form but you may have to include additional forms depending upon the type and amount of income earned and deductions claimed. Examples are forms for itemized deductions, profit or loss from a business, capital gains and losses, supplemental income and losses, charitable contributions, self-employment tax, etc.

Gather Tax Data - and the W-2 forms you receive from your employer. You may also receive 1099 forms that show dividends and interest earned in the previous year from a bank, mutual fund or other investment firm you do business with. You are responsible for reporting all the income from W-2 forms, earnings from the 1099 forms, tips, supplemental income and income from a business or hobby. You may also receive 1098 forms that show amounts and points pertaining to a mortgage.

Preparing Your Return - you should use a checklist to make sure you have all your records on hand. Follow the directions in your booklet or online tax program as you fill out the appropriate lines.

Remember to sign and date your return. Attach your W-2 statements and all required forms when mailing it to the IRS and your payment voucher with any payments. You may need to send your completed tax return in a specific pre-addressed envelope depending upon whether or not you are owed a refund.

Check for Errors - whether you do your tax by hand, use a computer program, send it in electronically or hand it over to an accountant or tax service. It may be as simple as mistyping your social security number, omitting a signature or incorrect math. It is better to spend a few extra minutes checking your return the first time instead of receiving a letter to inform you about an error. Make sure to send your return to the appropriate IRS processing center.

Follow These Suggestions - to assist you as you do your taxes. Round money amounts to the nearest dollar as it reduces the chance for errors and makes calculations easier. Use last years' form as a guide but watch out for changes in your income, the tax forms or the regulations. Always file on time and include a check if you owe money. If you include a check write your social security number (and your spouse's SS#), the tax form number and tax year on the face of the check. Keep a copy of your tax return for your records in case you need to clarify an issue. Keep your records separated from year to year in a separate folder. Get organized early and do not wait for the last minute to fill out your return in case you need to obtain additional information or forms.

Estimated Taxes - are paid quarterly if you do not have enough tax being withheld from your wages. The general rule is you have to pay estimated tax if your withholding doesn't cover 90% of your tax liability. If you have significant amounts of investment income (or other types of income that aren't subject to withholding) you may incur a penalty if you don't make quarterly payments of estimated tax.

9 - Selected For an IRS Audit

Do not panic, do not feel that you will be thrown in jail or fined five million dollars. As long as you have been truthful on your tax return and have documentation to back up your data you have nothing to worry about. An IRS audit is a review of your tax return to determine if it is accurate. You are not being accused of anything. However, the burden of proving that your return is correct is on you, the taxpayer. Here is some information that will help you prepare for the audit -

Why Were You Selected - is a question that everyone asks. Do not take it personally as it is usually for one of three reasons: (1) Professionals, such as lawyers and doctors, are selected because they usually run their own business and do their own bookkeeping. (2) The IRS computer program picks up an unusually large deduction. (3) You are selected because you are in a cash business and many people in these businesses do not declare all their income.

Which Deductions Will Be Challenged - will depend upon your income. Certain deductions must exceed a minimum percentage of your income before you can claim them. This currently pertains to medical deductions, casualty loss deductions and miscellaneous job expenses. The IRS may also question your charitable contributions if you deduct more than the average for your income bracket. You may also be asked about other deductions if they are above the norm.

Type of Audit - which you will be involved with will be spelled out in the letter from the IRS. Read the letter carefully so you can determine what you are being asked to do. There are three different types of audits: (1) a correspondence audit is for minor mistakes, a letter will tell you what documentation you need to send them through the mail (2) a field audit is one in which the auditor comes to your business or home to verify the accuracy of your return (3) an office audit is one where you physically need to appear at an IRS facility on a specific date and time, bringing the documentation that is being asked for in the letter.

Professional Help - such as, your attorney or the CPA who prepared your return can accompany you to the audit. If your situation is very complicated and technical you will benefit from having an expert on your side. If it is only a minor issue you will need to weigh the cost of hiring a professional versus having someone along just to ease your anxiety.

Appeals - can be filed and reviewed if you disagree with the auditor. If you do not reach an agreement with the appeals office you can file a formal appeal and take your case further up the judicial system. If you lose the appeals process the IRS will charge you for the additional tax plus interest.

Audit Advice - and some tips. If you are unable to support one of your deductions, admit it and pay the extra tax. Always be truthful. Do not volunteer more information than you are being asked. Be positive and have a good attitude. Keep good records and hold onto them for at least seven years. Educate yourself on your rights as a taxpayer. When you receive a letter for an audit, respond promptly. You may ask for a postponement if you need more time to gather the records and data to substantiate any entry on your return. If you write any correspondence, keep a copy.

Common Mistakes - are incorrect social security numbers, computed incorrect tax owed, wrong child tax credit, wrong refund or balance due, choosing the wrong filing status, no proof of purchase, not indicating a rollover as tax-free, filling out Schedule D when you do not need to or not claiming a seller's mortgage points. Not all of these mistakes lead to an audit but you should be aware of them.

10 - Selecting Medical Insurance

Although it can be a major expense, not having any medical insurance can cost you more. Without medical insurance you run the risk of financial ruin by having one major accident or serious illness. If you are employed you may be offered several group medical, dental and vision plans through your employer. If you must buy medical insurance on your own read each policy carefully before considering it. You need to know exactly what conditions and illnesses are covered and what procedures are excluded. In order to make correct choices take the following items into consideration -

Indemnity Plans - also called traditional or fee-for-service plans are the most familiar and flexible form of health care insurance. You can go to any doctor or hospital and submit medical bills to your insurer for reimbursement. Deductibles and co-insurance will be applied to the charges submitted on your claim.

HMOs - Health maintenance organizations offer comprehensive care however they usually restrict your choice of doctors to ones that belong to their organization. HMOs are the least costly of all the health care plans. They emphasize preventive care and may require you to select a PCP (primary care physician - a doctor who participates in the HMO and responsible for managing your health care and referring you to specialists).

PPOs and POSs - Preferred Provider Organizations and Point Of Service plans allow you to go to doctors in and out of their network. It will cost you less to see doctors in the network as they have contracted with the organization and agree to a discounted fee.

High Deductible Plans - are the newest form of cost-effective medical plan. The plan provides major medical health care protection for catastrophic expenses. They are characterized by tax-exempt Medical Savings Accounts and a high deductible providing you with tax favored money to pay for medical expenses that exceed the amount of your deductible and allow for the build-up of savings to pay for future medical expenses.

Copay - or co-payment is a partial payment the patient pays in addition to the insurance premiums. It is paid by the member to help defer the cost of health care benefits. They are typical in HMO plans that require a separate co-payment to be paid for each doctor visit, emergency room visit or prescription drug.

Deductible - is the amount of money you pay before your insurance company will begin paying your covered expenses. Your plan may contain both individual and family deductibles. Most deductibles are yearly although some can be for a lifetime.

Co-insurance - is the percent of your service charge that your medical insurer will pay after you have met your deductible. The percentage varies by the type of procedure or service and your plan benefits. You are responsible for the remaining percentage.

Maximums - place a limit on the total healthcare benefits available to you. Most often they are applied over a lifetime - typically, up to one million dollars but your plan can also contain yearly maximums. If you develop a catastrophic illness or have a major operation you could get close to reaching the maximum limitation.

OOP - out-of-pocket amounts are limits as to how much you must pay out of your own pocket. After you reach the maximum the insurer pays 100% of the covered expenses.

COBRA - gives you the option of keeping your existing health insurance if you lose or leave your job. Under COBRA (a federal law) you can extend your coverage for up to 18 months. COBRA also ends when you begin a new job with health benefits.

Medicare and Medigap - Medicare provides health coverage to Americans over age 65 and permanently disabled people under 65. Generally, you are eligible for Medicare if you are 65 and receive Social Security. Medigap polices are offered to seniors by insurance companies to supplement their Medicare benefits.

11 - Buying Life Insurance

Ever think about the welfare or the standard of living your family will be able to afford or what financial resources your loved ones will be left with in the event of your death? Life insurance is a contract that you make with an insurance company that promises to provide your beneficiaries a certain amount of money upon your death. You pay for the insurance by periodic payments called premiums. The amount of the premium is based on your age, gender, medical history and the dollar amount of life insurance you select. Here is some information that will help you select a policy -

Do I Need Life Insurance? - You should consider life insurance if you (1) have a spouse (2) have dependent children (3) have an aging parent or disabled relative who you support financially (4) you have a sizable estate or (5) own a business.

Other Reasons - for buying life insurance are (1) more cash value policies have a tax deferred status and you do not pay taxes on the accumulation until you actually retrieve funds from the policy (2) you can borrow or withdraw money on the cash value you have earned on a permanent life policy - this can help for college tuition or buying a home (3) you can use the money you get from life insurance to pay estate taxes and funeral expenses. Life insurance does not go through the probate process; it goes directly to your beneficiaries.

How Much Do You Need? - The rule of thumb is to purchase life insurance equal to 5 to 10 times your annual salary. When determining the amount you need to consider expenses for college tuition, care for a disabled child or parent and your family's living expenses. Subtract the assets you have already to come up with a realistic figure.

What Are Your Options? - There are several types of life insurance. First assess your need and decide if you require permanent insurance for long-term needs or term insurance for the short term. Permanent insurance has higher initial premiums but guarantees a fixed premium, guarantees a cash value, guarantees a death benefit and grows tax-deferred. Term insurance has lower initial premiums that increase with your age, has no cash value and offers only temporary coverage.

What Type to Buy? - You will decide on either a universal or variable life insurance policy. Universal life insurance is flexible and permits the policy owner to adjust the death benefit and/or premium payments. Variable life insurance is for people who want to tie the cash value of their policy to the performance of the stock market. You decide how your premiums are to be invested among several investment options however you are always at risk to market changes.

Life Insurance Tips - are plentiful. If you are interested in term insurance look for one that is guaranteed renewable so you won't have to shop around for a new policy. If you have no dependents or do not need life insurance, don't buy any. Shop around for a good priced policy while you are healthy. People who smoke or pose a health risk pay higher premiums. If your employer offers a group life insurance program it is usually less expensive than getting it on your own. Compare different types of coverages, the quality of insurance companies and their prices.

Review Your Policy - at least once a year. If you have a life situation change you should contact your insurance agent or company representative. It may have a significant impact on your insurance needs. Life changes may be a marriage or divorce, a child or grandchild who is born or adopted, a significant change in your health or that of your spouse or domestic partner, taking on the financial responsibility of an aging parent, purchasing a new home, refinancing your home, a loved one who requires long-term care or coming into an inheritance.

12 - Buying Disability Insurance

Disability insurance provides you income when you become sick, hurt or cannot work. It allows you to pay your bills and maintain your standard of living. If an accident or illness leaves you disabled, your income will probably stop. Many employers provide disability insurance options for their employees or you can buy a policy from a private insurance company. Even though you may be in good health you never know if you will ever need this type of insurance. Statistics on disability from the HIAA Source Book of Health Insurance Data show that the two highest categories of disabilities are 18% due to back injuries and 12% from emotional or stress-related problems. Here is some information that will help you select a policy -

Being Disabled - should be carefully defined in your policy. The definition can vary. Some plans pay when you are unable to perform any work in your own occupation and others pay only if you are unable to engage in any work for which you are trained for or experienced at.

Short Term Disability - provides income for the early portion of a disability, usually the first six months. Policies can vary from two weeks up to two years. Short term disability is often included as part of an employee's benefit package.

Long Term Disability - provides income for an extended period of time until the person is able to go back to work or turns 65 years of age. Some companies provide long-term disability insurance for their employees or offer coverage under plans you must pay for.

Non-Cancelable or Guaranteed Renewable Polices - ensures that you can renew the policy as long as the required premiums are paid on time. A non-cancelable policy gives you the security that premiums cannot be raised. With a guaranteed renewable policy your premium can be raised.

How Much Disability Insurance Do You Need? - It all depends on your cost of living and the standard of living you are accustomed to. Normally you should plan on allocating 60% of your total income after taxes. If you purchase disability insurance with after tax dollars your disability benefits will not be taxed. To calculate how much coverage you will need, add up your monthly living expenses (mortgage payments, property tax, rent, car payments, utilities, food, clothing, loan repayments, expenses for entertainment, etc.). Do not include any work related expense as you would not be at work to incur any.

Social Security - disability benefits may also be given to you if you are eligible and have a steady work history. These payments usually increase each year to keep pace with inflation. You would need to contact your local social security office to determine your eligibility, your spouse's eligibility or eligibility for any dependent child. The SSA maintains a strict set of rules for eligibility and a formula used to determine the amount of disability payment you would receive.

State Disability - is limited to very few states. These programs are generally short term and have low benefit ceilings. They may offer a way to offset a portion of the economic loss but do not come close to meeting the long term disability needs of a moderate to high income earner. Check with your individual state to determine what, if any, benefits are available.

Cost of Living Riders - is additional disability insurance that many insurance companies allow you to buy. As your income increases you can purchase additional insurance coverage without proving medical insurability.

Benefits Will Start - after a waiting period. The waiting period is usually 90 days but can be as low as 60 days or as long as 365 days. The longer the waiting period, the lower the cost of your premium.

13 - Making a Will

A will can be written as a very simple document that ensures that your property and personal effects will be distributed according to your wishes after your death. It is a legal document that designates the division of a person's estate after their death. Anyone with sound mind and over 18 years of age can write a will, however your state may have additional requirements. Here is some information and items that you may wish to think about as you contemplate writing your will -

Do You Need a Will? - Everyone needs one however only half of all Americans die without one. Without a will the court decides and distributes your property according to the laws of your state. You may not be aware of the size of your estate and can inadvertently leave property and assets to those you do not wish to. If you have young children it is important to have a will because you are able to designate a guardian for them in the event of your death. Without a will, the court will appoint a guardian.

What's In a Will? - The basic elements of a will are (1) your name and place of residence (2) a description of your assets (3) names of your spouse, children and other beneficiaries (4) specific gifts (5) establishment of trusts (6) name of your executor (7) an alternative guardian (8) your signature (9) witnesses signatures.

The Guardian - you select for your child will probably be the surviving parent. You also need to name an alternate guardian in case neither you nor your spouse is able. The guardian you choose is someone over 18 and willing to assume the responsibility. It is a good idea to talk to the person ahead of time and get their consent. If you do not name a guardian and/or alternate guardian the court may chose someone you would not have chosen to entrust the care of your child.

The Executor - is the person who oversees the distribution of your property and assets according to your will, makes sure your creditors get paid, pays taxes, notifies Social Security and other agencies of the death, cancels credit cards and magazine subscriptions. Most people choose their spouse or an adult child. You can also name a relative, a friend, a trust company or an attorney as your executor. If you do not name an executor the probate court will appoint one. Probate is the legal procedure for the distribution and proof of wills, guardianships and the settlement of the estate.

Preparing Your Will - starts by organizing your objectives. Have on hand an inventory of your assets and an estimate of your outstanding debts. Prepare a list of family members, friends and other beneficiaries. Use all the information you have gathered to consider how you want to distribute your assets. Be as clear as possible on names and specifying assets to avoid any confusion later on. To finalize and legalize your will it must be signed in front of witnesses.

Keep Your Will - in a safe place that is accessible to others after your death. If you had a lawyer help you prepare your will have them retain a copy. If you name a trust company as executor, they will hold your will in safekeeping. You can keep it in your safe deposit box, but be aware that some states will seal your safe deposit box upon your death, so this may not always be the best place to store your will. You can also store it in a fireproof box. Make sure a close friend or relation knows where to find it.

Updating a Will - will probably be needed several times during the course of your life. For example, a change in marital status, the birth of a child or a move to a new state should all prompt a review of your will. You can update your will by amending it by way of a codicil (an addition or supplement to a will to change, explain or add provisions) or by drawing up a new one. Generally, people choose to issue a new will that supersedes the old document. Be sure to sign the new will, have it witnessed and then destroy the old one.

14 - Starting Your Own Business

You are tired of the rat race, working for others or are part of a big corporation. You long to "go it alone" and you have a great idea for starting your own business. First you will need to time the market and develop good strategies to succeed. Being organized is your best asset. Then you will need to think about ways to finance your venture and successfully market your product and ideas. Here is some information that you may wish to think about -

Develop a Business Plan - to be your road map to help you establish your business. Think about what type of business you wish to own and what your major goals are. Research businesses that interest you that are already in the marketplace and see firsthand the competition you will face. Think about where to locate your business. Think about the current market, what type of customers you wish to attract for your product or service and how you will attract them. Ask yourself how your product or service will be unique enough to surpass the competition.

Name Your Business - with careful thought and consideration. The name should give people some idea of the nature of your business and should also project the image you want to have. Names can be simple, sophisticated, or even silly. Try to select one that will grow with your business and not limit you in the future. Along with a name, many businesses also develop a logo that provides a graphic symbol of the business. Once you come up with a name, make sure it is not already in use.

Financing - your business may require you to invest some of your own money. You may want to look for potential investors, loans or other sources of financing. To get a loan you must first write a proposal detailing all the costs you plan to incur and the capital you will need to cover it all. You will also need to develop a financial plan.

Tax and Legal Reasons - will dictate what form your business may take: (1) sole proprietorship when you are the owner and are solely responsible for all profits and losses (2) partnership of two or more people working as co-owners who share the profits and liabilities (3) corporation limits personal liability as the corporation itself functions as the legal entity (4) S corporation has the advantage of a corporation but income or loses are reported individually of the owners or stockholders. Consult with an attorney and an accountant to decide what form of business would be right for you.

Develop a Marketing Strategy - to sell your product or ideas. Perform market research to determine your target audience. Then identify what is unique about your product or idea and develop a strategy to advertise it to your target audience. You can attract new clients or customers by offering free workshops or lectures at community organizations or events. Think about hosting a website or networking to get the word out to build your customer base. Create business cards and brochures to pass around.

Price - your product or service to cover your costs and to return a profit. If you price your market lower than you can handle you will not make a profit and will slowly go out of business. If you price your market too high you will not get many customers. When pricing, remember to be competitive while you consider your costs and overhead.

Producing and Distributing - your product or service involve other considerations. Always be aware of what price you pay for your supplies or raw materials. Look for competitive prices among your suppliers. Find the least expensive way to get your product or service to your customers. As your business grows you may need to hire a staff to handle sales, service, manufacturing, purchasing, distributing or administration.

The Small Details - (1) obtain a Federal tax identification number (2) obtain a state sales tax identification number (3) retain an attorney and accountant or CPA for the business (4) obtain any necessary licenses or permits (5) keep abreast of new business tax rules (5) obtain insurance coverage (6) decide on an accounting system.

15 - Buying a Car

Buying a car today can make you dizzy because there are so many decisions to make. In order for you to make the right choice define the reasons why you need or want a car. Then you have to do your research and determine your preferences and what will fill your needs. You should also search for a good price or financial deal. Here is some information that you may wish to think about -

What Do You Need a Car For? - Determine the size of the car by the primary user of the car: is it just for yourself or for your family too? Do you want a sports car or one that is durable and strong enough to be used to haul lots of stuff? How often will you use the car: occasionally or every day? Will you do a lot of highway driving or be using it just around town? The car's comfort, gas mileage, engine power, safety features and total performance must be considered.

Researching - what you need and investigating your choices ahead of time will save you lots of time, aggravation and money. Look at car magazines or the Internet to see what models the car manufacturers currently produce. If you time it right and models for the next year are being showcased, check out if they are worth the newer price. Get to know and make a list of all the features and options you want. Pay attention to prices.

Cars Cost - more than their purchase price. Do not forget to add in gas, maintenance, taxes, auto insurance and the cost of repairs. New cars will come with a warranty for a specific number of miles or years. Make sure you are prepared to absorb all the costs to maintain the car as the years go on. Look at projected figures that compare car maintenance costs and their resale values. Make sure to check out the new hybrids.

Money - may determine many of your decisions. As you add more features and go up the line the price increases. Make sure you can afford what you want or arrange pre-approval on a car loan from a bank. Once you are set on a price range, do not wavier from it or you may overextend yourself and buy a car you cannot afford.

Shop Around - and compare prices. Look for cars that have all the optional features you want. Take a test drive and ask about the warranties and car performance. Then try to strike up a good deal. Buying last years model will save you money. Shopping at the end of the month when salespeople try to fill their quotas may also get you a better deal. If you belong to AAA or other such car clubs, take advantage of their service that finds you the best quotes in your area.

Used Cars - are lots cheaper than new cars but you need to consider the age and wear on the car. Has it been in an accident? Does it run well? Has it been well maintained? How many owners has it had? What major services have been done or parts replaced in the car up to this point in time? Is it still covered under a warranty? Make sure to have a mechanic check it out. Here again you will need to assess your needs, estimate what you can spend and do your research.

Leasing a Car - has the advantage of not requiring a down payment and lease payments are usually lower than when you purchase a car. The disadvantage is that you will not have any trade-in or resale value at the end of the contract period. You should still compare leasing deals between dealerships. Like any contract, make sure you review it carefully and read all the terms and fine print, before signing.

Auto Insurance - is a necessity and many states require you to carry a minimum level. You pay premiums to an insurance company as a way of sharing the risks of driving and in return your coverage protects you against the risk of sustaining a large financial loss. Shop around and compare prices among the auto insurance companies that operate in your state. Many insurance companies offer you lower rates if you combine your auto and homeowner insurance with them. You will be quoted cheaper rates if you have a good driving record or do not drive over a certain amount of miles per year.

16 - Renting an Apartment

This may be your first place to live on your own or it may be just a change of living space. Whether you are going to a new location or staying in a town or city you are already familiar with, finding an apartment is still a major decision that requires special thought and research. Here are some points that you may wish to think about -

What Are You Looking For? - Are you clear on what you are looking for before you begin your search? What size apartment do you wish? Do you wish to live in a large apartment house, a townhouse or private home? How many rooms do you wish? Do you want any special conveniences: access to a laundry room, storage room, doorman, garden or balcony? Do you need to be close to your place of work, in a good school system, close to public transportation or concerned about safety? Although you need to feel comfortable do not spend above your budget. The more you spend for rent, the less you will have for other living expenses such as food, dining out, entertainment and savings.

How Do You Find an Apartment? - Start with networking and word-of-mouth. Ask friends, relatives or co-workers if they know of an apartment that may be or will soon be available. Check your local newspapers in the classified ad section or the bulletin boards in your local stores. If you do not mind paying a fee (usually one month's rent) you can engage the services of a real estate agent or an apartment locating service. Sometimes landlords pay this fee.

Check Out Your Neighbors - and find out who lives next door, above and below. After you sign the lease it may be too late to find out your next-door neighbor plays loud music, the people upstairs give dance classes and the downstairs neighbor holds parties on work day evenings. If you think that your neighbor's lifestyle may impact yours look into finding a different apartment.

Apartment Layouts - vary, no two are the same. A great view, walk-in closet, wall-to-wall carpeting or large spacious rooms can make you fall in love with a place. Other differences are the source of heat, air conditioning, appliances, elevators, intercom system, the location and size of closets and windows around the apartment.

Inspect the Lease - and the apartment before you sign anything. Look around the building and apartment for physical damage because you do not want to be held responsible for damage you did not cause. Also look for safety violations: smoke detectors, appliances, outdoor lights, locks on doors and windows, fire extinguishers, carbon monoxide detectors and exits in the hallways.

Sign the Lease - once you have decided to rent the apartment. This is a legally binding agreement between a landlord and a tenant. It must specify the name of the landlord, the address of the apartment, the rent amount, when the rent payments are due, where to send payments and the term of the lease. It may also contain additional rules for subletting, who is responsible for making repairs, if pets are allowed, who pays for heat and utilities and what happens if you break the lease prior to the expiration date.

Security Deposits - are usually the equivalent of one or two months rent. It assures the landlord that any damages to the apartment while you are a tenant will be covered. The money and interest is refundable to you when you fulfill your lease agreement and leave the apartment in good condition. Prior to moving out of your apartment get your security deposit or ask if you can apply it towards your last month's rent.

Apartment Insurance - is very inexpensive yet gives you lots of protection. It covers damage to personal property from fire or theft. If you are forced to live somewhere else while your apartment is being repaired, your expenses will be covered. It provides you personal liability in the event you are sued over an injury to someone who is in your apartment. It is a good idea to think about what type of policy suits your needs and situation before you shop for apartment insurance.

17 - Buying a Home

You are about to buy a home and be a part of the American dream. If you have been renting, you can say good-bye to monthly payments that you never get a return on. By buying your own house, condo or co-op apartment you will be building up equity and will most probably be able to sell it at a higher market value. It is an investment in real estate. First you need to make some decisions on location, price and features. Here are some items that you may wish to think about -

How Much Do You Wish to Spend? - The price range you decide to look for will dictate many of your choices. A particular neighborhood may be too expensive for you or you may decide on a smaller home within the expensive neighborhood. It is good to get a handle on your net worth to consider your total assets. Then you can figure out how much you feel is comfortable for you to borrow. Lenders typically want you to put down 5% to 20% of the purchase price. The traditional guidelines cap total housing expenses (mortgage, insurance, property taxes and maintenance) at 20% of gross income. Online calculators are helpful in your decision making.

Real Estate Agents - are familiar with local neighborhoods, schools, shopping, recreation and transportation. Finding a highly recommended realtor in the neighborhood you are interested in can be very helpful and can save you time. However they do charge a realtor fee on the purchase price of the home, usually up to 3%. You can also do all the research yourself through resources on the Internet, local papers or looking in your neighborhood for sale by owner signs.

Location - is very important. If you have school age children the quality of the schools will be an important factor to you. If you must travel to work, commuting time, accessibility to local highways and public transportation alternates will be important. You may care about the distance from local services, shopping and entertainment. If finances are a concern, property taxes, common charges, co-op fees and assessments will make a difference. Municipal services: water, sewer, recreation, trash removal can add on additional costs.

Your Ideal Home - should include many of the items you care about. Make a list before you start a home search of what you would like to have. What style of home would you prefer? Do you want a new or older home? What size home would you like and how many bedrooms and baths? Do you want a basement, attic, garage, front yard or back yard? How much property would you like to own? How much are you prepared to pay for utilities and home insurance?

Financing a Home - should not bankrupt you. After you figure out how much you can spend, consider shopping around for a home mortgage. Decide how long of a loan period you wish to have, 15 and 30 years are the most common. When comparing lenders consider interest rates, points, loan application fees, mortgage insurance and document preparation costs. When figuring out the total costs consider attorney fees, transfer tax, title insurance, survey and home inspection costs among many others.

Professional Advice - should be obtained for your big purchase. Make sure you enlist the services of a reliable home inspector or engineer to examine the structure of the home and the electrical, plumbing, heating, etc. systems. The inspection may reveal defects such as a leaky roof or underground oil tank, the presence of mold, radon or termites. All this information is good to know prior to negotiating a final price for the home and to ensure that you know what you are getting into.

The Closing - is when all the progressive steps in buying a home from the acceptance of the offer, title search, home inspection, survey, buyer's loan application to approval, etc. come together in a final transaction. All the documents are ready to sign, the buyer is ready to hand over the purchase price and the seller is ready to transfer title and hand over the keys.

18 - Making Home Improvements

Once you have found your ideal home and lived in it for a while you begin to think of how it can be made better, bigger or more convenient. Making plans to redo or renovate a home can get pretty pricey. It is good to spend time thinking about what you really want versus the cost for the change. As you go through the process here are some things to think about -

Why Are You Thinking of the Change? - Is it just that your kitchen, bathroom or décor is out-of-date? Do you need to replace broken or inefficient fixtures or appliances? Is your family growing and you need more space? Do you feel that putting money into home improvements will improve the resale value of your home?

Are You Moving or Staying? - You need to evaluate your future plans if you are staying in your home. You may want to change something but may not get its' value back when you sell or give up your home. Enhancements that buyers are likely to find valuable are adding or remodeling a bathroom, improving a kitchen, adding on a room or landscaping. If you are modifying your home prior to a move you have no assurance that your improvements will be liked or appreciated by new buyers.

Maintaining Your Home - may initiate projects to improve your home. You may just wish to add on a family room, install replacement windows, complete a basement or perform general upgrades to an older property such as new flooring, siding or painting. A leak in the roof may require replacement of your roof or a plumbing problem can get you to start thinking about remodeling the bathroom. Maintaining the working order of the various systems in a home are important to your comfort and the home's resale value.

Who Does the Work - depends on how much you are willing to spend. Do-it-yourself projects are more economical than hiring professionals. If you have the time, are handy and knowledgeable then by all means go for it. If you do not have the experience it may be cheaper in the long run to hire a plumber, electrician or carpenter. Working on home systems you do not have any experience with can bring more repair costs into the picture.

Architects - design and plan additions to homes from the ground up. They can plan major structural changes such as adding or taking out walls, building rooms, garages or creating complex home remodeling designs. Architects are professionals and usually charge an hourly fee or a flat fee and provide an estimate of the total cost. Interview a few architects and compare their style, ideas and prices.

Contractors - oversee the everyday aspects of your home improvement project. They hire and supervise workers, obtain the materials, get permits and make sure inspections are completed on time. Get proposals from several reputable contractors based on the work you wish to have done. When pricing contractors, make sure to give them each the same plan, so you can easily compare the costs. Ask your neighbors or others for reputable contractors they have used for their homes and inspect their workmanship. Make sure their estimates include carting away what they are ripping out.

Designers - to landscape the outside of your home or to design the interior of your home can offer very specific advice. They can help you select the colors, styles and types of items to fit your personal style. Then they can save you time by narrowing down your choices. Your designer can also save you additional money because they usually can get professional discounts.

Funding Your Project - may come from monies already planned for in your household budget or may require you to accumulate additional saving. You may need to delay a project until you have saved enough to finance it. Or, think about taking out a home improvement loan or line of credit. Think carefully before you okay plans and then don't change your mind as changes midway on a project can increase labor costs dramatically. A small degree of change is inevitable as new projects usually encounter modifications or unknown situations.

19 - Selling a Home

You may be preoccupied with thinking about your new home. You may be hesitant to leave memories behind you or eager to start a new adventure. Whatever your situation is, you are faced with selling your old home. It is a good idea to place your home on the market as far in advance as possible giving you time to find a buyer offering you a good price. Realize that setting closing and moving dates must be well coordinated, as you may be moving into a new home on a specific date. Here are some things to consider that you may wish to think about -

Home Appeal - will lure potential buyers inside. Before you place your home on the market try to make as many easy improvements as you can to make your homes' interior and exterior inviting. Clean all the windows, floors and bathroom tiles, shampoo carpets, wash the curtains, repair dripping facets, oil squeaky doors and spruce up the landscaping. Keep all rooms neat and organized. You may even decide to repaint or re-carpet (a definite added plus) a room. Set out colorful flowers, scented potpourri and try to create a pleasant appealing atmosphere. Baking cookies or a cake helps by leaving a really nice scent in the house.

Selling Your Home on Your Own - can save you a broker fee or commission but be prepared to put in the time. You will be responsible for placing advertisements, answering phones, taking messages, setting up appointments and showing your home to strangers. An agent can do all that for you and help you establish an asking price, promote your home and place it with a multiple listing service, weed out buyers who cannot qualify for a mortgage and help you negotiate a fair price with the buyer.

Setting a Fair Price - is dependent upon the neighborhood, current economic conditions, supply and demand of the real estate market, local schools, average home prices in the area and any extras your home may have (pool, central air-conditioning, fireplace, hot tub). Of course, you will want to get the highest price you can but remember that the buyer wants to get the lowest price they can. Check out the sale of homes similar to yours in the neighborhood. Pricing your home fairly and reasonably should attract many more potential buyers.

Negotiations - may take place between you and the buyers. You may be lucky and have several interested buyers competing among themselves. Regardless of the number, it is a good idea to check into the buyers' debt and credit history to determine if each is a viable buyer. When people sell, move and buy there is usually a domino effect. It is wise to negotiate a closing and move-in date that is applicable to both parties, have it written into the contract and make sure everyone sticks to it. If one party or attorney changes a date after the contract is signed, all parties must mutually agree to it.

Temporary Living Space - should be a consideration if you are selling your old home and your new place of residence is not yet ready. Many people make prior arrangements to rent an apartment on a temporary basis (for a month or two) just for this type of contingency plan. Until a closing is completed anything can go wrong or be delayed. The buyer may also be selling their house and dependent on certain dates and events to take place. It is a small price to pay for the peace of mind it will give you.

Legal Representation - is a must whether you decide to sell your home through a real estate agent or by yourself. There are just so many little things to look out for. An attorney experienced in real estate transactions will negotiate the contract for you. A contract should contain the sales price, spell out exactly what is included in the sales price, the date of settlement and move-in date, contingencies of the sale, the time limit for the buyer to secure a loan, allow the buyer inspections (engineer, termites, radon, etc.) and determine which closing costs are to be paid by the seller and which by the buyer. Everything important should be in writing. The contract should be witnessed and signed by both parties.

20 - Choosing Child Care

You may have to go back to work or with all your other responsibilities do not have sufficient time to spend all day with your child. You are set on finding a safe caring environment for your child that offers age appropriate activities that will challenge and enrich their intellect. Infants require all-day day care but older children may require care for only a few hours before or after school until you are able to get home or during holidays or summer vacations. These are some things you may wish to think about -

Child Care Centers - seem to sprout up everywhere. They provide care for groups of children and are especially designed and equipped for children. Some centers provide a structured curriculum and do some preliminary education. All centers must meet state standards and be licensed by the state. If you are lucky you may work for a company that provides a child care center on the premises or sponsors one nearby. This will allow you to spend time with your child during your lunch or look in on them whenever you wish.

In-Home Care - may be more costly and harder to find than a day care center. You may decide to have a nanny or babysitter come to your home or may bring your child to their home. It may be more convenient for you to have your own caregiver, or if you travel a lot, may be your only alternative. If you take your child to someone else's home make sure your child will have a safe and comfortable environment.

Summer and Holiday Camps - can be found for all age groups. Your local YMCA may sponsor one at your child's school. Because of all the working parents today many schools schedule before and after school programs that are also in effect during school holidays. Summer camps are various: some are sleep away, some are co-ed and others are single sex, some have a theme or devoted to a particular sport and some educational.

Check Into All References - to insure that you will be leaving your child with someone that is responsible, patient and levelheaded. You can assess these qualities by checking references. If you wish to hire a nanny or caregiver interview them and do a background check. If you are looking at a day care center or camp check that it is licensed or registered. Find out how many children are cared for and what are their age groupings. Find out the adult-to-child ratio in each group.

Start Your Search - by telephone to perform interviews and find out what facilities are available in your area. Look through your local newspaper in the advertisement, classified and situations wanted sections to find child care providers. To help you narrow your choices find out what they would do in various situations, what special training they have, if they know first aid and CPR, how much they charge, their hours or availability.

Personally Visit or Interview - the remaining choices. Ask questions, lots of questions. If you are visiting a day care center ask about a typical day, activities your child will do, playing outdoors, staffing, licenses and liability insurance. If you are interviewing a potential caregiver watch how your child interacts with them, their disposition and openness to answering questions.

Babysitting Cooperatives - may be one final possibility. Cooperatives provide structure for the often spontaneous shared babysitting that happens between friends. Parents in the co-op exchange babysitting in a structured, organized fashion. The advantage to co-ops is that they save money and provide you with babysitters whom you know and trust. The disadvantage, in these busy times, is that you will have to plan on doing a regular amount of babysitting each month.

Make Your Choice - by considering the level of supervision, safety of the environment, personal attention to your child and the activities that they will be engaged in. Weigh all the factors you feel will contribute to the overall quality of care your child will receive. If at any time you do not feel comfortable with your present arrangement, change your childcare situation. Your desire is to trust your caregiver not to spend time worrying about your child's welfare when they are not in your care.

21 - Deciding Where to Live

There may be a time in your life when you need a change, a big change. It may be when you first decide to move away from your hometown, or for a better opportunity or for retirement. Regardless of your reasons, relocating to a new place requires lots of research, thought and planning. Here are some factors you will want to consider -

What Suits You? - If you could overlook the usual constrains of family obligations, friendships, a job and sentimental attachment to a familiar area where would you like to live? Somewhere in this country is a place that suits you. It is better than the one in which you now live in. You may wish for a location that has better weather, living in a state that has lower taxes or a city that offers more job or cultural opportunities. How do you go about finding it and what do you look for?

Cost of Living - is a big factor. Living in a city is more expensive than living in the rural countryside or a suburb of a city. Prices for apartments within a city are higher the closer you get to the center and cheaper the further you travel from the center. When you look at prices compare your household income to the cost for taxes, housing, food, transportation, entertainment and health care.

Jobs and Opportunities - are more plentiful in a city. The greater the population, the more jobs will be available. However if you work in a specific industry certain parts of the country may cater to it more than others. Look into prospects for local employment given your career, experience, training and education.

Crime - is more prevalent in larger metropolitan cities than in smaller cities, towns or rural areas. The sheer number and density of people is the main factor. Statistics show that there exist more violent crimes and property crimes in larger cities. However, no one area can be completely safe. Compare crime statistics in the areas you are interested in and take a look at the local newspaper for incidents.

Health Care - and the supply of health care facilities many also be a factor to you. Getting quality health care and having a wide choice of medical doctors and special services may be very important to you and your family. As you get on in years the quality and proximity of medical services may become more important to you.

Transportation - getting in or out of your area may be a factor to you if you need to travel or commute often. Investigate public transportation alternatives, inter-city options such as access to major airports, train stations, bus stations and interstate highways. There are many locations that provide no public transportation and you must have your own vehicle.

Education - for your self or your family may be very important. Look into the quality of the public school system and nearby colleges and universities. Beware that property taxes may be higher in communities that provide high quality education opportunities. If private education is important to you make sure there are schools nearby.

Arts and Culture - are important assets of a location. Museums, public libraries, sport venues and theatres can enhance your life, plus provide entertainment. For the sports minded look into recreational activities, ski slopes, golf courses, nearby lakes, state and national parks.

Climate - can play a big role in your decision. You do not want it too hot or too cold, you want it just right. Decide if you wish to enjoy all four seasons of the year or can be happy enough to live in a place that enjoys a constantly mild temperature year round. Different areas of the country are more prone to earthquakes, hurricanes and tornadoes.

Research - locations that meet your criteria. There are many books that compare cities and locales in various parts of the USA. They contain facts and statistics about the quality of life. Scan the Internet for information on new locations and get in touch with the local Chamber of Commerce for specific information.

22 - Selecting a College

You are being faced with your first adult decision. In case you feel overwhelmed and do not know where to begin, read on. There are many decisions to make but for the most important ones you need to be honest with yourself about your feelings and opinions and try not to be swayed by friends or family. These are some things to think about -

What Interests You - is the most important thing to discover. By looking at a combination of factors; school courses, what you like spend time doing, what you enjoy learning more about and after school activities you can begin to explore what interests you. Spending time doing an activity in the field will help you determine whether or not you wish to pursue it in your future.

What Are Your Priorities - in selecting a college? Are you looking for a school strong in academics or a special program in engineering, architecture, education, criminal justice or art? Do you wish to be at a single sex college, one that offers Greek life (fraternities and sororities), far away or close to home, a public or private college? Do you wish to live on campus? Would you enjoy a college in a rural area, city or suburban setting? Are you looking for a great teacher-to-student ratio and small classes?

What Your Major Is - will dictate your choice of colleges. Not every school offers every subject or concentration in a major. Think about what you possibly will be interested in learning more about and make sure you look for a college that offers courses on it. If you are looking for something different, explore student-designed majors. Looking forward to an occupation; be realistic. In today's world occupations in the health care and service industries will be more in demand. Explore how you can best utilize your skills and interests to find your own nitch in the working world.

The College Search - can be a time consuming process, however, it helps to know what you are looking for. There are so many search engines on the Internet to help you zone in on the exact criteria that you want. You can select by major, size, state, public, private, single sex, location, fraternities or sororities, etc. or any combination. There are also many books and magazines published on the topic.

College Visits - should be arranged when you have narrowed down your search. When you actually visit a college and are on campus you are able get to know firsthand if you like it or not. Attend an open house, go on a campus tour, sit in on a class, pick up a college newspaper, look at the dorms, eat in the cafeteria, visit the library, talk to the students and ask plenty of questions.

College Interviews - should be scheduled at colleges that either require you to have an evaluative interview or you just want to know more about the college's programs and how you can fit in. Any interviews should be scheduled through the college admission office beforehand. If you have a personal resume, bring it along with an agenda of questions to ask.

Be Prepared for Admission Tests - the SAT or ACT test, depending upon which part of the country you live in. Check which test the colleges you are interested in accept. These tests are divided into verbal and mathematical sections to test your knowledge and comprehension. Different colleges require additional SAT II tests in specific subjects for admission, so check it out.

College Application - should be filled out correctly and completely. It is a good idea to have someone check it over for errors before you send it out. Many colleges accept electronic applications or the common application that you fill out once and send a copy to all colleges you wish to apply. Recommendations should be asked for at the beginning of fall in your senior year. Don't forget to include your essay, any additional materials and your check for the application fee to the college.

Note: Read my other book *College Knowledge – The A+ Guide to Early College Planning.*

23 - Changing Your Job

Changing your job is a reality in today's market. It is predicted that today's work force will change jobs seven to ten times in their careers. If you decide to change your job take some time to develop a strategy that will help you land a better job than your current one. Perhaps you are looking for more money, a promotion, a new career or just a change of scenery. Here are some items you may wish to think about -

Assess Your Current Job - to determine how happy you are. Look into the reasons why you are uncomfortable or dissatisfied with your job. Ask yourself what aspects of the job would give you a greater degree of satisfaction, challenge you, be less stressful and give you more opportunity to advance or earn a higher salary.

Career Change - always passes by your mind when thinking about changing your job. People always believe the grass is greener on the other side. Many of us decide our life's passion when in the midst of a different career. When making a new transition it is often the time for you to think about going after something new, something else or just going back to school. Many a job layoff has motivated someone to take a different course.

Staying Within Your Company - and switching jobs is easier than going outside your company. Many companies have internal bulletin boards and human resource departments that post new opportunities and jobs that become available. Most companies would rather hire and promote from within before going outside to the public. Ask friendly co-workers in different departments to keep their eyes open for you.

Job Placement Agencies - help increase your number of job opportunities and save you time. They can help to match your skills and abilities to companies who are looking for them. You can also find many Internet bulletin boards that list jobs and many companies include a job posting page on their website. The hiring company usually pays the fee directly to the job agency.

Networking - with friends, family and members of professional organizations is one of the best ways to find a job. Chances are excellent you already know people who can help or hire you. Talking to people of influence who understand your strengths is more effective than calling a stranger. Most people prefer to hire someone who personally knows you or is recommended by someone they know, trust and respect.

Timing Is Everything - as it helps to be at the right spot at the right time. As we cannot control time we need to make the best of it. While you are waiting to land that new job check newspapers and employment ads everyday, use the Internet to find websites that offer job openings, widen your job search, talk to others in your field, go on job interviews and use networking resources.

Resumes - get you to the next step, the interview. Prepare your resume and make it as professional looking as possible. Reread your resume for grammatical and spelling errors. Consider reading a book on resumes to see some examples. Find someone in your industry to comment on it. One page is better than two pages and shows how you can streamline yet show off all your assets. An organized impressive resume can go far.

When You Leave - your old job obtain all that you have coming to you. Schedule an appointment with your company's benefit counselor or staff to discuss all your options. Your health insurance will end but you can get COBRA medical and dental insurance for up to 18 months. Find out if you have any money accrued towards a pension or other type of employee retirement plan. Ask abut money in your 401K, 403(b) or 457 plan and if you need to do a rollover or can keep it there. Find out about payment for unused vacation days, when you should receive your last paycheck and whom to contact if you have a question after you leave. Most often your employee handbook will contain many of these answers.

24 - Caring for Your Elderly Parents

Making decisions for or with your parent(s) may be one of the hardest things you may have to do. Emotionally it is tough to handle. Instead of them making decisions for you and your welfare the tables have turned. The responsibility of your decision may seem a burden but once you educate yourself on the options it becomes easier. These are some things you will want to find out about -

Talk to Your Parents - about their concerns. Do not wait until one or both of your parents become ill, incapacitated, or unable to take care of them self. It will be easier to intervene and prevent problems if you have talked to them regularly about their wishes, needs, desires and finances. This can be difficult in families where the subject of money was always taboo but waiting until a crisis occurs can cause stress, heartache and money losses. Planning ahead helps ensure that your parent's wishes are carried out and reduces disagreements among siblings regarding exactly what your parents would want done.

Today's Options - are always expanding. It used to be that seniors had only one choice, spend as much time making do on their own then enter a nursing home when they could no longer care for themselves. Today, they can decide to live in a retirement community, an apartment complex of senior citizens, an independent care facility, a personal care center, an assisted living community, a life care community, in a nursing home or can decide to hire a nurse or personal assistant and remain in their own home. Each option has its advantages and disadvantages.

Financial Considerations - will probably dictate many of the options. Will your parent's personal resources, such as income, social security, pensions and savings, cover all the expenses? Do they have long term care insurance and what does it cover? Do they have Medicare and additional medical and/or dental insurance coverage? Are you willing to assume or share some of the financial responsibility? Have they used up most of their assets and eligible for Medicaid assistance?

Health Considerations - is the next most important factor. Depending upon the physical health of your parent(s) and their mental capacity will determine what sort of facility or community would be good for them. For someone who requires constant medical supervision a nursing home or personal nurse would be appropriate. For someone who is mentally alert and physically able a recreational and educational atmosphere would be best. Seniors who are stimulated to be active, both physically and mentally, tend to feel more satisfied, happier and less depressed.

What Services to Look For? - Each facility or community will offer different services. You should ask about meals or availability to shopping centers, laundry, housekeeping, emergency and medical services. They may provide additional services for nursing, physical therapy and recreational therapy. Find out what recreational, educational and social activities they sponsor. Some centers are even connected to colleges so seniors can partake in or continue educational courses or degrees.

Take Your Parent(s) On a Visit - to the facility or community prior to making a major decision. It is hard enough having to relocate yourself but much more difficult if you are not happy with your new surroundings. Make sure your parent(s) is agreeable to the move. Talk to them frequently about any doubts they may have and try to explain why it may be best for them. Sometimes getting their medical physician or trusted friend on your side can help.

Make the Transition - an easy one by being very patient. Older people are less adaptable then younger ones. Give them plenty of time to adjust to their new surroundings and offer as much of your time and assistance that you possibly can. Call them often and try to visit them frequently. If you do not live close by have a friend, relative or senior caregiver service look in on them occasionally. Make sure that they have everything they need and so they do not feel like you no longer take any interest in them.

25 - How and When to Retire

Some people can't wait to retire. They look forward to days of doing what they enjoy most, a hobby, a sport or just reading a book. Others wish to retire but cannot because of financial reasons. While others who can comfortably retire, fear it. They see retirement as the end of a road and are not ready to adapt to a life change. As you get closer to that retirement age here are some things you may wish to think about -

To Work Or Not To Work, That Is the Question? - People used to wait until age 65 to retire from their job and get the customary watch for working 40 years at one company. Today people are faced with all types of options. If they cannot financially afford to retire right away they can decide to work part-time, start a new career, or start up a business from a lifetime hobby. If they can afford to retire they can decide to go back to school, take educational courses just for fun, play a sport, travel, take up a new hobby, partake in an old one, or get involved in lots of other leisure activities.

Can You Afford to Retire? - Having wisely saved your money you now have the option of retiring. If you did not save well and feel you do not have enough you will have to wait awhile before your dream of retirement comes true. When you figure how much you have to live on consider your pension, 401K plan, IRA, Roth IRA, stock gains, dividends, bond interest and all the income from your assets or supplemental activities. Evaluate your cost of living, life expectancy and use one of the many financial calculators to determine how far your money can go. Review all your investments and decide if you should rollover any accounts into a tax-free Roth IRA.

Your Life Style - will determine how much you will need and spend. The figure tends to vary but most financial planners advise 75% of your working income. Meaning when you retire, if you plan to continue with your same lifestyle you should have at least 75% of your working income available to you. Costs for work expenses, clothing and transportation will decrease. Costs for travel, entertainment and health may increase. Many people decide to retire and simplify their style of living to save on expenses. They may relocate to a state with a lower tax rate, buy a smaller home, cut down on dining out, travel less or try to economize on generally everything.

Enjoying Your Retirement - may entail filling your life with an acquired interest or new activity. You must give careful thought about what you wish to do with your time. You may decide to devote some time to volunteer work and give back something to your community. You may decide to take advantage of your time to travel places you have dreamed about or visit old friends. You may decide to take educational courses to learn a new skill or gain knowledge on a topic you have always been interested in. You may decide to become more physically active, now that you have the time and enjoy or take up a new sport. You may decide to spend more time with your children or grandchildren. Or, you may decide to just relax, mow the lawn at your leisure, read more books or go to more movies.

New Issues - concerning seniors will confront you that you may not have thought of before. You may decide that your home is too much to care for or too large for your current needs and you should downsize. You may wish to look into long-term care insurance for peace of mind. To ease the physical load of home ownership you may wish to hire professionals to care for your lawn, plow the snow from your driveway or occasionally clean your home. Or, you may wish to check out reverse mortgages, discounts for seniors and tax benefits to increase your stream of income.

Your Decision Is Never Final - if you decide or wish to change or try something new. Do not feel that you must make one decision and are stuck with it. You may decide to go back to work or move back to where you used to live. You are allowed to try new things and decide if they are for you or not. As long as you pay attention to your health and stay healthy you can do anything. So learn to eat right, do moderate exercise, keep your mind active and ENJOY!

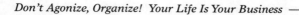

EPILOGUE

Done with the book already? You must be very organized by now. Hopefully you picked up several ideas and suggestions on how to organize your life and how to plan ahead of time. Now you need to begin putting them into action. Once you practice the techniques that you have learned you will become more organized, get lots of things done, schedule activities and always be on time. You will no longer feel like you are on a treadmill, speeding through tine. You will have a prioritized plan set for meeting all your goals. You will have learned about the different aspects of your life and how keeping things organized, planned and scheduled can keep you on track.

Organization and time management skills are not innate nor do they happen by accident; they must be learned and practiced. Being organized is a process to be mastered or refined over a lifetime, so do not expect instant results. As you go through life you will be able to apply many of the techniques you have learned in this book. Constantly ask yourself how you can improve and work at your maximum efficiency. Always prioritize your goals and maintain a positive outlook. But most of all avoid being critical of yourself and others. Remember, only you are in control of your life, your accomplishments and your future and have the ability to make choices. Success and happiness is within your own grasp so constantly have fun, do things you enjoy and fill your life with meaningful experiences and personal achievements.

I hope this book has taught you how you can manage your life the way today's most successful businesses do. Always look for new answers to life's challenges. Identify new opportunities for personal organization and success. Organize the various areas and functions in your life so you can devote quality time to each of them. Gain insight into a framework for making your personal decisions that is focused, productive, realistic, flexible, creative, responsive and organized. Know that you can live a happier, more fulfilling productive life by following the examples of successful businesses. Learn how to carry on the business of your life and head yourself on the road towards a successful and profitable future.

Regina Muster

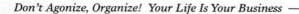

Appendix 1

WEB SITES
TO REFERENCE

Organizing Tip Sites:

1. www.betweenfriends.org

Uniquely created for moms, the site is devoted entirely to tips for busy moms. But you do not have to be a mom to look through all the advice and information the site offers. Their motto is *"Achieving a balanced life through working smarter, not harder"*. The site contains articles and tips on time management, household hints, organization, parenting, money, business and self-improvement. They have a monthly newsletter that you can subscribe to with tons of new hints, featured articles and recommended resources.

2. www.hint-n-tips.com

The website is an exchange center for practical hints, tips and information. The site is divided into household, food & drink, pets, motorcycling, vehicle and computer repair & maintenance, motoring, travel advice, finance & investing, career, beauty, business, garden care, appliance care & repair, health, plumbing, leisure, security, safety, pets and you will find much, much more.

3. www.getorganizednow.com

Full of organizing tips, tools, checklists, articles and ideas the site offers free idea packs, an email newsletter and discussion forums. Each month, on the first of the month, they release a new monthly checklist that contains 10 items for you to complete each month. The site gives you access to their *"Get Organized"* store filled with organizing books, tools and systems.

4. www.organizetips.com

The focus of the site is about helping to organize your daily life. It contains a daily planner, house maintenance section, *"Chart the Course"* section that includes printable checklists, home office help, hints on how to use and set up Palm Pilots, organizing articles, a moving planner, a wedding planner, a time management section plus a section on organizing items such as books and time planners.

Organizing Product Sites:

1. www.a1priorites.com
Offering organizing ideas for time management and for daily living the site highlights their products including planners for keeping track of your plans and all types of calendars geared for students, families and businesses. They offer free monthly newsletters, checklists and menu planners. Here you can also find sections on organizing household papers, email strategies and setting personal goals.

2. www.officemax.com
Sponsored by Office Max the site offers organizing and office supplies, calculators, software technology, furniture and drafting tables. Among the various COPYMAX services they offer are custom stamps, labels and calendars. They have sectionalized their site by specialty shops: digital bookstore, art and farming, wireless phones and phone plans, downloadable software, high speed/dial up Internet and by industry: legal, real estate and supplies for a small business center.

3. www.orgainzingyourworld.com
Providing organizing solutions, organizing services, organizing products and organizing resources for your house, desk, computer and business this site is your one stop supermarket for organizing everything at home and at work. They offer books and software products. You can also *"Ask the Organizer"* service. They are a resource center for locating and referring independent professional organizers.

4. www.staples.com
Sponsored by Staples the big office supply store, the site contains thousands of supplies; calendars, organizers, forms, paper, envelopes, folders, furniture, file cabinets, bookcases, desks and shelving. They also offer organizing technology: computer printing supplies, faxes, PDAs, scanners, telephones and custom printing: business cards, letterheads and holiday cards. You can either place an order online or use their local store finder to locate a Staples store near you.

Time Management Sites:

1. www.balancetime.com
This website claims to double your personal productivity in less time and stress if you use their methods and techniques. They teach time management and personal productivity seminars, speed reading, executive coaching, seminars, classes, workshops, keynotes and consulting anywhere in the U.S. with life long support to students and graduates. A free newsletter is also offered.

2. www.businesstown.com
Presenting information from the business point of view the site teaches you how to control and manage your time. There are sections on the secrets of time management: procrastination and saving time, business planning: how to start and how to run a business, managing people: motivation, getting started: steps to success, letters and forms, getting paperwork in order and time management.

3. www.timemanagementtraining.com
At the Time Management Training Institute you can receive time management training information. They provide instruction on the basics of time management. Their seminars and courses for managers, sales personnel, administrative assistants and executives are scheduled in cities all around the USA. Participants will focus on tasks that help them to concentrate on working on goal setting activities and learning how to apply time delegation techniques and time management skills to manage their time and life.

4. www.time-management-tips.com
The site includes free management tips and documents how to identify time wasters, understanding time, keeping a time log, making distinctions between urgency and importance, types of tasks, effective decision making, setting goals, identifying interruptions, regaining control, effective delegation and empowering others. They offer training courses available on both e-Book and multimedia CD-ROM.

Goal Setting Sites:

1. www.about-goal-setting.com
Offering free tutorials and resources on goal setting the site contains a 20-minute goal setting tutorial that you can go through on your own. They address why setting goals works, setting of financial goals, mind mapping (note taking and planning), managing time, procrastination and tips for speeding up your reading. Each section contains a list of even more websites to use as a resource.

2. www.goalsforamerica.com
The website provides tips, articles and a free newsletter for setting and managing all your personal and professional goals. Health, family, career, leisure, relationship and personal goals are the main areas of concentration. You can go through a step-by-step goal setting process for any short or long-term goal. If you decide to register for their services you will be sent email reminders that arrive at the time when you should be working on each task.

3. www.mindtools.com
Backed by Mind Tools, here you can discover the essential skills and techniques that will help you to excel in your life and career. You can learn more than 100 of the most important thinking skills in time management, stress management, memory improvement, information assimilation, practical creativity, managing complexity, decision making, project planning and communication skills. Each of the essential areas provide reference to books and other resources to extend your knowledge.

4. www.topachievement.com
Besides providing articles on setting goals and e-book specials, the site gives you a new *"quote of the day"* for inspiration. It contains a listing of power words - to use to help achieve your goals. They provide powerful goal setting techniques in seven easy steps, host a discussion board and maintain an encouragement chronicle full of stories for you to get inspired by.

Finance Sites:

1. www.fidelity.com

Brought to you by Fidelity Investments, a leader in mutual funds. On the site you can perform research on stocks, bonds, options, IPOs, annuities and all types of fixed income investments. They offer guidance on retirement, estate, college, tax planning and charitable giving as well as servicing their customers and accounts through Internet transactions and their products and services.

2. www.kiplinger.com

From Kiplinger, a publisher devoted to personal finance and business management. The website contains sections on the basics plus how to build up your financial knowledge. They offer tips and tools for investing, the latest rates and money saving tips for your finances, planning to put your financial goals into action, doing research for big purchases, calculators, financial advice from experts and tons more.

3. www.money.com

From the editors of CNN and Money magazine this site contains separate sections on real estate, automobiles, your home, stocks, mutual funds, jobs, the economy, world business, technology, Fortune 500 companies and the best employers. Their financial tools include calculators for mutual funds, savings, retirement, mortgages and asset allocation, to mention a few. In *"Money 101"* they explain many of the basics of managing your finances.

4. www.vanguard.com

Brought to you by the Vanguard Group their web pages for personal investors are loaded with information. In their *"Plain Talk"* section they offer personal financial planning guides on savings, retirement, college, investment basics and taxes. You can research all types of investments, create a watch list, investigate insurance options and compare costs. Their customers are able to track their accounts and perform buy and sell transactions online.

Tax Sites:

1. www.irs.gov
On the official Internal Revenue Service government website you can find all the tax forms, advice, instructions and information an individual will need. The site also provides highlights of what is new in the current tax season, addresses tax refunds and relief, free tax return preparation, tax solutions, late filing, refunds, time extensions, tax shelters, tax incentives, withholding calculators, tax counseling for the elderly, how to obtain a copy of a prior tax return or an extension, etc.

2. www.hrblock.com
This is the site of the H&R Block professional tax preparation service. They offer tax programs, office services, tax software and professional help for doing your taxes. The site offers tax advice and planning tips. They have calculators to figure your withholding, AMT, etc. There is a section devoted to the tax effects of specific life changes: having a baby, adopting a child, getting married and looking for a job.

3. www.turbotax.com
Brought to you by Intuit, the maker of TurboTax software, the site offers lots of tax tips and resources, as well as tax forms, a tax estimator, tax preparation checklist, tax law changes and ways to maximize your tax deductions. Within their customer support section they offer their other major software products. Their Quicken software lets you see your complete financial picture and integrate with Turbo Tax.

4. www.wwwebtax.com
On the World Wide Web Tax site you will find IRS forms, instructions, tax tables, publications, rate schedules, charts, worksheets and answers to practically every IRS tax question in their Master Index of tax topics. They offer tips and strategies on how to avoid an IRS audit. You can check the status of a tax refund. The site allows you to e-file and print your IRS tax return for a fee. They offer a tax discussion group and IRS and government tax links.

Travel Sites:

1. www.fodors.com

Fodor's, the publisher of travel guides for all over the world, brings you this site to help you find the trip you want. They offer information on destinations worldwide, hotels, restaurants and historical sights. Their tips and feature articles highlight novel locations and unique travel information. They also offer many bargain deals and specials. You can book your travel tickets, hotels, rental cars and travel packages through the site.

2. www.frommers.com

Providing expert travel guidance for more than 2,400 destinations around the world on this site you can research travel trips and get advice before you travel. You can book your air, lodging, cruise, auto or rail. Inside their *"Community Section"* you can swap stories with other travel enthusiasts, share your own experiences or learn from someone else.

3. www.ricksteves.com

Rick Steve's Europe Through the Back Door guidebook series is a great resource when traveling abroad. His website features travel news, tips and information plus a travel store where you can stock up on his books, bags and travel accessories. To plan your trip the site offers a section on European festivals as well as information for all the counties in Europe, Eastern Europe and Russia.

4. www.travelocity.com

This is the most used site for travel deals. Here you can search and buy airline tickets, make hotel reservations, set up car rentals and book a vacation or a cruise. They are famous for their last minute deals and packages. You can get travel information and check on the status of your flights. Their destination guides allow you to print out a customized mini-guide. Their travel tools provide you with photos, video clips, a map center, a weather center and a currency converter.

Party Planning Sites:

1. www.alltimefavorites.com
The website is an event planning resource for weddings, conventions, bar/bat mitzvahs, festivals and parties or events of any kind. The site is arranged by sub-categories within main categories such as entertainment, flowers, invitations, photographers, party rentals, transportation options, etc. You can enter a product or service you need and search for a price quote from a local vendor.

2. www.eventplanning.com
Brought to you by Hospitality Networks you can view resources for wedding, party and special event planning in various cities. You can look into their bookstore, make a map, get driving directions, find many planning tips and chat with others about your special event. You can also perform searches on the many links posted by planners and supplies across the USA and even subscribe to their e-magazine.

3. www.partydirector.com
This site allows you to select a region within the United States and search for local caterers, banquet halls, DJs, entertainers, party planners, florists, balloons, limousine services, musicians, clergy, officiants, party favor providers, party rentals, party supplies, photographers, printers, calligraphers and travel services. They also provide information on planning weddings, party themes, baby & bridal showers, etc.

4. www.partypop.com
Here you can enter some basic information and get ideas for seating arrangements. You can find party vendors in your area and professionals in the party, wedding and event industry. You can find or get hundreds of ideas for a theme for your party. You can get information on all types of events: anniversaries, baby showers, bachelor, bachelorette, bar/bat mitzvahs, birthdays, bridal showers, confirmations, engagements, family and school reunions, school proms, sweet sixteen parties and weddings. There is also a budget calculator to help you get a rough idea of your cost.

Being Healthy Sites:

1. www.healthfinder.com
This site is brought to you by the U.S. Department of Health and Human Services. Here you can find a comprehensive health library for men and woman, organized by age, by race and ethnicity: for parents, caregivers and health professionals on prevention, wellness, diseases and conditions. The section on health care gives you information about doctors, dentists, clinics, hospitals, long term care, nursing homes, health insurance, prescriptions, Medicare, Medicaid, etc.

2. www.mayoclinic.com
Sponsored by the Mayo Foundation for Medical Education and Research the site contains a section devoted to healthy living. Here you can find a collection of information on children's health, fitness, food, nutrition, sleep, your working life, health decision guides, men's and women's health. The section labeled *"Tools"* offers interactive self-assessments to determine your health status and calculators to estimate your risk of certain diseases.

3. www.surgeongeneral.gov/beinghealthy
From the Office of the Surgeon General the site gives you information from many reliable resources offered by the Federal government and nonprofit organizations. Under their *"Healthfinder"* section you can find information on general health and perform online checkups. Information is organized for kids, parents and educators. They have links to other resources from the Office of Public Health and Science.

4. www.webmd.com
If you hit the WebMD Health tab you will be presented with information on current trends and news about health, diet and exercise. You can explore lifestyles, diet, food, healthy skin, energy and nutrition information. Here you can also find medical information concerning specific diseases, conditions, symptoms, drugs, herbs and a medical library, as well as health quizzes and calculators.

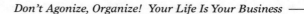

Appendix 2

GLOSSARY OF TERMS

Action Plan
An action plan expresses an objective in terms of specific actions or operations. It specifically states what steps or tasks will be accomplished to achieve the objective. It includes a schedule with deadlines for significant actions, resources necessary to achieve the objective and methods to measure the objective. Preparing action plans addresses potential problem areas, considers the impact of the actions and ultimately increases productivity. Using an action plan can help you stay organized, coordinate activities and keep projects on schedule.

Asset
An asset is any real or personal property or resource of a person or business. The definition of an asset includes savings accounts, checking accounts, stocks, bonds, mutual funds, real estate, automobiles, a home, a vacation home, boats, airplanes or a business enterprise.

Asset Allocation
Asset Allocation is the ratio of stocks, bonds and cash in a portfolio. It involves diversifying a portfolio among different investment classes: stocks, fixed income alternatives such as bonds, cash equivalents, real estate and other tangible assets. The right asset mix relative to an investor's risk tolerance can generate high returns while effectively managing risk.

Associations
Associations are made between what we learn and the environment we are in, between the information and our mental states and between the information and our stream of thoughts. When things are associated in memory, thinking of one helps bring the other to mind. When you are having difficulty recalling new material you can help bring it to mind by thinking about what you have associated it with. In other words, you can retrace your mental path.

Body Image
Body image involves our perception, imagination, emotions and physical sensations about our bodies. It is ever changing; sensitive to changes in mood, environment and physical experience. It is psychological in nature and influenced by self-esteem more than by

actual physical attractiveness as judged by others. It is not inborn but learned. This learning occurs in the family and among peers, but these only reinforce what is learned and expected culturally.

Bonds
Bonds are a form of indebtedness that are sold to the public in set increments, normally in the neighborhood of $1,000 by corporations, the federal, state and local governments. Not only is the borrowed amount paid back but also a little extra in the form of interest for the privilege of borrowing the money. In return for loaning the debtor the money the lender gets a piece of paper that stipulates how much was lent, the agreed-upon interest rate, how often interest will be paid and the term of the loan.

Budget
A tool used by individuals, businesses and governments to predict flows of money over a period of time, usually a year. A household budget lists all the sources of money for that household, such as wages from a job, rents, etc., and all the ways in which money will be spent, including costs for housing, school, clothes, food, phone bills, etc. An *actual budget* is simply the amounts that currently come in and go out while a *projected budget* is an expectation of future ins and outs.

Business Plan
A business plan is a document that is written with two objectives in mind: (1) To clearly identify, define and explain a business opportunity. (2) To detail how the entrepreneur will take advantage of this business opportunity. During the process of developing a business plan entrepreneurs not only acquire a more intimate knowledge about their businesses, their customers and their markets, but they also get the chance to work out all the "bugs" first on paper thus increasing their chances of successfully implementing their business objectives.

Carry-on Allowance
The carry-on allowance is the amount of luggage that can be carried onto an airplane subject to certain standards. Each airline has their own standard and number limit. The size limitation of your luggage is calculated by adding the total outside dimensions of each bag, that is, length + width + height.

COB

If you and your family have coverage, under more than one insurance plan a coordination of benefits (COB) provision eliminates duplication of payment for services. Under COB, the plan that pays first is the primary plan. The secondary plan pays after the primary plan. The end result is that each insurance company pays a fair share but the combined payments by both plans will not exceed the maximum allowable reimbursement.

COBRA

In 1986 Congress passed the Consolidated Omnibus Budget Reconciliation Act (COBRA). The law provides continuation of group health coverage for up to 18 months. It allows former employees, retirees, spouses and dependent children the right to temporarily continue health coverage at group rates. Group health coverage for COBRA participants is more expensive than coverage for active employees, as the employer formerly paid a part of the premium but less expensive than individual health coverage.

Cost of Living

The amount of money needed to buy the goods and services necessary to maintain a specified standard of living. Cost of living is closely tied to inflation and deflation rates. In estimating, the costs for housing, food, clothing, rent, property taxes, fuel, electricity and furnishings as well as expenses for communication, education, recreation, transportation and medical services are generally included.

Credit Report

A credit report is a document that contains information about who a person has borrowed money from, how well he pays his bills and how much debt he owes. There are three major credit reporting agencies that have a credit file on you: Equifax, Experian and Trans Union. They do not share information with each other and most lenders do not subscribe to the services of all three agencies. Therefore your credit report with each agency will differ as to the completeness of information.

Deduction

Within the United States' income tax system a tax deduction is an item which is subtracted from gross income to arrive at the taxable income. There are many types of deductions. Common examples of tax deductions for individuals are mortgage interest paid on a primary residence, loan interest, charitable contributions, business expenses, union or professional dues, medical expenses above a certain percentage of total income, cost of tax advice, software and books, work uniforms, moving expenses, casualty losses, state and local taxes, capital losses, etc. Each of these deductions may or may not be appropriate given a taxpayer's filing status and income. All tax deductions allowed by the federal government are also allowed by all the state governments. Each state government may allow additional types of expenditures to be tax-deductible.

Disability Insurance
Disability insurance pays benefits when you are unable to earn a living because you are sick or injured. Like all insurance, disability insurance is designed to protect you against financial disaster. Most disability policies pay you a benefit that replaces part of your earned income (usually 50 to 70 percent) when you can't work.

Diversification
Diversification is spreading one's money among different investments. It is a risk management technique that combines a wide variety of investments in order to reduce the impact that any one security has on the whole portfolio's performance. A diversified mix of investments can lower an investor's overall risk without necessarily reducing their potential return.

Education IRA
This type of IRA shares the name with traditional and Roth IRAs. They share the benefit of tax-deferred growth and with a Roth; they share the opportunity for tax-free withdrawals. But they are not really IRAs in the customary sense since they are designed to help pay college expenses not retirement costs. Each IRA must be set up for a specific beneficiary, annual contributions are limited and there is a salary cap limiting who can make contributions.

Estate Planning
Developing plans and taking action during your lifetime to ensure that your wealth will be accumulated, preserved and upon your death distributed in the desired fashion is estate planning. This process requires an extensive knowledge of trusts, wills and taxes.

The objective of estate planning is to ensure the orderly transfer of as much of an estate as possible to heirs and/or beneficiaries. It encompasses the making of a trust or will, decisions on ownership of assets, power of attorney, using the unified gift and tax credit, gifting, making charitable contributions, setting up a charitable trust, probate, etc.

Estate Tax
These are Federal estate and state inheritance taxes that may be payable when property is transferred at the time of death. The goal of effective estate planning is to minimize the amount of estate taxes that must be paid. Estate tax planning encompasses the knowledge of gift tax exclusions, charitable gifts, trusts and types of ownership.

Executor
An executor is the administrator of an estate designated in the descendents will or if the descendent died in testate (without a will) through a court appointed administrator. Their job is to collect assets, pay bills, resolve legal and tax issues. Many times a spouse, child or close friend is named executor. With complex and time consuming estates the use of a lawyer or one with professional skills is either named executor or called for consultation.

Expenditures
Expenditures are monies spent on living expenses, to purchase assets, pay taxes or repay a debt. A *fixed expenditure* is an equal payment each period, typically each month, such as a mortgage, installment loan payment or insurance premium. *Variable expenditures* are payment amounts that are always changing such as food, clothing and entertainment.

Fraud Alert
A fraud alert is a free service that requests creditors to verify your identity before opening a new account. It is designed so you will get a telephone call any time anyone applies for credit, opens up a new account or applies for a loan in your name. Then you can decide whether to approve it or not. You will need to contact each of the three major credit bureaus to place a fraud alert. Each alert lasts for a limited amount of time.

Goal

A goal is something towards which effort or movement is directed, it is an end or an objective. It is something you tell yourself that you are going to do. In order to make a goal you must do three things: make sure your goal is realistic, make a realistic date when you want your goal to be completed by and make a plan to keep you organized while completing your goal.

GPS

The Global Positioning System (GPS) is a satellite-based navigation system made up of a network of 24 satellites placed into orbit by the U.S. Department of Defense. GPS was originally intended for military applications, but in the 1980s the government made the system available for civilian use. GPS works in any weather conditions, anywhere in the world, 24 hours a day.

Guardian

A person who has the legal responsibility for providing the care and management of a person who is incapable, either due to age (very young or even very old) or to some other physical, mental or emotional impairment, of administering his or her own affairs. In the case of a minor child, the guardian is charged with the legal responsibility for the care and management of the child and of the minor child's estate. The legal guardian will be under the supervision of the court and be required to appear in court to give periodic reports about the status of the child and their estate.

Identity Theft

Identity theft occurs when someone steals personal information about you to obtain money or credit. The thief may apply for credit in your name by opening loans and mortgages or applying for credit cards in your name. They may also make purchases you are responsible for paying or change the billing address on your credit card accounts. Identity theft is now the most common type of consumer fraud as it provides a low-risk, high-reward gamble for criminals.

IRA

An individual retirement account is a tax-deferred personal retirement plan open to any working America to which a person may contribute a specified amount each year. The tax-deferred advantage of an IRA is that your investment grows much faster than it would in a taxable account and the sooner you begin contributing, the larger it can grow. As a plan to encourage personal savings the Employee Retirement Income Security Act (ERISA) invented it in 1974 and named it after Ira Cohen, an IRS actuary.

IRS Audit
The IRS performs an audit as an investigation to determine whether the information provided to the government on a tax return is correct. As a result the audit can determine whether the proper amount of tax was paid. The burden of proof is on the taxpayer. They have to prove to the government that all of the information on the return (the amount of income, exclusions, exemptions, deductions and credits) is true and correct.

Keogh Plan
A Keogh plan is a defined-benefit or defined-contribution plan that can be established by a self-employed individual for him/herself and his/her employees. Similar to IRAs, the earnings in a Keogh plan accrue on a tax-deferred basis except that you can contribute substantially more. Small businesses offer Keogh plans instead of 401K plans.

Liability
Liabilities represent debts that are owed and must be repaid in the future. They could result from department store charges, bank credit card charges, installment loans, rents, car payments or mortgages on housing and other rest estate. Some liabilities are due immediately, as soon as you receive the statement or bill, while others are more long term and may be paid over a period of months or years.

Life Style
Life style is a pattern of behavior that conforms to an individual's preferences towards household formation, participation in the labor force, utilization of leisure and their use of available resources. Individuals make long term decisions that guide their preferred pattern of daily behavior. People within different life style groups have taste variations and preferences that affect the choices they make everyday.

Long Term Care Insurance
This insurance covers the cost of medical, personal and social services provided at home, in a community center or in a nursing home for those with catastrophic illnesses. The longer you live, the greater the risk that you will need long term health care. Companies that sell long term care insurance each differ on what is covered and payout restrictions.

Long Term Disability
Long-term disability comes into play if a disabling illness or accident prevents you from working and earning an income. It picks up where short-term disability leaves off. Once your short-term disability benefits expire, generally after 3 to 6 months, the long-term disability policy pays you a percentage of your salary, usually 50 to 60 percent. You then receive benefits until you reach age 65. Long-term disability policies either offered to you by your employer or purchased privately, act as income protection.

Marketing
Marketing is the analysis of customers and competitors to gain an overall understanding of what each segment wants, targeting the most profitable segments, positioning products and doing what is necessary to deliver on that positioning. It involves decisions that are made for all advertising tactics and strategies based on the market analysis.

Mnemonics
Mnemonics are devices that aid in the memorization of something. These devices come in many varieties and forms: such as rhyme, acronyms and mnemonic techniques. They help you remember large amount of information, words, numbers, spelling, telephone numbers and lists of various items.

MRD
MRD stands for the minimum required distribution you must withdraw from an IRA once you turn 70 1/2. The penalty for failing to take the minimum is steep; you may lose half of what you failed to withdraw. There are two methods for determining your minimum withdrawal. You can base withdrawals on your life expectancy and that of your beneficiary at the time of your first withdrawal or you

can recalculate the divisor each year. Once you choose a method you must stick with it for subsequent withdrawals. The method you choose will also affect how payments will be made to your beneficiary.

Mutual Fund
A mutual fund is a collection of stocks, bonds or other securities owned by a group of investors and managed by a professional investment company. These companies offer a widely diversified portfolio of securities as well as a variety of investor services. When investors put money into a fund it is pooled with money from other investors to create much greater buying power than they would have investing on their own.

Net Worth
Net worth is the amount of actual wealth or equity an individual or family has in owned assets. It is the amount of money that would remain after selling all owned assets at their estimated fair market values and paying off all liabilities. Your net worth is your total assets (what you own) minus your total liabilities (what you owe).

Networking
Networking is a process of gathering helpful information and developing relationships from a network of contacts in a conversation on a particular topic of interest. It is a method of communicating with others by introducing a topic for discussion to obtain new ways of looking at things, different points of view and information. The aim of networking is that during the conversation or discussion you may offer information that is helpful to someone else or someone else may offer helpful information to you.

Outsource
Outsourcing is the transfer or delegation, to an external service provider, the operation and day-to-day management of a business process. It takes place when an organization transfers the ownership of a business process to a supplier. The organization does not instruct the supplier how to perform its task but focuses on communicating what results it wants to buy and leaves the process of accomplishing those results to the supplier.

Paired Associates

A paired associate is a type of memory technique that assists in remembering. It is the ability to memorize a list of paired items, such as pictures and names, common objects and nonsense syllables, or words and corresponding visual scenes. The first word in the pair is used as a cue to memory to the second word in the pair.

PDA

A PDA is a digital organizer or personal digital assistant that can be comfortably held in your hand (it is also called a handheld). Much like traditional computers, PDAs consist of a display screen (the screen is usually a touch screen and is called a LCD display), a processor and memory. Calendars, notepads and address books are common features on a PDA but many also download email and other materials from a computer or the Internet. Some synchronize or copy certain files from a computer to the handheld device. Popular PDA brand names are Palm Pilot and Blackberry.

Personal Financial Planning

The objective of personal financial planning is planning that covers the key elements of an individual's financial affairs and aimed at the achievement of his or her financial goals. It encompasses the short and long range results that an individual wants to attain such as controlling living expenses, managing one's tax burden, establishing savings and investment programs and meeting retirement needs. One of the major benefits of personal financial planning is that it helps you to more effectively control your financial resources and gain an improved standard of living.

Personal Image

One's personal image is how you visually represent yourself to the outside world. It is what you are first judged on whenever you meet someone. It consists of your sense of style, appearance, how you dress, your voice, what you say, body language, hairstyle and even your manners. Self-confidence and assurance is also projected into the total image.

Portfolio

A portfolio is a collection of securities assembled for the purpose of meeting common investment goals. Developing a portfolio of security holdings is an important part of investing, it enables you to diversity your holdings. A good portfolio combines personal and financial traits with your investment objectives to give your investments structure.

Recall
The most popular kind of memory is recall. It involves a search of memory and then the comparison process once something is found. Recall is coming up with the information from memory yourself such as the name of a person you recognize. It is the recollection of a telephone number you have just heard, a list of items you are to purchase at the store or a list of dates you learned in history class.

Recognition
Recognition is memory that uses two mechanisms: familiarity and retrieval. When provided with information we double check our memory if we have seen it before. It includes matching, feelings of familiarity and recognizing someone you know. An example of recognition is when a history teacher gives four dates and learners are to choose the one that goes with the specific historical event.

Reproductive Memory
Reproductive memory is the true recollection of information that was physically presented originally. Reproductive memory stores simple facts and reproduces the events as they were experienced.

Retirement 401K Plans
Known as a defined contribution plan, a 401K plan allows employees to contribute a portion of their paycheck in pre-tax dollars to a retirement fund. The employee selects how the money is to be invested among the choices offered by the company, such as mutual funds, money market accounts or company stock. One great advantage of many 401K plans is the employer matches all or part of your contribution. Employers vary on how much they contribute. All the money in a 401K account grows tax-deferred.

Retirement 403(b) Plans
These retirement plans are similar to 401K plans however they are only for teachers, healthcare workers and non-profit employees. In the interest of their employees school boards and hospitals set up 403(b) plans and administer them through insurance companies that push tax-sheltered annuities. Some 403(b) plans allow other choices such as mutual funds while others do not.

Retirement 457 Plans
These retirement plans are similar to 401K and 403(b) plans however they are only for governmental group employees. They generally work the same way; to defer pre-tax compensation to help you meet your retirement goal.

Revenue
Revenue is income from sources as earnings from a salary, wages, tips, commissions, dividends, interests, retirement benefits and government benefits such as social security.

Risk Tolerance
Risk is defined as uncertainty with respect to economic loss. There is always the risk that an investment will not hit its target. Some investments are riskier than others. Your risk tolerance is how much risk you choose to accept and is a measure of your comfort zone when it comes to bearing an economic loss.

Rollover
A rollover is simply the transfer of funds from one instrument to another without incurring tax penalties or realizing a gain. It is an employee's transfer of retirement funds from one retirement plan to another plan of the same type or to an IRA without incurring a tax liability. The transfer must be made within 60 days of receiving a cash distribution. The law requires 20 percent federal income tax withholding on money eligible for rollover if it is not moved directly to the second plan or an investment company.

ROTH IRA
They are IRAs that are tax-deferred and also tax-free if you follow the rules for withdrawal. Withdrawals from a ROTH account are completely tax-free if your account has been open at least five years and you have reached the age of 59 1/2. You are also able to continue contributing for as long as you have earned income and you are not required to begin withdrawals at age 70 1/2, as you are with traditional IRAs.

Short Term Disability
Short-term disability pays a percentage of your salary if you become temporarily disabled, meaning that you are not able to work for a

short period of time due to sickness or injury. A typical short term disability policy provides you with a weekly portion of your salary usually 50 to 60 percent for 13 to 26 weeks.

Spreadsheets
Spreadsheets are computer programs that work with numerical data the same way that word processors work with textual data. A spreadsheet is the computer equivalent of a paper ledger sheet that consists of a matrix of columns and rows. It is used to organize and calculate numbers. You can change numbers and a spreadsheet will automatically recalculate. A spreadsheet performs tedious calculations that make number manipulation and recalculations easy, without error and faster than can be done by hand.

Stocks
Stocks are pieces of the corporate pie, when you buy stocks or shares you own a slice of the company. A corporation's stockholders, sometimes thousands of people and institutions, all have equity in the company or own a fractional portion of the whole. They buy the stock because they expect to profit when the company profits through capital gains. A stocks value can change at any moment depending on world events, market conditions, investor perceptions, politics or a host of other issues.

Tax Form W-2
You should receive a separate W-2 form from each employer you worked for during a tax year showing your total pay and other compensation, the income tax, social security tax and Medicare tax that was withheld during the year.

Tax Form 1040
This is the main tax form that is filed with the IRS yearly. It contains information on your wages and other sources of income as well as your deductions and credits. There are schedules attached to the 1040 form that may need to be filed to report interest, dividends, deductions, self-employment income, capital gains, etc.

Tax Form 1098
If you paid mortgage interest, including certain points, during the year you should receive form 1098 from the mortgage holder. The

statements show the total interest you paid during the year. If you purchased a main residence during the year then it will also show the deductible mortgage points.

Tax Form 1099
If you received certain types of income you should receive a 1099 form. There are separate forms that report income from interest, dividends, state income tax refunds, barter income, OID (original issue discount), early distribution of pension funds and real estate transaction proceeds.

Tax Planning
Tax planning is aimed at reducing taxes immediately, as well as in the future. It involves looking at an individual's current and projected earnings and developing strategies that will defer and/or minimize taxes. Tax plans should reflect the form in which the tax reductions are to be received; earned income, investment income, passive income, tax sheltered income or capital gains.

Total Assets
Total assets is the total value of all items owned by an individual such as bank accounts, stocks, bonds, home and automobiles. The goal of most individuals is to accumulate their assets and increase their wealth while maintaining a desired standard of living.

Will
A will is a legal document that transfers your property after you die and names the people who will settle your estate, care for you children who are minors and administer any trusts the will establishes. A will has to be a formal written document that meets the legal requirements of the state where it is prepared.

Working Smart
In essence there is no real definition of *"working smart"*; however it can be interpreted as working in a systematic, methodical, articulate and efficient manner. By focusing your approach, narrowing your definition and specializing, *"working smart"* requires less effort, time and resources.

INDEX

COLLEGE KNOWLEDGE:
THE A+ GUIDE TO EARLY COLLEGE PLANNING
By Regina Helene Muster

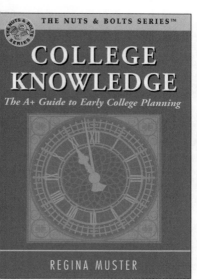

SBN 0-9748765-8-5

• Teaches students how to get organized and plan for success, as early as freshman year.
• Helps students discover their inner passions so they can align their goals with the best possible colleges for them.
• Coaches students on how to present their abilities and credentials in the best possible light in order to gain a competitive edge when it comes to college admissions.

College Knowledge is a step-by-step guidebook with a personal touch and a positive attitude that takes the guesswork out of college selection and application. Written by Regina Muster, a computer programmer who went through the process with her daughter, Jenna Mehler. College Knowledge features a highly organized approach for navigating every aspect of the college journey.

The guide offers practical advice on topics such as:
- writing a personal profile and resume
- selecting a college based on class profiles
- being your own personal college counselor
- what to do if you do not get enough financial aid
- understanding what information is on a school transcript

must read! This is the perfect resource for getting a head start on the college search d admissions process. College Knowledge is a well-organized, thought provoking and mprehensive guide. I strongly recommend College Knowledge for every high school eshman considering higher education."

Susan Baka Rautenberg
High School Counselor
Annandale, New Jersey